TATTOOED:
THE SOCIOGENESIS OF A BODY ART

Tattoos have become increasingly popular in recent years, especially among young people. While tattooing is used as a symbol of personal identity and social communication, there has been little sociological study of the phenomenon. In *Tattooed: The Sociogenesis of a Body Art*, tattoo enthusiasts share their stories about their bodies and tattooing experiences. Michael Atkinson shows how enthusiasts negotiate and celebrate their 'difference' as it relates to the social stigma attached to body art – how the act of tattooing is as much a response to the stigma as it is a form of personal expression – and how a generation has appropriated tattooing as its own symbol of inclusiveness. Atkinson further demonstrates how the displaying of tattooed bodies to others – techniques of disclosure, justification, and representation – has become a part of the shared experience.

Cultural sensibilities about tattooing are discussed within historical context and in relation to broader trends in body modification, such as cosmetic surgery, dieting, and piercing. The author also employs research from a number of disciplines, as well as contemporary sociological and postmodern theory, to analyse the enduring social significance of body art.

MICHAEL ATKINSON is an assistant professor in the Department of Sociology at McMaster University.

MICHAEL ATKINSON

Tattooed

The Sociogenesis of a Body Art

UNIVERSITY OF TORONTO PRESS
Toronto Buffalo London

© University of Toronto Press Incorporated 2003
Toronto Buffalo London
Printed in Canada

ISBN 0-8020-8777-9 (cloth)
ISBN 0-8020-8568-7 (paper)

∞

Printed on acid-free paper

National Library of Canada Cataloguing in Publication

Atkinson, Michael, 1971–
   Tattooed : the sociogenesis of a body art / Michael Atkinson.

   Includes bibliographical references and index.
   ISBN 0-8020-8777-9 (bound).   ISBN 0-8020-8568-7 (pbk.)

   1. Tattooing – Social aspects.   I. Title.

GN419.3.A84 2003   391.6′5   C2003-901041-4

This book has been published with the help of a grant from the Humanities
and Social Sciences Federation of Canada, using funds provided by the Social
Sciences and Humanities Research Council of Canada.

The University of Toronto Press acknowledges the financial assistance to
its publishing program of the Canada Council for the Arts and the Ontario
Arts Council.

University of Toronto Press acknowledges the financial support for its
publishing activities of the Government of Canada through the Book
Publishing Industry Development Program (BPIDP).

Contents

Preface

In the early 1990s, I wandered into a dank tattoo studio on a pier in downtown Halifax. It had not been the first time I had sauntered into a tattoo parlour, and definitely not my first encounter with tattoo artists. On this cold and blustery day in the middle of February, I entered into the first significant agreement I had ever made with my skin. With a very dear friend of mine, with whom I have shared some of the more impetuous and potentially destructive moments of my life, I decided to join the ranks of 'tattoo enthusiasts' – a relatively small band of individuals devoted to marking the skin in an ancient and deeply human way. As I describe in this book, *a tattoo enthusiast is simply a person who has a personal/cultural fascination with tattoos, and at some point in the life course decided to become tattooed.* My friend and I did not know anything about the process, had not deliberated about the designs we were going to choose, nor about the locations on our bodies that were to be tattooed. With naive trust and a sense of adventurousness, we clumsily flipped through the designs available in a decrepit photo album sitting on the artists' front counter in the shop. After selecting a design, I sat down and rolled up my left shirt sleeve. Through the course of the hour it took to apply the tattoo I felt exhilaration, nausea, and a recurring twinge of shame. But at the end, I was tattooed.

Reminiscing about the experience just about every time I gaze down at the tattoo, I wonder if I would do it all over again. If the tattoos from my arms could be magically erased, would I begin to have my body tattooed once more? I thought a single tattoo would suffice, and that I would be satisfied in doing what I had always dreamed about that one time. But I have now been tattooed by artists across the country, with both of my arms adorned in tattoo sleeves. I know very few people with only one tattoo, and some of their experiences will be discussed throughout this work on tattooing. However, I would hazard a guess that in the years to come, they too will seek out tattoo artists on more than one occasion, filling in bits and pieces of their bodies with ink. I do not know when, or perhaps where, my predilection for tattooing will end. But I am certain I will continue to tattoo my body as part of chronicling my life.

My first academic encounter with tattooing occurred about ten years ago. Enrolled in a course in the sociology of deviance, I read a piece from Clinton Sanders's well-known work, *Customizing the Body: The Art and Culture of Tattooing* (1989). Contextualizing tattooing as an example of stigma management and secondary deviance, Sanders skilfully presented it as an exotic, disrespected, and marginal social activity. Needless to say, my own experiences with tattooing did not completely resonate with Sanders's representations. I eventually decided to pursue a small study of tattooing for a course in qualitative methodology during my Master's degree research. I quickly learned that sociologists, psychologists, and the majority of cultural anthropologists writing on the subject had advanced no description or explanation of what Canadians were doing with tattoos. Furthermore, even though we have witnessed a recent boom in academic interest in the subject, the lack of knowledge we have as an academic community about tattooing is only slightly overshadowed by our commitment to classifying tattooing processes within the broad category of social deviance or personal pathology.

Quite simply, we need to inspect critically and readjust our understanding of tattooing as a cultural form of expression. With this said, my own studies of tattooing have never been about political campaigning, claims-making, lobbying, or condemnation. From the onset of my research, my intentions were to venture into sociologically uncharted waters – by talking with tattoo enthusiasts in an attempt to grasp their experiences with this form of body modification, and eventually representing these experiences in the most respectful and responsible way I know how. In this way, I didn't want to produce another coffee-table book about tattooing, or another detailed description about what tattoos 'look like' in contemporary societies. The goal is to analyse tattooing practices sociologically, exploring how this body project is a deeply social act. I do not set my work on tattooing up as the definitive piece on the subject, nor do I imply we should regard it as a point of closure. Hopefully, this piece of sociological work will encourage others to muck around in this area, extending what I have done into other contexts, situations, and cultural settings.

Aside from my personal interest in the topic (that is, as someone who is tattooed and a sociologist trying to make theoretical sense of the practice), I possess a fervent sociological interest in issues of corporeality. My sister, now a lawyer in Toronto, began her academic career by completing university degrees in English. During her years as a student, she exposed me to critical readings of the body, often from postmodernist theoretical perspectives. At the time I believed textual deconstructions of the body to be academic gerrymandering, a sign and task of someone with little better to do than pontificate about the textuality of the physical self. Exploring this literature during my initial foray into the tattooing figuration, I found a wealth of sociological knowledge and insight about bodies and their cultural significance.

The sociology of the body is, for me, one of the most exciting, prolific, and innovative sub-fields within the discipline. Arising out of virtual obscurity in the 1980s, the subject of corporeality has never been more consequential in sociological research than now. Theory, methods, and substantive foci of investigation are all affected by our return to bodies. In writing this book, I cannot help but reflect upon the growth in research on bodies even since I began this research several years ago. An interdisciplinary journal, *Body and Society*, now exists as a vehicle for gathering and disseminating research on bodies, articles about corporeality in other journals continue to grow in number as do books on the subject, and courses in the sociology of the body are creeping into undergraduate curricula across the country. Furthermore, experts in typically marginalized sociological sub-fields such as sport, gender, and health/illness are now called upon for their theoretical insight, and long-standing theoretical dualisms such as the mind/body, self/society, and agency/structure separations are vigorously questioned through empirical research.

At the same time, I cannot help but wonder where and how the sociology of the body will develop in the future. We currently stand at a critical point in this area. Looking backwards, we see a path carved out by individuals establishing that bodies matter in sociological theory and practice. Viewing our current standing, we see scores of researchers rushing into the field, rapidly working to construct a bridge so that others may cross the divide separating modern and postmodern society. We should, however, carefully inspect the empirical quality, theoretical durability, and methodological strength of the planks providing this walkway. In clamouring to gather evidence about the impact of postmodernity on bodies, we seem to have forgotten that sociologists are in the business of conducting social research – research founded upon empirical evidence, methods with evaluative criteria, and theories that can be tested against lived experience. Taking the development and empirical testing of theory on bodies as a central concern in this research, I wish to continue the sociological investigation of corporeality demanded by sociologists of the 1980s and early 1990s, while warning others about the perils posed to the study of bodies by nihilistic, seemingly purposeless, or self-indulgent musings on the subject.

One of the most troubling criticisms that friends of mine have made of sociology is that sociologists have a tendency to describe that which is easily perceptible in exceedingly verbose and confusing academic texts. As a sociologist, I understand this concern, while simultaneously realizing that we simply must venture beyond 'common sense' understandings of human interaction. If we do not we are merely social commentators, aimlessly strolling city streets offering social opinion to those who might listen. In practice we walk a fine line, carefully developing concepts and theories to explain the nebulous collage that is the social world, yet retaining the integrity and voice of those we study (or those with whom we study social life). I sincerely question the benefit of sociological research that is solely geared toward pleasing the academic community rather than stimulating or benefiting other 'communities.'

The following discussion of tattooing is based on over ten years of personal involvement with tattoo enthusiasts in Canada. I have met many characters along the way, seen friends come and go, and questioned my own beliefs about tattooing. Deviant or not, tattooing is a deeply historical and unique form of human representation. As a species, we mark our bodies in order to signify our humanity, to express and communicate our sociality as we do through sculpture, architecture, painting, speech, dance, cinema, or gesture. For too long, sociologists have downplayed the (cross)cultural significance of tattooing, favouring depictions of the tattoo as a symbol of personal sickness, subcultural deviance, or social disrepute. Our cultural sensibilities toward this form of art are undergoing rapid change, however, and in failing to recognize the fluctuating nature of the tattoo as a cultural signifier, sociologists have misinterpreted the humanity ingrained in the practice and the relevance of tattooing across time and space. The discussion of tattooing constructed here is, then, not a totalizing, politically charged, perfect, romantic, or theoretically flawless account of individuals who at some point in their lives decided to become tattooed. It is simply a piece of sociological research, and I offer it as such.

The analytical orientation I adopt in this book is what sociologists refer to as a figurational approach to the study of group life. Figurational sociology points to how social life is best conceived of as a grid of interrelated actions and processes, and how individual lives are tied to others' through extensive chains of interdependency – literally, as a web of interconnected people. In this book, I undertake an analysis of the contemporary tattooing figuration in Canada to illustrate how the highly individualistic act of tattooing is essentially a group phenomenon involving a litany of connected social actors. Furthermore, the tattooing habits of Canadians are located within broad, and changing, social conditions and relationships within Canada and elsewhere. My goal is not to force a theoretically complex or abstruse understanding of social life onto tattooing practices, but rather to help understand why Canadians have rediscovered tattooing as a viable and meaningful form of corporeal expression. The process of 'figuring the tattoo' is concerned with exposing not only how tattoo enthusiasts' practices are linked together as a figuration, but also how movements and changes in the tattoo figuration are related to social practices and processes outside of the group.

Acknowledgments

There are dozens of people who helped make this book possible, and each contributed in different yet equally valued ways. First and foremost, this book would not have been possible if tattoo enthusiasts did not allow me to pry into their lives. I feel privileged to have shared time and space with tattoo enthusiasts in this study, and to have talked about our most private body-modification experiences alongside our innermost thoughts and feelings about tattoos. To the tattoo artists I have met over the course of the past few years: there are no words I can use to relate how much I appreciate your openness and honesty. I wear the reminders of my experiences in tattoo studios, and will reflect upon them with much nostalgia in the years to come.

There have been many others who provided critical assessment and support of this work at varying stages of its completion. I would like especially to thank Kevin Young for encouraging me to pursue this topic, and for providing constant faith in, and incredible insight regarding, my work. I would also like to thank Bob Stebbins sincerely for his guidance and advice regarding what I should do with the text. I have also been fortunate to receive keen recommendations and direction from Eric Dunning, Leslie Miller, Bruce Arnold, Billy Shaffir, Alan Smart, Dick Wanner, Arthur Frank, Kelly Hardwick, Brian Wilson, and Andy Hathaway – to each of you I owe a unique thank-you for reading my work, listening to my ideas, and giving me theoretical inspiration.

I also wish to acknowledge the efforts of Virgil Duff at the University of Toronto Press, who enthusiastically supported this book from the time I first submitted my proposal to him. My sincere thanks also go to John St James for his thoughtful editing of the manuscript of this book. Thanks are in order to the anonymous reviewers from the University of

Toronto Press and Aid to Scholarly Publications Programme / Humanities and Social Sciences Federation of Canada, who offered considerably constructive evaluations of the manuscript. I would also like to thank the granting agencies that helped fund both my initial research on tattooing in Canada and the publication of this book. The research discussed in this study was funded in part by the Social Sciences and Humanities Research Council of Canada.

   Finally, I would like to thank my father, mother, Jodi, and Bronwyn for their continued belief in my abilities and trust in my life choices – particularly, those that have led me to redesign my body through tattooing! Many thanks are also due to Scott Veldhoen for providing the photographs contained in this book.

TATTOOED:
THE SOCIOGENESIS OF A BODY ART

CHAPTER ONE

Tattooing as Body Modification

Recently, I watched a commercial on television advertising a revolutionary way to tone one's abdominal muscles. A person attaches a series of high-tech, scientifically designed plastic electrodes to the midsection and 'the muscles are stimulated into sending out fat-burning and muscle-producing messages.' The purpose of the apparatus is seemingly elementary: to rouse the muscles into a state of simulated exercise. The commercial shows several hulking men lying on a beach or lounging on chesterfields while their bodies are effortlessly shaped by the device. Similarly, young, bikini-clad women are shown relaxing in tanning beds or watching television while the machine works away their unwanted pounds.

The product, and commercial advertising of the product, underscore the simple fact that we are increasingly motivated to pursue new and innovative ways to modify our bodies. We live in an era in which people are expected socially to engage in a full gamut of body-modification practices, from the routine (e.g., a haircut) to the physically traumatic (e.g., breast augmentation). Body modification products and services abound in everyday life. Grocery stores, hair salons, diet centres, exercise gyms, fashion retailers, laser eye-care offices, and health spas all offer commodities and strategies oriented toward changing our physical bodies and bettering our lives. We are, in a sense, a culture of body modificationists, with our hunger for altering the corporeal only frustrated by the limits imposed by our imaginations, financial resources, products at our disposal, and scientific-medical technologies.

Since the late 1980s, sociologists have become increasingly mindful of the frequency and rapidity with which people deliberately modify their bodies. Through perhaps one of the most focused and insightful exegeses of the topic, Shilling (1993) conceptualized body modification as intentionally designed 'projects,' and contended that such undertakings are integral in formulating identity over the life course. He argued that bodies exist in a continual process of becoming – as their sizes, shapes, appearances, and contents are subject to ongoing transformation.

One of the most visibly en vogue, and clearly contested, body projects in the new millennium is tattooing. It is estimated that approximately 15 to 20 per cent of North Americans are now tattooed (Atkinson and Young 2001). This prevalence is historically unparalleled in Western cultures and somewhat surprising given previous estimates, which suggested the participation rate to be as low as 4 to 6 per cent (Sanders 1989; Steward 1990). Though tattooing was associated almost exclusively with the social underbelly (Grumet 1983; McKerracher and Watson 1969; Paine 1979; St Clair and Govenar 1981), existing research illustrates how it now cuts across categories of age, gender, socioeconomic status (i.e., education, income, occupational prestige), ethnic background, religious affiliation, and sexual orientation (DeMello 2000; Irwin 2000; Myers 1997; Vail 1999). With the influx of people (both artists and their clients) into the tattoo 'scene' (Irwin 1977), and a contemporary shift in cultural understandings of tattoos, the practice is undergoing unplanned transformation in North America.

For the most part, though, we still know very little about contemporary tattoo enthusiasts' fascination with this body project, cultural sensibilities about the practice, or collectively shared understandings of tattoo art. This is particularly true in the Canadian context, since there have been no sustained analyses of Canadian tattooing. Given the ongoing renaissance in Western tattooing – a collection of activities and events altering the membership base of tattoo enthusiasts and ushering in a new era of professionalism in tattooing (DeMello 2000) – it seems that an empirical look at where tattooing has come from in the recent past could shed some much needed light on the contemporary appeal of tattooing for Canadians.

This book is, then, organized around two main sociological problems. First, I am principally concerned with explaining why a noticeable number of Canadians are tattooing their bodies at this juncture in our cultural history. With a plethora of less permanent and more normative methods for manipulating bodies readily available, why has tattooing become undeniably *de rigeur* among Canadians? In my effort to locate the current study in the ongoing historical development of the Canadian *tattoo figuration* – the term 'figuration' referring to a collection of social actors bound together by chains or webs of interdependency (Elias 1994) – a primary concern is how long-term social transformations in Canada (both within and outside of the tattoo figuration) have influenced individuals to become more curious about, fascinated with, and accepting of tattoos.

Second, and conjointly with the first problem, this book examines how individual *habituses* (Bourdieu 1984, 1990; Elias 1994, 1996; Mauss 1973) – what one might call 'personality structures' or 'second natures' – fluctuate over time. Specifically, through the critical inspection of stories about tattooing provided by contemporary tattoo artists and their clients, key segments of the text are devoted to detailing how tattoos are sought out as a form of personal expression. Attention is given to how tattooing corresponds with the ongoing 'psychogenic' development of individuals, and how the experience of being tattooed is grounded in fundamentally interdependent, highly rationalized, and deeply affective structures of interpretation. Cultivating an analysis of tattoos as concurrent markers of independence (qua individuality) and interdependence (qua group affiliation), I centre my focus on the processes through which tattoos become reflective of specific personality structures toward, and cultural sensibilities about, the body and its modification.

What is offered in this book is, then, a theoretical/empirical analysis of Canadians' tattooing habits. For readers new to this subject (tattooing and/or sociology!) this text describes and analyses some of the most pervasive trends in contemporary Canadian tattooing from a 'figurational' perspective. For those possessing a familiarity with tattooing, this book is intended to encourage you to reflect upon your own tattooing experiences, and those of others around you – to see yourself linked to other enthusiasts who share your penchant for the practice. In either case, my aim is to underline how tattooing body projects are deeply social, personal, and meaningful communicative acts. In what follows in this chapter, some attention is given to how figurational sociology helps shed light on tattooing body projects, and to where this book fits into our understanding of bodies and their modification.

What Is Figurational Sociology?

The principles of figurational sociology were initially assembled through the works of Norbert Elias. A German-born Jewish sociologist who spent portions of his life in Germany, England, Ghana, and the Netherlands, Elias produced a series of masterfully written and poignant sociological texts, including *What Is Sociology?* (1978), *The Court Society* (1983), *Involvement and Detachment* (1987), *The Society of Individuals* (1991a), *The Symbol Theory* (1991b), *The Civilizing Process* (1994), and *The Germans* (1996). Through these works and others, Elias outlined a detailed program for studying how social 'figurations' (his replacement term for the word 'society') transform over time, and how life is experienced through interdependent social relationships. Eschewing the idea that individuals could be studied as separate, isolated entities, Elias spent decades arguing that social life is characteristically *interdependent* by nature. His axial concept of the social figuration points to how individual behaviours are accurately conceptualized as an outcome of, and process in, collective social activities spanning long-term historical processes.

A figuration, then, is a complex web of social relationships based on individual and group interdependencies – such as a family, a school, a workplace, a community, an economy, or a political sphere (Elias 1994, 208). In the sociological literature, such theorizing shows considerable similarities to the attempts to bridge the agency/structure dichotomy by the analysis of multiplex networks and network densities (Friday and Hague 1976; Krohn 1986; Laumann 1976). This line of thinking also shows considerable similarity to Simmel's (1964) understanding of social life as a 'web of organic and rational group affiliations.' Like Simmel, Elias suggested that individuals are best understood in mutual (but not necessarily equal) relationships (Elias 1978, 1991a, 1994). In studying humans in the mutually related and mutually oriented sense, he moved away from strict analyses of the situated actor or all-encompassing social structures, and toward individuals in a plural rather than singular sense:

> The network of interdependencies among human beings is what binds them together. Such interdependencies are the nexus of what is here called the figuration, a structure of mutually-oriented and dependent people. Since people are more or less dependent on each other, first by nature and then by social learning, through education, socialization, and socially generated reciprocal needs, they exist, one might venture to say, only as pluralities, only in figurations. (Elias 1994, 214)

Given these conceptualizations of human group life, figurational sociologists contend that social researchers benefit by abandoning their mainstay conceptualizations of 'society' in favour of the study of interdependent human agents (Elias 1991a, 1994; Dunning 1999; Maguire 1993, 1999; Sheard 1999). To this end, Elias advocated what may loosely be compared to Kasarda and Janowitz's notion of a 'systemic model' of societies in which 'a community is viewed as a complex system of friendship and kinship networks and formal and informal social associational ties rooted in family life and ongoing socialization processes' (1974, 329). Elias was not the first theorist to use the term or concept of interdependence; however, he provides the most sustained and empirically based arguments on the importance of human interdependencies by placing the concept at the centre of his theory rather than treating it as a conceptual footnote.

Elias is perhaps best known for his exposition of Western 'civilising processes' (Elias 1994, 1996). Although often misunderstood by social researchers as a theory of progressive or evolutionary social development (see Salumets 2001; van Krieken 1998), Elias's research on civilizing processes is centrally concerned with how a series of shifts in social interdependencies (spanning several centuries) has had a cumulative impact on social behaviours and individual personalities – such that social life has become more safe, rationalized, status-oriented, and predictable, while individual behaviours are more linked to the activities of others, responsive to others' needs, sensitive to socially aroused feelings of shame and guilt, and reflective of a common repugnance toward outwardly uncontrolled affect. Indeed, much of figurational sociology is associated with Elias's description of how life in Western cultures like those of England, France, and Germany became highly controlled (socially, physically, and emotionally) as relationship chains between individuals lengthened and diversified (Elias 1978, 1991a, 1994). Rather interestingly, through the inspection of how social life changes as interdependencies between groups are altered, Elias maintained a key focus on how the body became targeted as a locus of social control. For figurational sociologists like Elias, much can be learned about the form and content of a historical era by examining the prevailing body norms (including body-modification norms) and practices within a given figuration of actors.

Elias's emphasis on long-term civilizing processes lead to his extended exposition on the 'sociogenesis' of Western cultures. In order to make analytical sense out of any contemporary social behaviour (like tattooing), figurational sociologists commence by inspecting how such behaviours are formed, transformed, and understood over time, mainly as a result of shifting social interdependencies between people (Mennell

1992; Salumets 2001). Quite simply, we can only understand a given social behaviour if it is contextually embedded within long-term social processes. For example, we may fully grasp the factors leading to the commericalization of modern sport if we first appreciate the social relationships that first helped to produce organized sport, along with the longer-term processes through which sport became institutionalized, rationalized, taught, and watched as a 'professional' activity (Dunning 1999; Maguire 1999). In a similar way, I argue in this book that any attempt to interpret cultural interests in tattooing must begin by reviewing the history of tattooing on this continent, as well as the current sociogenic changes that are influencing how we view our bodies and the act of tattooing.

Accompanying the study of sociogenic change is the examination of psychogenesis – in plain terms, the development of personality structures within specific figurations (Elias 1991a, 1996). A dominant principle in figurational explanations of social behaviour is a belief that individual/collective personality structures are largely products of the social environment. Through the process of socialization, individuals come to rely less heavily on biological impulses or emotions in guiding their actions, and more on those lessons about behaviour acquired in social figurations. Of course, these lessons are specific to cultural groups and are reflective of sociogenic trends over long-term historical periods. Through Elias's analysis of the body (1994) as a text of civilization, he underscores how changes in personal orientations toward the body and its display, for example, are products of changing social interdependencies between people (see also Kemple 2001). To grasp how individuals' thoughts, feelings, and actions (including body-modification attitudes and habits) come to be formed, we must first recognize how the ongoing psychogenic development of individuals is largely influenced by social forces.

Through his study of psychogenesis in the civilizing process, Elias (1983, 1994, 1996) described such personality structures as socially learned 'second natures' or *habituses*, and suggested that through ongoing socialization processes individuals learn seemingly taken-for-granted ways (i.e., habits) of experiencing, utilizing, and interpreting their bodies. Elias's exposition (1994, 1996) on the habitus formation process outlines how one's conceptions of corporeality are incorporated into everyday physical habits such as wearing clothing, eating behaviours, sexual displays, and the expression of emotion. In the study of tattooing, much can be learned about how tattooing behaviours, and preferences for tattoos, are formed as part of the habitus – a socially learned second nature. Here, we must search to uncover how tattoos become socially/individually meaningful for people, and how involvement in tattooing becomes second nature. While the taste for tattoos has been described as an 'addiction' by some (Vail 1999), it is probably more accurate to conceive of one's preferences for tattoos and their display as forming ongoing and reflexive social processes that are evident in everyday physical activity – just as brushing one's teeth, wearing shoes, or exercizing figures into the daily regimen as learned habits.

Yet a critical point that Elias made is that in studying the development of interdependent human existence, sociologists have typically jettisoned the need to inspect psychological development within specific figurations (1994, xiii). To remedy this tendency, Elias questioned how individuals' changing locations, statuses, and roles in a figuration, or what I refer to in this book as degree of *figurational embeddedness*, has an influence on the construction of their personality structures:

> The web of social relations in which the individual lives during his more impressionable phase, during childhood and youth, imprints itself upon his unfolding personality where it has its counterpart in the relationship between his controlling agencies, super-ego and ego, and his libidinal impulses. The resulting balance between controlling agencies and drives on a variety of levels determines how an individual person steers himself in his relations with others; it determines that which we call, according to taste, habits, complexes, or personality structure. (ibid., 454–5)

Elias argued that with the study of sociogenesis must come the study of psychogenesis, and discussed this connection throughout his work as 'the hinge' (1991a, 182). The result is a more complex understanding of how social, cultural, and biological factors interweave:

> The structures of the human psyche, the structures of human society and the structures of human history are indissolubly complementary, and can only be studied in conjunction with each other. They do not exist and move in reality with the degree of isolation assumed by current research. They form, with other structures, the subject matter of a single human science. (ibid., 36)

For Elias, while individuals are born with certain innate drives and impulses (such as anger, aggression, fear, sexual desire, and excitement) these drives are largely influenced over the life course by an actor's social position and biography in a figuration (Elias 1994). Unlike other sociological theorists who tend to portray these biological tendencies as completely muted or constant after a certain point in the life course (e.g., Gottfredson and Hirschi 1990), Elias argued – much like Sampson and Laub (1993, 2001) – that both unlearned and learned personality characteristics are *mouldable*. Therefore, we must look to the chains of interdependency bonding individuals together in social figurations (e.g., family, school, peers, leisure, and work relations) and the antici-pated or unanticipated impact of these chains on personality structures throughout life. Van Krieken captures the importance of simultaneously studying interdependency, figurations, sociogenesis, and psychogenesis quite well:

> The structure of human life could only be understood if human beings were conceptualized as interdependent rather than autonomous, compris-ing what [Elias] calls figurations rather than social systems or structures, and as characterized by socially specific forms of habitus, or personality-structure. He emphasized seeing human beings in the plural rather than the singular, as part of collectivities, of groups and networks, and stressed that their very identity as unique individuals only existed within and through those networks of figurations. (1998, 55)

What is especially pertinent in the examination of contemporary tattoo-ing practices in Canada is how 'pro-tattooing' ideologies are creeping into our collective habituses, and how broad social changes in the rela-tionships between people are leading us to become more accepting of (and fascinated with) tattooing body projects.

For some reason or other, figurational sociology has received only marginal attention in North American sociological research. While the central tenets of figurational sociology have been rigorously applied in the sociology of sport (Dunning 1999), and in British, German, French, and Dutch research on nation states (Blomert 2001), few soci-ologists in Canada have explored figurational sociology as a viable the-oretical framework. Even fewer have tapped into figurational sociology to inspect body-modification practices. This has been, in my opinion, one of the largest oversights in sociological research on the modified body. By connecting some of the more salient principles of figura-tional sociology with dominant theoretical understandings of the body, a powerful series of concepts can be stockpiled – each providing considerable insight as to how Canadians' tattooing practices may be decoded.

Bodies, Body Modification, and 'Other' Theories

While the tenets of figurational sociology provide a sound theoretical framework for structuring the analysis of contemporary tattooing practices, other sociological theories can be drawn upon for their key conceptual ideas about body modification. Each teaches us something about how body modification practices are socially meaningful, and why individuals develop specific body-modification habits.

Almost two decades have passed since Bryan Turner's seminal work, *The Body and Society* (1984), helped rejuvenate an interest in corporeality within sociology. Following Turner's lead, social theorists are now considerably more aware of the myriad ways bodies are constructed, modified, and understood by people (Harvey 1989; Strinati 1995; Vigarello 1995). Although sociological concerns with corporeality are multi-layered, it appears the general 'turn to' bodies in theory and research has been fuelled by two major trends.

First, the contemporary explosion of studies about body modification has been inspired by the ascendance and widespread exploration of several burgeoning streams of theory. While authors may debate the specific aetiology underlying the growth in research on bodies, feminist theories (Bartky 1988; Bordo and Jaggar 1989; Butler 1990, 1993; MacKinnon 1987; Martin 1994; Sedgwick 1994), Foucauldian post-structuralism (1977, 1979, 1980, 1987), postmodernism (Baudrillard 1983, 1988; Derrida 1976; Lyotard 1986), phenomenology (Kleinman 1979; Merleau-Ponty 1962), and dramaturgy (Goffman 1959, 1963, 1967) are enduring influences. By emphasizing different foci of inquiry and promoting divergent interpretations of bodies, these theoretical perspectives collectively advocate an exigency for studying the body as a *text of culture* – that is, how bodily shape, size, appearance, movement, and experience influence and are influenced by one's interaction with others in a particular culture (Bordo 1989, 14).

Second, the growing sociological interest in bodies is also driven by a recognition that long-term, and ongoing, sociogenic transformations in Western societies have fostered new sensibilities about what constitutes normative or otherwise appropriate bodily construction and display. Giddens (1991), for example, suggested there is escalating disbelief in dominant cultural meta-narratives that establish universal guidelines for understanding the nature of bodies (e.g., religious, moral, medical-scientific). Individuals are now more reflexive and simultaneously uncertain about how their bodies can be used as a means of personal representation.

Expanding upon this idea, Maguire (1999) argued that the cross-cultural exchange intrinsic in globalization processes effectively erodes barriers between cultures. As a result, traditional uses and understandings of the body in Western cultures are now widely questioned and uncertainties about the body exacerbated. Similarly, Beck (1991) contended that the post/high-modern epoch is characteristically an era of risk in which individuals are more conscious of the multiplying social (e.g., discrimination, poverty, crime) and biological (e.g., AIDS, pollution) perils that highlight a necessity for meticulous bodily monitoring, maintenance, and defence. In a related way, Featherstone (1991) noted how the heightened attention granted to bodies both inside and outside the academy is reflective of cultural constructions of bodies as sites of commodity consumption. As bodies can be altered, modified, or restructured with the aid of a wide range of commercial products, individuals are able to explore a multitude of ways for manipulating their bodies and literally repackaging their selves (Falk 1994).

Yet as researchers devoted to the study of body modification generally concur (see Eichberg 1998; Williams and Bendelow 1998), many sociologists in the first two-thirds of the twentieth century ignored the imperative of positioning bodies centrally in sociological theory, in favour of a Cartesian separation between the mind and the body (e.g., Homans 1961; Mills 1956; Parsons 1937). With some notable exceptions (e.g., Goffman 1959, 1963; Simmel 1957, 1971; Spencer 1908), bodies vanished in mainstream sociological theory until the late 1970s. While Elias continued to position the body as a central subject of sociological investigation during this period, other sociologists were ignoring the centrality of the flesh. Apparently transcending the need for studying how corporeality ties into socio-logic, sociologists pursued theoretical and empirical analyses of either the *self* (and self-consciousness) or *social structures*. In an extension of the project of Enlightenment philosophers, individuals were considered as minded beings with innate capabilities for reason, rationality, self-reflection, and foresight, with the sociological significance of embodiment eschewed. Elias (1991a, 1994) referred to this trend as the predominance of the *homo clausus* ('closed personality') perspective in sociological theory, in which the mind and the self are ritually separated – the body viewed simply as an empty vessel or container for the all-important self.

The resurgence in bodies (and their modification) as subjects of theory and research in the past two decades, however, has transformed our sociological appreciation of corporeality. In this process, new 'lines of sight' for interpreting body projects have been offered. Importantly, then, in an era when tattooing is booming, theoretical understandings of bodies are equally proliferating. Therefore, one would be more than remiss to ignore the wealth of insight on body projects provided by sociologists of the body in an examination of tattooing. Yet scarce attention has been given to theories of the body, or empirical research on embodied experience, in existing research on tattooing. In piecing together a figurational explanation of tattooing in the current era, I borrow heavily from extant research on the body as a means of 'fleshing out' a more rounded conceptual understanding of the tattooing process.

Rekindling a Sociological Interest in Bodies

In any review of the literatures on body projects, several of the sociological sub-disciplines should be lauded as pioneers in the study of how we actively modify our bodies. To be sure, they offer individuals interested in the subject of tattooing (including figurational sociologists) much critical insight about body-modification processes. Although body modification is now investigated from within a variety of sub-fields within sociology, research in the areas of health and illness, sport, and gender is especially noteworthy. Perhaps most significantly, these 'bodies' of research point to a series of ongoing sociogenic trends that influence how we view body-modification processes. These trends become particularly relevant in the process of understanding why so many Canadians are now turning to tattooing as a form of self-expression.

In a diverse collection of substantive research, work in the sociology of health and illness elicits a recognition of the voluntary (e.g., dieting, exercizing, or preventative therapies) and involuntary (e.g., through surgeries and in response to disease and decay) manners by which bodies are modified. Homing in on the authority over bodies and their modification assumed by members of the medical/health care industries, Freund and McGuire (1999) offer a general critique of the 'medicalisation of everyday life' and of the hegemony that doctors and other medical experts wield in constructing and promoting understandings of bodies. Even more generally, sociologists of health and illness have explained North Americans' escalating concern with bodies by pointing out that our society is ageing, and thus is more attuned to corporeal issues. In seeking to gain greater biological control over the body, we invent new devices and medical technologies to sustain or improve impaired bodies (Williams and Bendelow 1998).

North Americans may now choose from a proverbial shopping list of implants, prostheses, vitamin supplements, exercise regimens, and apparatuses/tools to limit the toll taken on the body by natural break-down. As a result, our ability to fix bodily dysfunction (simply *postponing* the effects of ageing) is greater than in any other historical period. Being, and especially looking, healthy is an option and expectation for most members of society as the technology and services exist to sustain the biological integrity of our bodies (White, Young, and Gillett 1995). In this way, body-modification practices are engrained in our collective habituses, and undertaken as habitual activity. Not only do medical advancements alter how we experience corporeality, they buttress exist-ing medical discourses that construe bodies as physical entities to be probed, mapped, invaded, dissected, modified, and cloned (Critical Art Ensemble 1998; Kroker and Kroker 1987; Shogan 1999). In this process, the body becomes more aptly regarded as a series of interchangeable parts rather than a unified entity – or in any sense composite elements of a self.

In ways closely linked to research on the replaceability of body parts, sociologists of health and illness also inspect the ways in which bodies are modified in preventative defence of or response to traumatic ill-nesses such as AIDS, cancer, heart disease, or other chronic physical pathologies (Aggleton, Hart, and Davies 1989; Crawford 1994; Juengst and Koenig 1994). Here, the study of body modification revolves around the methods (e.g., biological, medical-technological, or inter-personal) that people adopt in reclaiming traumatized bodies. For example, Frank (1991b) and Sontag (1991) both advocated the study of patients' narratives about their experiences with illness as part of devel-oping theory about the relationships between bodies, selves, societal institutions, and medical discourses. This research equally points to the ways in which body modification becomes a part of one's second nature, a learned response to illness and a tactic for recovering (physically and socially) a damaged body.

In building upon themes proffered in the sociology of health and ill-ness, sociologists of sport strive to discern how 'athletically modified' bodies are inextricably connected to identities. Considering issues in hyper-muscularity in sport (Klein 1993), gay bodies in sport (Pronger 1990), gendered bodies in sport (Dworkin and Wachs 1998; Hargreaves 1986; Lenskyj 1986; Messner 1992; Young 1997), technology and sporting bodies (Blake 1997; Brohm 1978; Cole 1998; Hoberman 1992; Rintala 1995), or the release of emotions through sport (Elias and Dunning 1986; Maguire 1993), sociologists of sport have accepted a mandate to study how athletic performance is framed by (and itself frames) broader cultural constructions of the body. Employing a variety of theories and covering a multitude of substantive areas, sport-related research challenges those inspecting the sociological relevance of corporeality to venture beyond a mere spectatorship of sporting bodies (Hall 1996). Research shows that just as the meaning of sport in our society is disputed, athletes' experiences with body modification in sport are equally subject to situated definition and interpretation.

One of the most illustrative lines of inquiry explores how athletes learn to define and collectively articulate bodily pain and injury (White and Young 1999). Expanding upon the literature in the sociology of health/illness that analyses the sociality of corporeal injury and technologies of physiological recovery, sociologists of sport delve into an aspect of life typically shunned or silently managed. The sociology of sport teaches that the injured body is as damaged socially as it is physically scarred, bruised, or broken. As athletes' identities (and material livelihoods) are heavily tied to bodily performance *and* appearance, a disabled athletic body is an outward signifier of a discredited self (Burstyn 1999). Sociologists of sport typically contend that the consideration of how physical capabilities/limitations are socially constructed and understood is central in developing embodied sociological theory. Furthermore, in linking research in the sociology of sport to the study of tattooing, such understandings of the body clearly point to the primacy of the marked body in situated social spheres, and indicate how the outwardly marred flesh carries specific meanings (enabling or stigmatizing) in such contexts.

Perhaps the most common field within which the study of body projects has prospered, the sociology of gender is built upon a foundation of embodied theories and concepts. Born out of debates concerning naturalism and gender – or, the study of how socially experienced differences between the sexes are constructed as natural derivatives of biological differences – feminist deliberations on how bodies are socially defined through outward markers of masculinity and femininity have led to a re-evaluation of how cultural discourses shape body habits. Feminist research underscores how women's bodies are texts upon which cultural codes of femininity are produced and contested, as female body projects involve either the ongoing maintenance of hegemonic ideology about femininity or the conscious attempt to subvert patriarchal ideology through bodily resistance – or both (Ollenberger and Moore 1992; Scott and Morgan 1993; Wolf 1990).

Feminist research on the social construction of bodies adds much to our understanding of how daily body habits are replete with cultural norms. Discussing the processes by which culture is inscribed upon or performed through the body in everyday practice and movement – what de Certeau (1984) referred to as the act of 'intextuation' – feminist researchers articulate how patriarchal standards of beauty and sexuality are imprinted on women's bodies as a means of social control (Davis 1994, 1997b; Haug 1987; Sanford 1992). Drawing heavily (and some-times almost exclusively) upon the works of Foucault (1977, 1979), fem-inist researchers expose how masculine authority in Western cultures is partly maintained through the active biological (i.e., medical) and social (i.e., norms, values, beliefs) control of women's bodies (Cole 1993; Deveaux 1994; Duncan 1994; Eskes et al. 1998; Lenskyj 1994; Segal 1994). Quite simply, the female body is socially constructed, moni-tored, regulated, and maintained according to dominant notions of femininity. Organized around unattainable images and styles of respect-able yet sexually desirable femininity, traditional body codes promulgate the idea that feminine bodies are both passive and powerless: 'It is no coincidence that this sexual ideal (of the slim, soft, innocent body) is an image which connotes powerlessness. Admittedly, the actual ideal is not of a demure, classically "feminine" girl per se, but a vigorous and imma-ture adolescent ... [I]t is not a shape which suggests power' (Coward 1985, 41).

A central theme in the feminist literature is, then, the indomitable relationship between bodies and social structures of power/authority. Feminist and pro-feminist researchers insist that gender is a key (and perhaps the principal) component in shaping one's body-modification habits over time, and that the cultivation of such habits reproduces rela-tions of power in a society. Feminist authors such as Bordo (1989) have maintained that culturally accepted women's body projects (such as breast augmentation or excessive dieting) are best viewed as exagger-ated or caricatured expressions of dominant ideals of the female body, since these body projects express traditional images of the female body and existing relations of power in excess.

However, feminist researchers also note that body projects may be carefully orchestrated by women to subvert dominant gender codes. While feminist scholars remain attentive to, and unequivocally captious of, body projects that reaffirm and reproduce hegemonic masculine codes of traditional femininity (i.e., docile, subordinate, yet hyper-sexual), the study of body projects that undermine dominant cultural ideologies is now more common. For example, Miller and Penz (1991) suggested that the 'unnatural' strength cultivated by women through bodybuilding breeds both physical and social power, ultimately challenging masculine hegemony. Through the study of radical forms of cosmetic manipulation, Davis (1994, 1997a) illustrated how women may contest figurational codes of feminine beauty by engaging in certain forms of dramatic plastic surgery. These theatrical body modifications are vulgar or grotesque when compared to conventional images of the beautiful female body. For some women, modifying the body in these ways creates an avenue of self-exploration and personal emancipation.

In the rare analyses of women's participation in tattooing, authors such as Sanders (1991), Wroblewski (1992), Mifflin (1997), and De-Mello (2000) have stated that tattooing, branding, and scarification body projects (typically markers of hyper-masculinity) confront 'hegemonic masculine' (Donaldson 1993) constructions of the feminine body. Pitts (1998) has suggested that, for many women, radically or subversively modifying the body becomes a vehicle of liberation in the process of reconstructing one's self-identity. Described as a 'liminal rite of passage' (ibid., 73), participating in non-normative body projects like branding or piercing signifies the movement from a former powerless self (regulated and controlled by men) to an empowered self (liberated through profane body practices). In Cohen's terms (1972), women may employ tattooing, piercing, or branding in the process of 'winning space' in a culture.

Complementing research on the social construction of femininity, empirical investigations of how body projects are employed as a method of exploring masculinities are steadily increasing in number (Connell 1995; Edward 1997; Hearn and Morgan 1990; Johnson and Meinhof 1997; Kimbrell 1995; Kimmel and Messner 1992; Scott and Morgan 1993). This movement toward acknowledging masculinity in its plurality has been somewhat validated by the creation of a journal devoted to the subject (*Men and Masculinities*). Advocating research on a variety of masculinities, queer theory has repositioned the study of male bodies by focusing on how dominant figurational constructions of masculinity tend to marginalize certain types, forms, or expressions of the male body (Pronger 1990). In particular, gay male bodies are culturally and institutionally subordinated in relation to heterosexual constructions of gay bodies. In this respect – as evidenced in research in the sociology of sport focusing on the construction of masculinity in sport cultures – gay bodies are appropriately viewed as cultural texts upon which codes of acceptable masculinity are produced, reproduced, negotiated, and contested (Morgan 1993). For others, particularly those criticizing the tendency to conflate the sociology of gender with women's studies, analyses of masculine bodies reveal the limitations and constraints (preventing the outward display of emotion and feeling, bodily experimentation, physical/affective relationships with other men) imposed by dominant cultural constructions of masculinity upheld by both men and women.

These are only several of the main theoretical, conceptual, and substantive themes related to body modification (e.g., body projects, bodies as social texts, culture/identity/body links, intextuation, authority/power/discourse) generated by existing research. In this study of tattooing, I recognize the direction provided by other sociologists as a theoretical and conceptual terrain upon which a study of body modification seen through a figurational perspective may be mapped. I consider others' research on body projects a springboard for formulating figurational questions relating to mainstream or non-mainstream forms of body modification like tattooing. These questions would include:

- How, why, and by whom are particular forms of body modification promoted as normative or non-normative?
- How, when, and by whom are body-modification practices constructed and/or interpreted as acts of cultural reproduction or resistance?
- How do one's body-modification practices relate to social position (i.e., gender, class, socio-economic status, religion, sexual orientation, ethnicity)?
- How, and when, is body modification linked to the (re)construction of identity; and is body modification central in cultivating collective identities?
- How are intersubjective understandings of bodies and body modification achieved?
- How do cultural and/or individual sensibilities toward body modification develop over time?

Taken separately and together, each of the sociological sub-disciplines noted above offers rudimentary answers to these questions (based on varying theoretical lines, and substantive foci, of inquiry). While the above questions pertain directly to my sociological interest in tattooing, a relatively untapped theoretical framework, figurational sociology, is employed in this book to recast and (re)address each in a slightly different manner. As an approach that champions theoretical integration, development, and synthesis, I argue that figurational sociology engenders considerable understanding of contemporary tattooing practices in Canada.

Admittedly, then, one of the primary goals of my investigation of tattooing is to encourage sociologists to press actively for theoretical innovation in and integration of research on all body-modification practices. However, it would be misleading to imply that my concern for theoretical and substantive integration in research on the body is the first of its kind. As a means of calling attention to the sociological relevance of bodies, integrating existing work on bodies, and summarizing main theoretical issues germane to the sociological study of corporeality, researchers including Turner (1984) and Frank (1990, 1991a) developed analytical templates for conceptualizing corporeal experience. While an extended discussion of the respective natures, thrusts, and merits of each typology might prove worthwhile, yet another examination of each typology would be needlessly digressive (see Maguire 1993). At this stage of research on forms of body modification like tattooing, it suffices to say that the project I outline in this book follows in the well-established tradition of theoretical integration.

Modifying Research on Tattooed Bodies

Through this introduction to the subject of body modification, I have deliberately selected, and judiciously ignored, some of the more central theoretical arguments and concepts applicable to any study of body modification. At best, I view existing research as a toolbox of theories, concepts, and lines of inquiry from which researchers devoted to the study of corporeality may construct analyses of body modification. When existing lines of inquiry are conjoined with some of the orienting principles of figurational sociology, we are provided with a treasure trove of information to be used in making sense out of contemporary tattooing habits. At worst, however, it seems that we have come to a cross-roads in theory and research on bodies. If one examines the analyses of body modification produced in the past decade, it is evident not only that *empirically based* research efforts on the body are ironically waning in number, but that sociologists have not held fast to the principles of testing, amending, or substantiating theories against empirical data. Quite simply, the conceptual tools we use to construct theories and interpretations of bodies are dwindling in number.

From the outset, the sociological portrait I present of tattooing in this text is shaped by my own sociological (and personal) interest in the practice, and by a deeply committed belief in the importance of exploring alternative theoretical lines of inquiry in order to inspect tattooing *sociologically*. One only needs to visit a shopping centre, church, or public park to locate hordes of tattoo enthusiasts. Since the early 1990s, tattooing has blossomed as a popular body project, ascending from being an esoteric cultural practice of marginal subcultures to one actively adopted by individuals from a melange of social backgrounds. While it would be careless to dismiss the long-standing association between tattoos and deviance in Canada, Canadians' attitudes toward tattooing are indisputably in flux. At the forefront of this study of tattooing is a recognition of the need to study such changing constructions and interpretations of tattooing, and an underlying concern to understand why Canadians are now participating in tattooing in unprecedented numbers.

To advance our collective understanding of Canadians' tattooing habits, we should first cull and integrate several important concepts from the sociological literature on body modification. Salient in the literature on corporeal alteration – irrespective of the theoretical stance adopted or substantive focus of investigation – is an awareness of the body as a *text of culture*. Along with the study of habituses, I take this to be one of the most important sociological revelations about (tattooed) bodies. Without a keen appreciation of cultural/bodily inscription processes, sociological investigations of body projects like tattooing commence on the wrong foot. To ignore that culture is literally written (or in the case of tattooing, drawn) on bodies would be irresponsible sociology. Too often do researchers focus on the textual nature of the body (i.e., as a communicative, de-centred, and commodified signifier) without attending to people's lived (i.e., interactive) experiences with corporeality. Semiotic analyses and textual deconstructions of bodies (Barthes 1972, 1975; de Saussure 1960; Lacan 1977; Lyotard 1986) have replaced sustained empirical analyses of people's experiences with their bodies. Unfortunately, through these readings of bodies, researchers' political allegiances, creative methods of analysis or narrative representation, and unwavering adherence to specific theoretical positions mystify and cloud lived experiences with the flesh.

We should also applaud researchers who locate current sociological analyses in *historical contexts*. Perhaps as a consequence of heightened reflection about culture at the new century's onset, postmodernist and post-structuralist arguments about the collapse of the time-space continuum (Borgman 1992; Dunn 1998; Strinati 1995), or the rising popularity of Foucault's genealogical method (Andrews 1993), contemporary sociological investigations reveal a revitalized concern for situating social processes historically. With good reason, figurational sociologists principally examine how social phenomena develop over long periods of time, and stress how interaction, cultural ideologies, and social organization are best understood in historical moments.

Equally, the devotion to body modification as a process of *personal identity construction* is another foundational pillar upon which research efforts on body projects should be structured. Given the litany of techniques of body modification available, we need to question when and why individuals select to alter their corporeality in the process of self-creation, redefinition, and representation. Using the body to signify and perform identity is a cornerstone activity in the social-communication process, and such a recognition is perhaps *the* point of departure in this current examination of tattooing. However, I am puzzled by sociologists' commitment to the analysis of body modification as a solely independent act, that is, a private search for individual identity (Featherstone 2000). Treating the self as a free-floating, unanchored, isolated, and extremely temporary phenomenon, their focus is directed to the ways in which body modification symbolizes intentional dislocation from others and a voyage to find one's 'real' or 'authentic' self (Balsamo 1996). This is one of the most theoretically misleading and empirically unreflective propositions replicating itself throughout current research on body modification.

Thanks to more recent postmodernist theorizing, individuals are encountered in research as such – *persons devoid of relationships of interdependency*, who seemingly exist outside of any web or chain of social networks. Individuality is conceptualized vis-à-vis body modification as a process of liberation from these networks of interdependency, which is only realized when an actor asserts his or her agency through body modification. Thus, individuality is synonymous with isolation and freedom from collectively held cultural norms, values, and beliefs. Body-modification projects such as tattooing are viewed as sources of identity (i.e., individuality) construction *because* they assert one's intention to be different and independent, or because they are conducted for deeply personalized and highly private reasons.

While the search for individuality through body modification should figure prominently into analyses of tattooing in Canada, the subject of contention I present here is the notion of achieving individuality through body modification outside of the group or collective context. Elias (1991a, 1994) staunchly argued that any definition of individuality, and the analysis of how individuality is experienced, that is dissected from broader figurations of interdependency denies that individuality is, and can, only be achieved within a group context. *Analytically removing the individual from the webs of interdependency within which he or she lives prevents us from grasping how individuality is achieved and understood by actors involved in interaction and self-representation.* Along these lines and others, the sociological understanding of tattooing remains in its infancy. The terrain of tattooing is, rather, open to be travelled across by researchers who are ardent about empirically investigating body-modification practices and who share an intent of generating historically grounded, theoretically integrated, and wholeheartedly sociological accounts of the tattooing process. In what follows, I offer but one sociological account of contemporary tattooing based on my personal (and sociological!) involvement in tattooing since the mid-1990s.

CHAPTER TWO

Tattoo and Sociogenesis

Tattooing has neither a long nor a storied past as a subject of sociological investigation, despite the fact that it has been practised in North America for generations. Yet predominant in most social, historical, and cultural accounts of tattooing is an association between the practice and social deviance. A cultural stereotype has long held that tattoos are marks of shame worn only by outlaws, misfits, or those fallen from social grace. According to historically dominant perceptions of the practice, wilfully marking the body with tattoos is the embodiment of a person's inability to conform with existing social norms, values, and beliefs. Consider the words of Lombroso-Ferrero: 'In modern times this custom [tattooing] has fallen into disuse among the higher classes and only exists among sailors, soldiers, peasants, and workmen. Although not exclusively confined to criminals, tattooing is practised by them to a far larger extent than by normal persons ... In a great many cases, the designs reveal violence of character and a desire for revenge' (1972, 46–7). Thus, the limited sociological analyses of tattooing have viewed the practice from a narrow viewpoint.

While the argument remains credible that in Canada and other Western societies tattoos, deviant images, and social stigma tend to go hand in hand, this proposition often limits the sociological analysis of tattooing as a powerful form of human expression (Atkinson and Young 2001; DeMello 2000; Friedman 1996; Gallick 1996). Debates about the changing status of tattoos have become common as tattooing and other more radical forms of permanent body modification have become clearly in vogue. While the image of deviance signified by tattoos continues to exist in North America, we must also recognize that tattoos are now considerably more open to interpretation and subject to situated definition.

Of central importance is how seemingly competing cultural definitions of tattoos transform over time. Thus, we must begin with a very simple recognition that tattoos are pregnant with a multitude of social constructions in any historical era. We should equally note that cultural conceptualizations of and personal experiences with tattoos are, however, largely influenced by socially pervasive constructions of normative body use and display in specific historical periods. Therefore, in deciphering how sensibilities about tattooing progress over time, we need to examine the conditions under which culture-specific prohibitions against body experimentation are relaxed or reinforced. Those investigating the sociological significance of tattooing have not sufficiently traced the development of cultural attitudes about tattooing over time, and as a result, our knowledge about the practice is needlessly fragmented and underdeveloped.

Equally important is a recognition that the historically pervasive stigma attached to tattooing in North America is an unintended consequence of certain nefarious subcultures' enchantment with tattooing. In fleshing out an explanation of how North American sensibilities toward indelibly marking bodies with tattoos have evolved over time, it is crucial to identify the unanticipated ways tattoos have been utilized and how motivations underlying such usage are manifest in contemporary tattooing practices. An examination of the history of tattooing on this continent makes it evident that established cultural understandings or 'preferred readings' (Hall 1980) of tattoos have crystallized in reference to the association between tattooing and socially marginal subcultures. In many ways, contemporary interpretations of tattoos (made by enthusiasts and non-enthusiasts alike) derive from historical uses and understandings of tattooing.

In the following, several of the 'historical moments' in North American tattooing are outlined. When we examine the ostensibly dissonant uses and meaning structures given to tattooing over the past one hundred and fifty years, it becomes evident why tattoos are best understood within generational moments. Key to this argument is the notion that dominant social constructions of bodies (and appropriate bodily display) prevalent in particular historical eras affect how and by whom tattooing is utilized. Yet before we may revisit and unpack the sociogenesis of North American tattooing, further development of the concept of the tattooing 'body project' (Shilling 1993) is needed.

Living in S(k)in: The Tattooing Body Project

Central to any body project is the process of physical alteration. Setting aside, for the moment, the need to study the affective and social-psychological experiences involved in modifying the flesh, we must commence by recognizing that body projects transform the corporeal in some manner. Transformation of the body may be achieved in a variety of ways: permanent or non-permanent forms of modification; disguizing or removing elements from the body; hiding parts of the body or embellishing components of the body; or using technology to enhance one's capability for movement or perception. According to the physical invasiveness, purpose, and outward display of the body modification, body projects may be bracketed into four subcategories: camouflaging, extending, adapting, and redesigning.

Camouflaging body projects are orchestrated by individuals as attempts to hide, cover, mask, or aesthetically enhance the biological body. Typical examples of this project would include, for example, applying make-up to the face, adorning the body with clothes or costume, wearing deodorant or perfume, or using mouthwash. Such projects represent cultural understandings about the body as an entity that may be 'cured' of its unsavoury or repulsive biological qualities (e.g., odours) in strategic ways. These projects are predominantly temporary and non-invasive, and usually undertaken on a daily/regular basis. Furthermore, body projects intended to camouflage the body are seen or read by others as an everyday method of presenting favourable images of the self, and typically conform to cultural codes about bodies and norms governing personal representation as a means of communicating a person's commitment to cultural body habits (particularly as they relate to dominant class, gender, and racial/ethnic constructions of bodies). Thus, camouflaging body projects are relatively standard, normative, and common techniques of body manipulation learned in socialization processes (Robinson 1998).

Conceptually similar to the process of camouflaging the body, *extending* body projects are geared toward compensating for or overcoming limitations of the natural (i.e., biological) body. The underlying purpose of the alteration shifts away from corporeal aesthetics to functionality or experimentation (e.g., psycho-tropic drug usage). While a carefully scripted presentation of self, in line with cultural standards about the body, often remains integral in extending body projects, of central importance are the innovative methods people concoct in the

process of enhancing bodily performance with non-invasive technologies (Rintala 1995). For instance, technological apparatuses may be
sought to help manage the physical limitations and social stigma
imposed by disability (e.g., wearing prostheses or contact lenses), may
serve as vehicles for interfacing with other forms of technology in work
or leisure settings (e.g., wearable technology for computers), or may be
routine tools or pieces of equipment essential in specific interactive
activities (e.g., using tennis rackets, running shoes, skis, baseball gloves,
or ice skates in sports contests). In all cases, extending body projects
involve semi- or non-permanent modifications of the physical body, and
are incorporated into one's overall sense of self in varying degrees (i.e.,
a prostheses figuring more prominently in one's self-conceptualization
than a computer mouse used at a workstation).

The third major type, the *adapting* body project, includes more permanent forms of body modification. In these instances of physical
reconstitution, parts of the body are removed or repaired for a host of
aesthetic (e.g., hair removal or weight loss) or medical (e.g., preventative mole removals, lumpectomies, or casts) reasons. The adapting body
project is guided by the overriding goal of physical maintenance –
reducing or eliminating parts of the body in one's daily regimen in com-
pliance with socially diffuse standards of bodily comportment and presentation, or as part of removing noxious conditions or pathologies that
jeopardize personal health and longevity (which may involve single or
multiple procedures). Some of these body projects are publicly displayed in the effort of swaying audience perception of the individual,
while others are anxiously hidden and silently experienced, since they
may invoke unfavourable or otherwise deleterious images of the self
(Frank 1991b). Deeply ingrained in adapting body projects are empha-
ses on the body as a site of personal representation, and the moral
imperative to be, and outwardly appear to be, healthy (White and Young
1997).

Redesigning body projects are the most invasive, dramatic, and least
common body projects. Including the tattooing process, redesign body
projects are those that literally reconstruct the body in lasting ways (e.g.,
contours of the flesh, durability of organs, strength of joints and liga-
ments, shape or integrity of bone structures, and pigmentation of the
skin). Although it would be tempting to describe redesigning body
projects as purely aesthetic forms of physical enhancement (e.g., breast
enlargement, hair transplant, rhinoplasty), they include those that vastly
improve corporeal performance capacities that have been breached by

physical trauma (e.g., a pacemaker, replacement joints, or other surgical implants). While other types of body projects involve foresight, planning, reflexivity, and self-awareness, redesigning body projects generally involve the highest level of commitment (Dull and West 1991; Balsamo 1996). Reaffirming (or sometimes flagrantly challenging) gender, sexuality, class, or ethnic codes, redesigning body projects are hyper-expressions of personal understandings about one's cultural location. In like manner to adapting body projects, redesigning body projects are outwardly displayed according to the (perceived) social reaction elicited in specific contexts of interchange; that is, people are often likely to display a redesigned body in contexts in which they would not be stigmatized or marginalized for their corporeal manipulations (Gillespie 1996).

What unites these categories of body projects is the act of inscribing sets of symbols upon the body that connote interdependency, social position, and personal difference within a figuration. Body projects are fundamentally acts of human interchange; that is, others may be involved directly by providing a body-modification service (e.g., hairstylists, physical trainers, or doctors), and people often participate in body-modification projects collectively (e.g., an exercise class, hair club, or weight-loss group). Moreover, body projects are frequently designed with the explicit purpose of being displayed to others (e.g., make-up, stylish clothing, or breast augmentation), and one 'takes the role of the other' (Mead 1934) in anticipating reaction to personal body-modification practices. To restate arguments made previously, to conceptualize a body project, like Shilling (1993) and others do, as solely a private form of personal representation is as theoretically misleading as it is empirically fallacious. In the process of reconfiguring our sociological understanding of body modification, we must acknowledge the interdependency involved in corporeal alteration.

We also find, quite centrally, the idea that body modification is predominantly learned behaviour. Each type of body project involves the creation, performance, display, and affirmation (or purposeful denial) of dominant cultural habituses, especially since they embody cultural constructions of gender, race, class, and sexuality. Through socialization processes we are exposed to socio-cultural ideas about body modification and use what we have learned from others (in conjunction with our own subjective emotions, thoughts, preferences, personal biographies, and experiences with the flesh) in forming a personal body orientation as part of the habitus. As a complex matrix of understanding, then, those cultural habituses learned through socialization processes are axial for understanding body-modification projects. In this sense, we may witness how culture lives in and is lived through body projects.

Take, for example, the process of cosmetic surgery. Some time ago, I purchased the inaugural edition of an Australian magazine, *The Art of Cosmetic Surgery*. By detailing the endless ways in which we may beautify our bodies through elective surgery – with the aid of plastic surgeons who have come to be viewed as skilled doctors and inspired flesh artists – the magazine brings to the fore the importance of both individuality and cultural conformity in body-modification processes. Plastic surgery is a deeply individualistic act, since it involves the creation of a new and unique look, allowing a person to become physically whoever they want to be in a figuration. Such individual projects are clearly dialogical with dominant cultural definitions of beauty, and to ignore that cultural ideologies are literally purchased and confirmed in the cosmetic-surgery process overlooks much of the sociological significance of the physical act.

There are some stark conceptual contrasts, however, between different types of body projects. First and perhaps most consequentially, some body projects are clearly more culturally normative than others. Body projects that reproduce and conform to existing middle-class standards about the body (again, especially as they apply to cultural constructions of gender, class, and race) are usually viewed as normative. In this respect, body projects that serve no other purpose than to shock audiences through the subversion of dominant cultural ideologies are much more subject to stigmatization (e.g., a man wearing heavy make-up or a dress, someone of white, European descent growing dreadlocks). Extending this idea, body projects underscored by the task of personal improvement and maintenance or role/status acceptance tend to be more culturally normative (Robinson 1998). We should, however, be careful not to assume that the permanence or invasiveness of the body project figures prominently in the degree to which an audience deems a body project deviant. For example, research on cross-dressing body projects indicates precisely the opposite (Garber 1992).

Second, some body projects are designed with the expressed purpose of public display, while others are only divulged to a select few. For instance, camouflaging body projects are specifically orchestrated for public-display purposes, since the goals underlying the projects are cultural conformity and status confirmation (Shilling 1993). On the other hand, body projects that may be reacted to negatively in situated contexts are routinely hidden or concealed. This may occur following medically related redesign body projects (Dutton 1995; Lorde 1985; Taylor 1983), as individuals attempt to hide outward signifiers of bodily breakdown or pathology denoted by remnants of surgical invasion (e.g., scars, colostomy bags, stitches, bruises). Hiding one's corporeal alteration also occurs in cases in which a body project may jeopardize one's social status within a group – as in the case of the post-operative trans-sexual who continues to 'dress like a man' at work to avoid stigmatization and discrimination from workmates.

Third, while all body projects articulate one's participation in a figuration of actors, and are equally elements of one's public identity, some are obviously more integral components of the self than others (Balsamo 1996). Extending body projects, for example, are not regularly incorporated into an individual's overall self/body conceptualization. They may be regarded as personal possessions, considered part of the 'extended self' but not conceived as actual parts of the body (Belk 1988). In their research on athletic shoes, Wilson and Sparks (1996) noted that owning and appropriately wearing certain brands of basketball sneakers within specific Afro-Canadian and African-American youth subcultures carries a degree of social capital within the groups. The shoes become extended elements of the self, as important as what one says and how one acts in front of others.

Criticizing more recent intersections between bodies and technological commodities, Haraway (1991) and Balsamo (1996) were highly sceptical of extending body projects, and highlighted the social ramifications of failing to grasp how corporeality increasingly encounters and interfaces with the mechanical as a hybrid human-machine. Camouflaging and adapting body projects (especially the more culturally routine) tend to be incorporated centrally into one's lasting sense of self (Shilling 1993; Woodward 1997). However, while they are primary in creating and presenting identity, they become quite taken-for-granted projects. One might argue that more radical, permanent, and invasive redesigning body projects have the most profound and deep impact on the self.

In the following section, key moments in the history of North American tattooing are introduced to provide a template for considering manifestations of tattoos and the meaning structures granted to tattooing in the current era. A brief analysis of the history of tattooing will establish a gateway for understanding contemporary tattooing practices. The social relevance of tattooing – as a body project centred on redesigning the body/identity – across several historical epochs is documented here in the process of describing how dominant uses/definitions of tattoos reflect fluctuating cultural body habits and preferences. To this end, the history of tattooing in North America is segmented into six interrelated and unintended moments: the colonist/pioneer era; the circus/carnival era; the working-class era; the rebel era; the new-age era; and the supermarket era.

The Unintended Sociogenesis of North American Tattooing

The history of tattooing in North America is a rich tapestry involving myriad social groups, each having a unique and indelible impact on cultural attitudes toward tattooing. When we examine the sociogenesis of tattooing on this continent, it is evident that current cultural understandings of tattoos have been formed in relation to long-standing stereotypes about tattoo enthusiasts confirmed by deviant social groups in the nineteenth and twentieth centuries, have been influenced by those engaging in 'identity politics' in the past forty years, and are affected by the current renaissance in tattooing practices.

The Colonist/Pioneer Era (1760s-1870s)

Social historians concur that the modern history of tattooing in North America (at least, among white colonizers) finds its roots in European sea travel – such as Captain James Cook's voyages to the South Pacific (Brain 1979; Ebin 1979; Sanders 1989). In the past few years, authors including Caplan (2000), DeMello (2000), and Gilbert (2000) have meticulously drawn together histories of tattooing in the West, and documented the impact of sea travel on the genesis of tattooing among white cultures in North America. Travelling to Polynesia, Micronesia, and Melanesia as colonizers, explorers, and imperial delegates (ca. 1784), Cook and his men encountered Tahitians, Samoans, Hawaiians, and Maori among whom tattooing had been practised for over four thousand years. This was not, however, Europeans' first encounter with tattooing, since they had been previously exposed to tattooed bodies in a number of ways. For example, Roman soldiers referred to Celtic warriors as 'Picts,' in reference to the vast war-inspired tattoos (full- or half-body tattoos done in blue or black 'ink') worn by the Celts. Similarly, Europeans of the 1600s often tattooed their bodies with religious iconography to indicate spiritual affiliation (Gathercole 1988). Furthermore, European seafarers encountered heavily tattooed natives far before Cook's voyages. Columbus wrote extensively about pagan natives adorned with permanent body markings. Still, it was Cook who first documented the pervasiveness of 'tattooing' (a derivation of the Tahitian term *ta-tu* or *tatau*) among South Pacific cultures.

The initial period of contact between non-tattooed European travellers and tribal cultures had profound effects on both the colonizers and the colonized. For European explorers (including those venturing to eastern parts of Canada), the tattooing practices of the tribesmen were raw and primal. Tattooing was a foreign ritual, frightening and profane in the way it transformed the flesh in such a painful manner. The explorers' fascination with tattooing grew to such an extent that by the late 1770s tattooed savages were exported to Europe as living evidence of primitivism in the New World (Caplan 2000; DeMello 2000). Martin Frobisher, among others, had established this tradition in the late sixteenth century. Upon returning from one of his voyages to the Northwest Passage, Frobisher brought a tattooed native woman to London as a spectacle of the wild New World. As Gray wrote: 'This arctic woman, and the succession of tattooed foreign curiosities who followed her to Europe, although a typical, upright member of her own society, represented to Europeans the radical self-expression, physical vanity, and exuberant sexuality they had denied themselves (or pretended to), in the service of their restrictive deity. The tattooed pagan became the wet dream of an overheated imagination' (1994, 88). Following Cook's and Frobisher's voyages, the spectacle of the tattooed primitive became more common as individuals including Prince Jeoly of Meangis and the Tahitians Omai and Tupai were paraded though European court societies, museums, dime stores, and taverns as human oddities ... 'live primitives' contrasting with the decisively continental character of each context. In an era of strict bodily/emotional control, early European sideshows involving tattooed 'wildmen' became a legitimate social outlet for exploring unbridled physicality, exotica, and perversion. While scores of European sailors returned home with Polynesian, Micronesian, and Melanesian tattoos, the European middle and upper classes were increasingly exposed to tattooing. Such body marking stood in dramatic contrast to regimented cultural codes about the body ingrained in European habituses (Elias 1983, 1994, 1996). In many ways, tattooed bodies reaffirmed Europeans' understanding of their own cultural advancement and progress, as the outwardly uncontrolled libidinal bodies of the 'backward' tribal cultures of the world articulated a brutality long overcome in Western cultures (Caplan 2000).

During the same period, European contact had an adverse effect on tribal tattooing practices. DeMello (2000), who has produced one of the most comprehensive analyses of the history of tattooing in Western cultures, described how cross-fertilization between the groups transformed tribal practices in several ways. For instance, by the 1800s tribal tattooing began to include European images such as ships, guns, cannons, and flags. Imagine the astonishment of individuals among the crowds at sideshows in England, France, and Spain who saw natives adorned with European flags, naval vessels, and even portraits of monarchs (Gray 1994; Lautman 1994). As another example, Kaeppler (1988) noted that before European contact Hawaiians used tattoos as a spiritual form of defence, believing the tattoo would protect the wearer from physical harm, much as Borneans believed that tattooing dark lines and geometric patters around one's feet would protect the individual from snakebite (McLaughlin 1973; Lautman 1994). With the introduction of firearms and other weapons of war to Hawaiian and other Pacific cultures, tattoos lost some of their spiritual status and were increasingly worn for decorative purposes.

Perhaps most notably, the Maori tattoo art known as *moko* would be irreparably damaged by European contact. Moko tattoos are facial designs worn by Maori men and women to indicate their lineage, social position, and status within the tribe (Eldridge 1990; Kaeppler 1988). The Maori tattoo is sacred within the culture, prominent as a marker of identity in life and significant in the afterlife as a vehicle for storing one's *tapu*, or spiritual being (DeMello 2000). Following Cook's voyages in the 1770s, Europeans developed an interest in the Maori tattoos to the extent that guns and ammunition were traded for Maori heads. Maoris were subsequently hunted for their moko tattoos and decapitated to provide souvenirs of the New World – an unproblematic matter for Europeans, since the tribal groups were collectively viewed as subhuman (Lautman 1994). Until it was banned in 1831, the trade in Maori heads escalated to the point that Maori men and women refrained from wearing any tattoos in the fear of being killed (Eldridge 1990). It would be almost a century until the Maori began to adorn themselves with the moko once again (see Caplan 2000; Gilbert 2000; and King 1972).

Throughout the first wave of contact with tribal tattooing practices, we might categorize European interest in tribal tattooing as a paradoxical mix of fascination, disgust, irreverence, and wonder. Sailors found tattooing their bodies to be a source of excitement and adventure, a keepsake from interaction with fabled tribes and exotic Others (Caplan

2000; DeMello 2000; Lautman 1994). Elite and popular European social circles equally envisioned tattooing to be an exotic source of entertainment, yet interpreted such exoticism to be spiritually vulgar and culturally uncivilized. Regardless of this paradox, as sailors travelled abroad and returned home with cultural artefacts inscribed upon their bodies, tattoos began sneaking into mainstream European, and eventually North American, figurations.

The Circus/Carnival Era (1880s–1920s)

Toward the end of the nineteenth century, white North Americans shared with Europeans a similar fascination toward and repulsion from tattooed bodies. Largely influenced by European constructions of the tattooed body as a symbol of primitivism, North Americans' early understandings of the tattoo were laden with stereotype, folklore, and racism. Notwithstanding the earlier exposure to tattooing experienced through interaction with native peoples of North America (Light 1972), the European treatment of the tattooed body as a source of entertainment had a noticeable impact on nineteenth-century North America.

At the Centennial Exposition in Philadelphia in 1876, some of the first staged exhibitions of 'primitive peoples' were presented to the public (DeMello 2000). While the rather esoteric tradition of tattooing was already well established among North American navy cultures (learned through exchange with British sailors and tribal cultures around the world), a majority of North Americans had no knowledge of tattooing practices. Living tableaux of Hawaiians, Samoans, and other Polynesian/Melanesian groups were offered in museums and at county fairgrounds in stark juxtaposition with modern life – a life characterized by science, technology, industrialism, urbanism, progress, and conservative moral dictums about the body and its appropriate display. Through the late nineteenth century, these human sideshows grew in popularity, eventually finding a niche on the carnival and midway scene. In 1901, the first 'freak show' involving tattooees at Buffalo's world's fair solidified in the cultural association between tattoos and carnivals in North America (Mifflin 1997).

During this period, carnival owners and sideshow operators mainly used natives (often taken as slaves by explorers and missionaries of the time) in their tattoo attractions. Set upon stages and wrapped in chains and loincloths, these individuals stood as the antithesis of modernity. As part of shows including wild animals and other forms of human exotica (e.g., people with dramatic forms of physical disability), the tattooed primitive represented the savage tribal world. P.T. Barnum, an entrepreneur in the freak-show business, brought one of the most famous of tattoo attractions to North America, Prince Constantine (Mifflin 1997). Reportedly having over three hundred and eighty tattoos, Prince Constantine was a legend of the carnival/dime-museum circuit. Reportedly making close to one hundred dollars per week as a tattooed savage, Constantine reigned as the king of the tattooed freaks and drew the attention of many Westerners, especially navy men and early American tattoo artists (Eldridge 1992, 1993).

In an unplanned development, heavily tattooed navy servicemen returning from voyages abroad started to sell themselves to carnivals as 'live wild men' during this era (Caplan 2000; Gray 1994; Lautman 1994). Seeking work in the carnivals and circuses, these men found financial reward in the growing public demand for tattooed freaks. Given their obvious European ancestry, these men could not be used as tribal primitives, and thus created alternative narratives about the acquisition of their tattoos. In reaffirming cultural stereotypes about tribal cultures, navy men and like-minded carnival workers often concocted elaborate tales of forced tattooing to explain their heavily tattooed bodies. By claiming to have been kidnapped and tattooed under duress by non-Christian savages (ironically, the Maori in particular), individuals such as 'The Great Omi' (a.k.a. Horace Riddler), John Rutherford, James O'Connell and others worked the carnival circuit, regaling audiences with carefully constructed stories of capture, torture, tattooing, and dramatic escape (DeMello 2000). Seemingly willing to ignore the extensive amount of American iconography involved in their tattoos (e.g., American flags or other service symbols), audiences were amazed by the visible markers of brutality signified by the tattoos.

As the demand for tattooees on the carnival circuits blossomed, the demand for professional tattooists also increased. Often regarded as the first professional North American tattooist, Milton Hildebrandt began tattooing in the mid-1800s in New York. He worked almost exclusively on servicemen and circus workers (McCabe 1997). Inspired by and enticed into tattooing by characters in the circus sideshows, early professional tattooists of the late 1800s and early 1900s such as Hildebrandt, Bert Grimm, Cap Coleman, Charlie Barrs, Tom Riley, Milt Zeis, and Charlie Wagner profited on Americans' burgeoning curiosity with tattoos (DeMello 2000). With the invention of the electric tattoo machine in 1891 by Samuel O'Reilly, tattoos could be applied easily and were considerably less painful. With this shift in technology, tattooists could take their trade on the road, could administer tattoos to clients more efficiently and with greater expertise, and (ironically) added a sense of modernity to the process.

In many ways, circus workers and tattooists existed in a state of symbiosis. Tattooists provided the circus workers and sideshow freaks with a steady supply of tattoos, while performers supplied the requisite demand to ensure that tattooing could be financially rewarding as a permanent occupation. In some cases, tattooists worked for the carnivals and sideshows, travelling with the troupe across the country. In other cases, tattooists would set up shop at a carnival when it arrived in a town, secretly tattooing performers in the off-stage areas of the fairgrounds.

As tattooed attractions at carnivals became banal to more discriminating and thrill-seeking audiences, owners and promoters developed new and innovative ways to shock the public with tattooed performers (DeMello 2000; Gilbert 2000). By the early 1900s, scores of circus and carnival performers were tattooed, and no longer could one earn a living simply as a tattooed attraction. Circus performers and carnival workers began to blend their shows, and as a result, tattooed dwarves, tattooed sword swallowers, and tattooed lion tamers displaced the 'live savage' in circuses and carnivals (Rubin 1988). To create an even greater sense of exoticism and eroticism around the tattoo, female tattooed attractions (and a handful of female tattooists) took centre stage. The wives or girlfriends of circus performers or tattooists were lured into tattooing through the promises of fame and fortune mythologized within the scene (Mifflin 1997; Sanders 1991). Framed in the stories of capture and forced tattooing common in the carnival for over a decade, the tattooed lady became the pinnacle of tattoo attractions in the golden era of circus acts (ca. 1910–30), eventually edging men out of the spotlight. Female tattooees such as Betty Broadbent, Artfullete, Serpentina, Pictura, Artoria, Lady Viola, and Princess Beatrice created, as Mifflin (1997) described, a 'double whammy' under the circus tent. Not only did women's participation in tattooing challenge cultural associations between the practice and masculinity; the sheer amount of the female body exposed in the performances titillated male audiences (Wroblewski 1992). The tattoo show became a form of soft pornography in which women would strip before the crowd, adding a libidinal element to the veritable peep show. Until the late 1940s, exhibitions in-volving tattooed ladies would be some of the most frequented and profitable shows on the midway.

In retrospect, the early carnival/circus had a lasting effect on North Americans' conceptualization of the tattoo as a form of social deviance. According to Bhaktin (1984), the carnival provides a context in which culturally repressed desires and emotions are explored in a controlled way (in this case, through viewing deviant others). Profane representations of the body during carnival allowed North Americans to experience subversive pleasures with and tortures of the flesh without sacrificing commonly held cultural understandings of corporeal respectability. The presentation of alternative body styles and pursuit of libidinal body play at circuses and carnivals actually reaffirmed dominant cultural ideas about the sanctity of the body. Marked bodies were depicted as vicious, savage, and, in some cases, prehistoric and subhuman. The tattoo sideshow became a vehicle for exploring deviant yet exciting body practices, a means of engaging in forms of corporeal subversion strictly forbidden in everyday life. Importantly, though, there arose out of this period a widespread association between tattooing and disrepute.

The Working-Class Era (1920s–1950s)

About the same time that circus shows were peaking in their popularity, the tattoo shop (referred to in popular vernacular as a 'tattoo parlour') became a fixture in downtown areas and neighbourhoods in North American cities such as New York, Chicago, Boston, Los Angeles, and Toronto. Many of the local parlours catered to military personnel and the working class. They were hidden down dirty alleys, crammed into the backs of barber shops or pool halls, and scattered across districts of the city characterized by poverty and crime. Frequented by carnival workers, servicemen, criminals, social outcasts, and pseudo-tough guys, the tattoo parlour (like the pool hall and the local tavern) became a social club where individuals existing on the fringe of society would meet and swap stories of adventure, grandiosity, and bravado (McCabe 1997). The shops were ports of call for servicemen, settings to prove one's masculinity to others, and a cultural centre for many working-class men. They were the locker rooms of the first half of the twentieth century, where aggressive sexuality and conquest over women were openly discussed and local men became legends in the neighbourhood.

Authors including DeMello (2000), McCabe (1997), Rubin (1988), Steward (1990), and St Clair and Govenar (1981) have masterfully documented the history of tattooing during this period. Among other insights, they have noted how tattooing moved out of the freak show and toward a distinctly home-grown American version of the craft. North American tattoo artists of this time were constructing their own unique tattooing genres, including the hyper-patriotic style now known as 'Traditional.' During this period, nationalistic images and emblems were incredibly popular as tattoos, denoting the wearer's love of country. While the customers were not (for the most part) members of the social elite, they expressed a sense of national pride held by fellow countrymen from all social backgrounds. As DeMello (2000) has commented in her analysis of American tattooing, many tattoos worn in post–First World War America represented the exuberance in American culture spawned by the global conflict (see Morse 1977; St Clair and Govenar 1981; Steward 1990).

Key technological developments affecting the practice of tattooing also occurred in the working-class era. Tattooists built upon O'Reilly's tattooing machine and constructed more precise and durable needles from new materials. Tattooist and wallpaper salesman Lew 'the Jew' Alberts promoted the idea of 'flash' in and around this time. Flash – reproduced sheets of tattoo designs – allowed artists to display their work on the walls of tattoo shops to clients and were sold to other tattoo artists as an encyclopaedia of designs (DeMello 2000). Commonly littered across the early flash sheets were military insignia, pin-up girls, dedications involving hearts and banners, cartoon characters, names of loved ones, skulls and daggers, eagles, snakes, and flags. Tattoo artists also developed and circulated 'proven' techniques for healing tattoos and methods for ensuring the ink would remain in the skin, including, for example, such rudimentary advice as 'Don't do nothin' to it!' (Gray 1994). During this period, some of the earliest tattoo parlours in Canada began to flourish. Following the military and urban working-class traditions in America, Canadian tattoo shops surfaced in urban centres and port cities such as Halifax, Quebec City, Montreal, Toronto, and Vancouver. While little written information exists to document tattooing in Canada during this time, oral histories of tattooing passed among current artists indicate that Canadian tattooing closely paralleled (in membership base and common tattoo imagery) developments in the American figuration.

DeMello (2000) has argued that tattoos were the least stigmatized in North America during this working-class era. They emitted an embraced sense of jingoism within America that was popularly regarded as a working-class expression of patriotism. Tattooing blossomed in urban landscapes across North America and key moments in the history of tattooing occurred, such as the onset of the artist-apprentice system of occupational training (in which an apprentice learns the trade over several years), the predominance of working-class men in the practice, and the mechanization and technologization of tattoo art. The membership base cultivated during this era and the eventual formalization of the tattoo parlour as a gathering place for marginal members of society firmly entrenched associations between tattooing and those lacking social grace. The tattoo ascended in popularity during this period, but retained a central component of disrepute. Interestingly, though, tattoos became normative body practice for servicemen and the working class in North America. Even though conservative codes about bodies and physical display were firmly embedded in the social fabric, the discredited practice of tattooing was a socially legitimate way of indicating one's class status to others. As a different set of social groups delved deeply into the practice of tattooing by the 1950s, the legitimacy of tattooing as a quasi-normative form of group expression would be almost completely dismantled.

The Rebel Era (1950–1970)

In the period directly following the Second World War, tattooing took a step backward toward social disrepute. As social groups brandished tattoos to advertise their collective discontent with society, the practice became popular among members of the social underbelly (Govenar 1988). Firmly entrenching cultural associations between tattoos and the fringe element in society, a full spectrum of social deviants adopted tattooing as a method of permanently expressing a politically charged disaffection with their cultural surroundings.

Arguably, the use of tattooing to symbolize social protest or political dissent is grounded in the history of tattooing in the prison context. As early as 450 BC, tattooing had been used as a means of labelling criminals. Greeks, for instance, referred to the permanent marks given to criminals as 'stigma' (Goffman 1963). In the study of the social history of tattooing we learn that agents of social control in countries such as Greece, England, Japan, and France originally used tattooing and forms of branding as a means of labelling individuals with a criminal or deviant identity (Brain 1979; Camphausen 1997; Caplan 2000; DeMello 2000; Ebin 1979; Gilbert 2000; Gray 1994; Grognard and Lazi 1994; Kitamura and Kitamura 2001; Martischnig 1987; Sanders 1989). Marks were inscribed on the body as a form of punishment for transgressing a variety of social laws or conventions. Garfinkel (1956) described such practices of exclusion as 'degradation ceremonies.' As the conduct of an individual is ritually denounced through hegemonic strategies (e.g., legal, political, moral), the actions of deviants are distinguished and separated from normative behaviour. The actions of social deviants were symbolically labelled as such by placing indelible marks on (in) the body. Not only, then, was it important to control socially disruptive *bodies* by taking them out of the general populace (Foucault 1977), it was equally important to further marginalize dangerous individuals with life-long marks of stigma – transforming them into discredited social actors.

Prisoners and other social deviants who involuntarily received tattoos eventually pursued lines of collective resistance to such pejorative labelling. These groups counteracted the punitive body projects by reclaiming the marks imposed on their bodies. For example, the ancient Japanese *irezumi* (which literally means 'the insertion of ink') style of tattooing developed in the eighth century (ca. 720), as a *yakuza* criminal underclass response to being tattooed or branded by prison authorities with words like 'dog' or 'pig' (Kitamura and Kitamura 2001; Martischnig 1987; McCallum 1988; Richie and Buruma 1980). Japanese criminals found a collective solution to the punitive marking by reworking the inscribed symbols and developing an underground tattooing style of their own (Kaplan and Dubro 1986; Kitamura and Kitamura 2001). French and English prisoners often tattooed dotted lines around their necks, writing 'cut here' in mockery of the institution's control over their lives (Caplan 2000; Gray 1994). The tattoo designs were transformed into a subcultural code of resistance shared among the group's members. Their bodies could not be freed in a literal sense, but could be freed symbolically through bricolage. The appropriated tattoo became a sign of resistance and represented what Hebdige (1979) might call 'noise' in a highly disciplined context in which bodies were expected to be docile and receptive to strict control (Foucault 1977).

However, as Gray (1994) and DeMello (1993) pointed out, with the widespread adoption of tattooing among prisoners, tattooed bodies quickly became symbols of a deviant Other. Even within the prison, styles developed differentiating 'convicts' (deviants who accept and relish their status as criminals) from 'inmates' (deviants who resist pejorative labelling processes). In this case, while prisoners and other social deviants transformed their imposed stigmata into something meaningful and resistant, they ironically reproduced their own disreputable status (Govenar 1988; Kent 1997).

Since the turn of the twentieth century, tattooing among North American prisoners has continued to grow in popularity as a method of creating specific identities and associations within the institution (DeMello 1993). Tattooing became most notable in the 1950s and the 1960s as the communicative encryptions largely served to denote gang affiliation within prisons (e.g., names or gang mottos, playing-card symbols or various weapons tattooed on the hands) or one's feelings of capture and confinement (e.g., a spider web encircling the elbow or a tear drop under the eye). Codes and styles developed in conjunction with techniques of tattooing common only in the prison. Fine-line (single needle) tattooing using black or blue ink (often acquired from pens or soot collected from burning carbon-based objects) predominated, and crude tattoo 'guns' (an intentionally menacing term) were patched together from pieces of transistor radios, guitar strings, pens, and electric razors (Govenar 1988).

As the popularity of tattooing grew in North American prisons, individuals from a diversity of social backgrounds participated in the practice. No longer was the tattoo the property of the white, urban, working-class convict within the institution. Chicano, African-American, Oriental, and Native American tattooing proliferated in prisons during this period, emanating outward into the urban area. By the end of the 1960s, prison tattoo styles and imagery had hit the street and would influence the dominant tattoo styles and practices for the next twenty years (DeMello 1993; Kent 1997).

Around the same time, motorcycle gangs claimed tattooing as a key signifying practice. An indigenous figuration to North America, motorcycle gangs (or in the preferred lingo 'clubs') picked up on the meaning structures given to tattooing within prisons. Since many club members had, at some point in their lives, been incarcerated, many bikers received their first tattoos in prison. Biker tattoos, like their prison counterparts, were laden with antisocial sentiment. Tattoos took on an even more mischievous and frightening character, as portrayed by the infamous FTW (Fuck The World) and EWMN (Evil, Wicked, Mean, Nasty), gang names, skulls and crossbones, marijuana motifs, and 'Born to Lose' tattoos commonly worn among motorcyclists of the era. For motorcycle-gang members, highly visible tattoos were both an encoded language of rebellion articulating disaffection with broader society and a lexicon of symbols instantly distinguishing motorcyclists from others in society (Eldridge 1992).

One of the most important outcomes of motorcyclists' interest in tattooing was the negative exposure tattoos received in popular media. By the late 1960s a full-fledged moral panic was developing around the social perils posed by motorcycle gangs (circulating around stories of murders, physical assaults, rapes, and robberies committed by bikers). Fuelled by cultural stereotype and exaggeration, cinematic and newspaper depictions of motorcycle-gang lifestyles defined such groups as outlaws who terrorized and pillaged local communities. Among the most immediately identifiable physical indicators of one's status as a biker/criminal were their tattoos. Supported by pop-psychological readings of the biker as a born criminal, tattoos were culturally decoded as a visible indicator of one's predisposition to crime (DeMello 2000). In the public eye, tattoos were (once again) the uncontested marker of the criminal, the outsider, the social miscreant.

Further investigating the genesis of tattooing practices in North America during this era, we learn that the signification of deviance emitted by tattoos was actively borrowed by growing numbers of radical or dissident youth subcultures of the 1960s (DeMello 2000; Gray 1994; Hebdige 1979; Sanders 1989). Numerous groups (e.g., urban youth gangs, Rockers, Modernists, Greasers, and Rockabillys) utilized tattooing for their own purposes of collective representation, and in so doing developed alternative ways of expressing the (sub)cultural significance of tattoos. Deploying the tattoo as part of rejecting class-based social norms, values, and beliefs, politically charged North American (and British) counter-cultures engaged in social critique, commentary, and rebellion through their corporeal manipulations (which tended to subvert working- and middle-class standards of respectability). In an epoch marked by extreme conservative understandings of acceptable physical representation – directly influenced by the expansion of the middle class – tattooing violated basic elements of North American cultural understandings of corporeality. However, it is important to recognize that the focal concerns for each of these groups and the degree to which they rejected mainstream class culture varied. Thus, while disparate groups similarly drew on the image of Otherness that tattoos represented, the encoded messages underlying the tattoos held different connotations in various subcultural contexts.

The period covering the 1950s and 1960s might accurately be referred to as the 'dark ages' of tattooing in North America. Tattooing moved away from the urban alleys and working-class communities and into criminal and outlaw spheres. Prisoners, motorcycle gangs, deviant youth subcultures, and political protestors latched onto tattoos in the process of outwardly representing feelings of discontent with society. Radically marking the body to achieve this goal drew attention to the social protestor in a culture where conservative codes about the body and its representation predominated. Consequently, deviance and the tattoo were synonymous during this era. Outside the context of the prison, this was a relatively new and unanticipated phenomenon in the world history of tattooing. For the most part, tattoos were marks of inclusion, a normative and culturally celebrated means of establishing one's status within a culture (and not merely a subculture or sub-group of actors). By the start of the 1970s, however, mainstream, middle-class North America had almost completely come to define the tattoo as a voluntary mark of social deviance (Sanders 1989). Toward the end of the decade, the meaning of the tattoo would begin to transform once again.

The New Age Era (1970–1990)

Cultural and social structural changes inside and outside of the tattoo figuration in the 1970s drastically redefined how and among whom tattooing would be practised in North America. For instance, as a product of cultural consciousness-raising generated by racially, sexually, and gender-based political movements, the body became a popular billboard for 'doing' identity politics (Dunn 1998). Recognizing the body as a key text of cultural exposition, those ultimately committed to challenging dominant social codes found in the body a highly political means of expressing and recreating identity. At the same time, the tattoo figuration was being restructured through an influx of new artists and clients. Shedding its almost exclusively blue-collar and criminal composition, the tattoo figuration now included people from all walks of life. Together, these movements would usher in a veritable renaissance in tattooing in the West (Rubin 1988).

Dunn (1998, 20) defined 'identity politics' as the process of aligning oneself with others who intersubjectively share feelings of marginality and oppression within a figuration. Eschewing or tearing asunder ascribed characteristics provided by dominant cultural hierarchies, individuals engaged in identity politics struggle to redefine personal (and collective) identity in the process of 'winning space' (Cohen 1972) in a culture. In this process, violating dominant norms, values, and beliefs that provide the ideological support structures for cultural practices becomes critical. The sexual revolution, the civil rights movement, and the women's liberation movement (which all gained cultural momentum in the 1960s) were collective enterprises oriented toward effecting social structural change, yet were at their roots social campaigns of identity politics – reclaiming and redefining collective identities (e.g., of race and gender) through the subversion of overarching hegemonic constructions of gender, race, and class. These movements begged North Americans to reconsider conservative, and ultimately oppressive, cultural ideologies and ways of life. As a result, an unprecedented level of social permissiveness grew, and individuals engaged in a smorgasbord of corporeal explorations heretofore denied as normative (or at least permissible) social practice in Western cultures.

Perhaps the most influential group (as an aggregate) to utilize tattooing in their identity-politics projects of the 1970s and 1980s were women. In her work on women's involvement in Western tattooing Mifflin (1997) notes that the period between the 1970s and 1990s involved a dramatic influx of women into the figuration (see also Atkinson and Young 2001; Sanders 1991; Wroblewski 1992). Casting off the circus sideshow or biker-moll attached to women's involvement in the practice since the turn of the century, women began to redraw themselves through tattooing. Approaching the body as a site of agency, self-determination, liberation, and sexual exploration, women's tattooing body projects stood in stark opposition to dominant constructions of the female form as frail and powerless:

> With the sexual revolution of the 1960s, when women began casting off their bras as they had their corsets a half-century earlier, tattoos were rescued from ignominy and resurrected in the counter-culture by women who were rethinking womanhood. The arrival of the Pill in 1961 had given women new sexual freedom; a little over a decade later legalized abortion secured their reproductive rights. Not surprisingly, the breast became a popular spot for tattoos – it was here that many women inscribed symbols of their own newfound sexual independence. (Mifflin 1997, 56)

Stressing the emancipatory nature of the tattoo, women highlighted how tattoos might be used as a means of permanently redesigning identity in a culture. The tattooed female form (outside of the highly sexualized, male-oriented circus show) articulated a voyage of empowerment and self-reclamation precisely because the tattoo was a pre-existing signifier of masculine deviance.

Several authors (Atkinson and Young 2001; Mifflin 1997; Wroblewski

1992) have agreed that the increased participation of North American women in the tattoo figuration through the 1970s and 1980s forever altered the practice on the continent. Like a pebble dropped in the middle of a placid pond, women's involvement in the practice stirred ripples across the entire tattoo figuration. Indeed, women challenged and undermined cultural constructions of femininity through tattooing, but similarly breached the integrity of cultural associations between the tattoo and the working-class male, the criminal, the sailor, the circus performer, the gang member, and the biker. As women demanded more feminine imagery than commonly found in traditional Western tattoo art, more personalized and sensitive treatment in the studio, and a higher quality of work, their participation in tattooing transformed the structure and ideologies underlying the practice. In doing so, waves of female tattoo artists (Sheila May, Vyvyn Lazonga, Calamity Jane, Ruth Marten, Jamie Summers, Jacci Gresham, Mary Jane Haake, SuzAnne Fauser, Kari Barba, Juli Moon, Patty Kelley, Pat Fish) and tattooees in the 1970s–1990s renaissance of the practice opened the door to redefine the practice culturally in unanticipated ways.

In her discussion of the tattoo renaissance, DeMello (2000) wrote that a curious and eager middle class contingent was similarly drawn to the figuration during this era. Until the 1970s tattooing had remained localized in urban street cultures, working class neighbourhoods, or deviant social settings. With the groundswell in tattooing practices (especially among women) in the 1970s, the middle class began encroaching on the historically working-class/outlaw terrain of tattooing. In line with the sentiments of self-exploration, physical experimentation, and mind expansion ingrained in the era, dabbling in and with the socially avant-garde – including tattooing practices – became chic for the middle and upper classes. As countercultural icons, popular rock musicians, and cultural heroes were seen with tattoos, the young middle class started to frequent local tattoo parlours. Neither identifying with nor understanding the dominant American tattoo styles (e.g., traditional) practised for over a century, the new middle-class clients demanded something more personal, less offensive, and customized of the tattoo.

Several journal articles, magazine stories, and book-length texts document the dramatic changes in the tattoo business during this period (DeMello 2000; Gumpert 1983; Rubin 1988; Vale and Juno 1989). Initially influenced by artists' (Don Ed Hardy, Cliff Raven, Spider Webb, Paul Rogers, Sailor Jerry, Lyle Tuttle, and Leo Zuluetta) exploration of tattoo styles from other cultures (e.g., Japanese, Bornean, Hawaiian,

New Zealand, Native North American, and African), North American tattooing began to take a turn toward internationalism and was thereby distanced from the more classically 'Traditional' styles. This trend was particularly appealing to the new middle-class clients, who did not wish to adorn themselves with images and symbols common in North American tattooing to date. Clients increasingly demanded a higher quality of tattoo art, asked for custom (one-time, designed-for-the-client) tattoos, and preferred more professional and reputable studios – cleaner studios, more hygienic conditions, artistically inclined tattooists possessing diverse repertoires of abilities, and friendly environments characterized by trust and respect.

As a result of changing demographics and stylistic trends within the figuration, a new generation of 'tattoo artists' (refusing to be called, in the working-class jargon, tattooists) arrived on the scene. Young people with art-school, graphic-design, and university training began popping up in tattoo studios across North America (Sanders 1989). These young men (and more women than ever before) came from a melange of social backgrounds and wielded enormous understandings of the physiological and social principles pertaining to corporeal movement, aesthetics, and display. Treating the body less and less as a canvas to be filled with tattoos and more as an integral part of the self, the young middle-class insurgence into the tattoo artist profession redefined many of the old ideologies held strongly in the trade (DeMello 2000; Vale and Juno 1989).

Artists were now more willing to listen to their clients and pursue emerging styles (e.g., tribal, skater, neo-fantasy, hentai/anime, and gothic), and moved their shops from the urban ghetto, harbour front, or periphery to the high fashion and youth centres of the city. The apprenticeship system became undermined in this process, and with the advent of many tattoo periodicals advertising the sale of tattoo equipment, younger artists were able to strike out on their own and establish upscale and professional studios catering to women and the middle class.

Some have argued that the most influential of the new groups of tattoo artists and enthusiasts in this renaissance era was the self-proclaimed tribalists or Neo Primitives. Groups such as the Urban/Neo/Modern Primitives (Atkinson and Young 2001; Myers 1997; Rosenblatt 1997; Vale and Juno 1989) have promoted an interpretation that encourages us to look back at the most primal and primitive uses of tattooing as symbolic acts of cultural cohesion and group identity. Including body modification as part of a homology of style, these individuals (with a core membership in the 18 to 35 year age range) ask to be treated as modern tribalists of the urban jungle. Rejecting both the traditional Western image of the 'marked' individual as deviant and the often dehumanizing way in which individuals are treated in modern urban life, they intend to capture the spirit of acceptance that tribal cultures (e.g., Melanesian, Polynesian, African, and Micronesian) exhibit toward tattooing. At present, it is widely accepted among tattoo artists that tribal styles are the most popular in the figuration. Acknowledging that the group is by no means completely homogeneous, Atkinson and Young (2001) have maintained that the Urban Primitive use of tattooing in Canada is directly opposed to Christian-based codes of bodily display that are part of the hegemony of Western cultures. In representing the focal concerns of Neo Primitives tattoos are used (at least) to signify a personal rite of passage; a marking of personal defence; an ability to endure pain; a challenge to conventional Christian notions of beauty and sexuality; and an exploration of alternative spirituality.

Throughout the 1970s and 1980s, more North Americans sought out and embraced tattooing as a personal form of expression than in any other historical period. Influenced by political movements that shook conservative understandings of the body to the ground, interpretations of tattoos were more varied and subject to contextual construction. As women and more 'respectable' social classes participated in tattooing it transformed into a practice of political identity construction. Shifts and restructuring of the professional organization within the tattoo figuration concomitantly occurred. New artists abounded, new styles were viewed on North American bodies, new equipment was supplied to artists, new techniques for learning the craft were being explored, and the construction of new studios brought tattooing into the spotlight of the urban mainstream. By the early 1990s, the 'supermarket era' (Polhemus 1994, 1996) of tattooing was in full swing.

The Supermarket Era (1990–present)

The dominant characteristic of the new era of tattooing – what DeMello (2000), Vail (1999), and others have referred to as the 'second renaissance' – is choice. In most major urban centres in Canada, including Toronto, Vancouver, Montreal, Calgary, Quebec City, Edmonton, Winnipeg, and Halifax, there are, typically, anywhere from five to a dozen professional tattoo studios. Where there were only a handful of artists operating in the cities twenty years ago, there are now scores in each.

Tattoo artists now proudly display stickers and banners in their windows pronouncing, 'Tattoos: Not Just for Bikers Anymore.' With the ongoing expansion of the clientele base (a term now preferred among tattoo enthusiasts), the practice of tattooing has become a highly competitive market economy. Clients are consumers, ready to exchange cash (or other commodities) for artistic consultation and the services provided by celebrity artists in their areas.

To take the city of Calgary as an example, in 1990 only a handful of recognized tattoo studios existed within the city limits. Now studios litter the city, with any number of independent artists operating out of their homes or other quarters. These studios are located in corners of the downtown core – infiltrating fashion districts such as the popular 17th Avenue and Kensington Road areas, existing alongside financial institutions in the city's centre, and situated in high traffic/tourist areas such as MacLeod Trail. Neon signs flashing 'TATTOO' are seen throughout the city. One no longer needs to travel into secluded or dangerous parts of the city to receive a tattoo. Tattoo studios are travelling to communities overrun by young, hip, affluent adolescents and professionals. Quite simply, the business is going where the demand and the money exists.

If it is true that the modern tattoo enthusiast can locate a local tattoo artist in most nooks and crannies of Canadian cities, it is equally true that clients now come from every walk of life. Unlike previous eras in which tattoos could only be acquired if an individual personally knew an artist or was brave enough to 'risk' entering a working-class tattoo parlour, tattoo artists now compete with one another for their clients (Sanders 1989; Steward 1990), who include men and women, people from all ethnic backgrounds and classes, and individuals possessing divergent sexual preferences, religious affiliations, and ideological beliefs.

With the expansion and diversification of the client base, tattoo artists must now be able to accommodate diverse tastes and preferences that clients possess for tattoos (Irwin 2000; Vail 1999). The flash displayed on artists' walls contain dozens of different tattoo styles and the portfolios artists keep of their work (available to any customer as a method of illustrating the depth and expertise of an artist's ability) contain dozens more. A common motto among tattoo artists in Canada decrees, 'If you can think it up, I can do it.' This sentiment represents broader cultural attitudes essential to the survival of any free-market economy (e.g., service first, the customer is always right). People are able to shop around for a tattoo artist they feel comfortable with and choose from thousands of images for their tattoo body projects. Individuality, freedom of expression, and self-exploration are overriding dictums for artists and clients. In a culture that privileges individual choice and the right to assume control over one's body, tattoo styles are now much more heterogeneous and personalized than ever before.

Interestingly, the tattoo style now referred to as 'neo-Traditional' (an updated version of classical American working-class tattooing) has had an upswing in popularity. As many tattoo artists and other devotees delve into the history of the art form and learn about the roots of North American tattooing (especially those unimpressed with or suspicious of New Age or Neo Primitive perspectives on tattooing), people are actively bringing back to life working-class tattoo styles and imagery. Perhaps as a function of the current era of cultural uncertainty and doubt brought about by globalization processes, political correctness, ethnic pluralism, and the breakdown of dominant cultural social-classification systems (race, class, gender), people are turning to tattooing as part of a collective quest for something uniquely (North) American. Therefore, while some might be quick to attribute the recent boom in the popularity of tattooing to hyper-individuality, the emergence of neo-Traditional indicates that North Americans continue to utilize tattooing in interdependent ways vis-à-vis the search for and expression of cultural affiliations (Atkinson and Young 2001). In many ways, by pursuing tattooing body projects, individuals may be actively and purposefully shopping for culture through their corporeal alterations.

Lastly, DeMello (2000) has addressed a much-neglected characteristic of the tattoo figuration in the current era. DeMello focuses on how, in a society that she argues is preoccupied with communication technologies, high-speed information systems have altered the sense of community in the tattoo figuration. Positing that tattoo periodicals, Internet newsgroups, World Wide Web pages, and highly advertised tattoo conventions bring tattoo enthusiasts together into an information-rich community of social actors, she emphasises how tattoo enthusiasts (regardless of their diversity) are much more cohesive as a social group. If tattooing has emerged out of the social shadows and into popular culture, DeMello argues, it has done so because people can learn on-line about the tattooing process, find out about artists through magazines, and contact artists all over the world. There is a level of dialogue between tattoo enthusiasts in the current era, and as individuals from all over the world begin to share their experiences with and stories about tattooing with others, the structure of the tattoo figuration continues to change in unplanned and unanticipated ways.

One of the most difficult questions I am often asked when discussing the history of North American tattooing is, 'Where do you think it will go in the future?' History, I often respond, dictates that this is impossible to predict. Among whom will tattooing be popular, what styles (if any) will predominate, or how will tattoos be applied in the future? We cannot forecast answers to these questions without engaging in pure speculation. The figuration has and will continue to transform in unintended ways. What we can say with some degree of certainty is that ongoing transformations within the figuration will most likely be directed by several major influences.

First, tattooing has been chiefly influenced by dominant (i.e., normative) figurational constructions of the body as a site of personal representation. In earlier eras of tattooing in North America, bodies were strictly regimented and controlled as a site of personal display. With cultural understandings of the tattooed body as a signifier of atavism and barbarism in effect, only a few of the more socially adventurous engaged in tattooing. This trend would persevere for approximately a century on this continent, until individuals would wage war against long-standing corporeal codes and regimens. Tattoos would eventually figure into these movements, and filter into popular culture toward the end of the twentieth century as normative standards about the body and its modification were commodified, blurred, confused, and in some cases erased.

Second, the social diffusion of tattooing is directly affected by the degree to which the practice is defined as a deviant social practice within a larger cultural context. Clearly, tattooing remained unpopular in North America, or conversely ascended in popularity, because of the image of deviance conjured by tattooed bodies. Tattooing has never been and perhaps never will be a completely normative social practice. Paramount, though, among the reasons or motivations for becoming tattooed that individuals develop is the deviant or 'outsider' status of the tattoo. Whether the tattoo enthusiast utilizes a tattoo to signify social protest, rebellion, disenfranchisement, or conformity (i.e., in eras categorized by attitudes such as 'to shock is chic'), the practice has retained an aura of marginality throughout its brief history in North America.

Third, the professional structure (principally artists and their studios) of the figuration both alters and is altered by fluctations in cultural body tastes and preferences, dominant perceptions of tattoos, expanding and contracting membership bases, and clients' preferences for particular tattoo styles. These factors influence the activities of professional tattoo artists in the figuration singularly and cumulatively. Future quantitative and qualitative changes in the structure of the figuration are difficult to predict. How can one, for example, predict with any accuracy the manner by which professional learning processes in tattooing will change or where tattoo studios will be located? Speculation would be nothing more than (un)educated guesswork, and not guided by empirical knowledge or informed analysis.

In a sense, we stand at a turning point in the history of tattooing in North America – in both our fascination with and sociological understanding of the practice. I would hope that sociologists choose to follow the path carved out by historians (within and outside of the tattoo figuration) in documenting the social significance of tattooing. For example, very little has been compiled about the history of tattooing in Canada. Although extensive similarities appear to exist between the Canadian and American tattooing trends, no one to date has documented the rich history of tattooing in Canada. Furthermore, whereas historians have assumed the mandate of chronicling the history of this most controversial form of urban art, sociologists have not followed suit with investigations of the practice as a form of human communication, social interchange, and cultural performance.

In the next chapter, I will review extant academic knowledge of tattooing gleaned from the limited analyses of the practice, and will suggest that we should jettison much of our commonly held theoretical approaches for studying the practice. Neither academic nor popular (media-based) representations of tattooing adequately depict the range of sensibilities toward tattoos currently shared and debated by Canadians. To that extent, alternative ways of seeing tattooing would invigorate the sociological approach to the activity and, hopefully, stimulate new discourses and debates about the social status of tattoos in Canada.

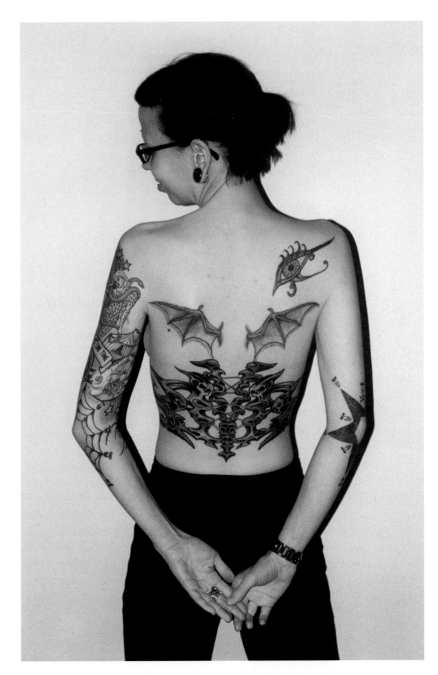

More Canadian women than ever are pursuing extensive tattooing projects.

Unlike in previous eras, many Canadian tattoo enthusiasts proudly display their tattooed bodies in everyday life.

Canadian tattoo art styles vary widely and include a full range of images and motifs.

An illustration of tribal tattooing and style.

An example of 'neo-traditional' tattoo art.

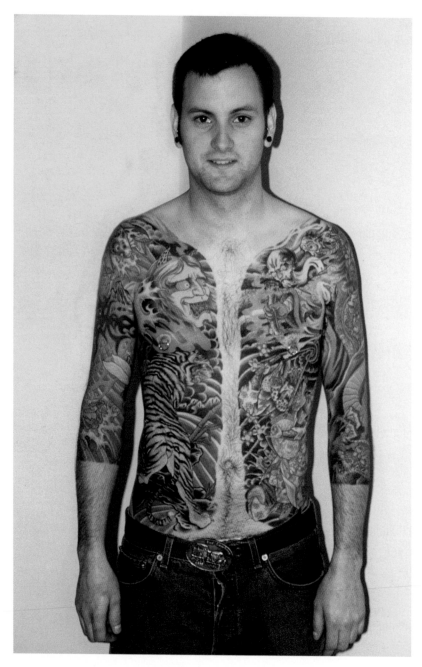

An example of a Japanese-inspired tattoo 'shirt.'

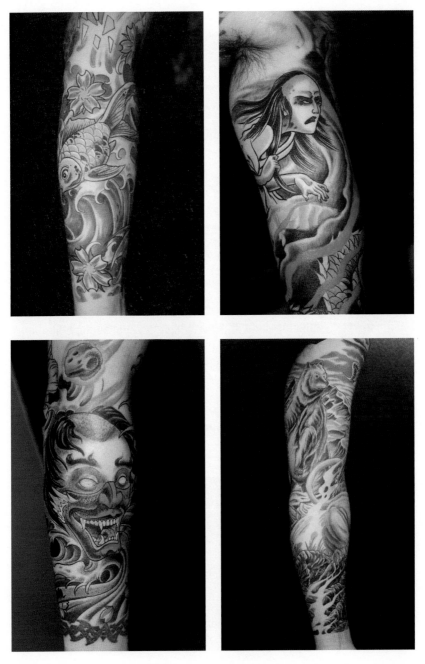

Tattoo 'sleeves' are becoming increasingly popular in Canada.

For some, tattooing is a process of bonding and affiliation.

CHAPTER THREE

Academic and Media Representations

As evidenced in the historical literature on tattooing in North America, understanding of Canadian tattooing practices is, in a word, lacking. Part of my own interest in tattooing stems from the pittance of knowledge we have accumulated about this aspect of human expression in Canada. Nonetheless, the extant academic research on tattooing in North America (although limited in its breadth and conceptual development) is a useful guide for anyone fascinated by the practice. To aid my own investigation of contemporary tattooing practices in Canada, I drew on research conducted on the subject in cultural anthropology, psychology, and sociology, and found it worthwhile to juxtapose academic musings on tattooing with popular media accounts of tattoo enthusiasm in the current era. While these bodies of knowledge do not sufficiently or wholly explain Canadians' interpretations of tattooing, they provide partial glimpses into the world of tattoo enthusiasm.

Cultural Anthropology: Marks of Inclusion

Through the 1970s and into the 1980s numerous anthropological texts examined the tattooing practices of such groups as the Dayak of Borneo (e.g., Vale and Juno 1989), the Maori of New Zealand (e.g., Gathercole 1988), Native North Americans (e.g., Light 1972), and Japanese groups (e.g., Richie and Buruma 1980). Among the more notable of these texts were Robert Brain's *The Decorated Body* (1979) and Victoria Ebin's *The Body Decorated* (1979). By documenting how tattooing is, in the terms used here, a redesigning body project oriented toward linking the individual to larger cultural webs, these authors investigated how tattooing is normative corporeal practice in many non-Western cultures. Tracing the origins of tattooing to 3500 BC, cultural anthropologists Brain and Ebin painted a very different portrait of tattooing than most Western authors. They highlighted the social significance of tattooing as an activity that fosters in-group cohesiveness and mutual identification. Analysis of the deviant aspects of tattooing is forsaken in these discussions, since the (tribal) groups studied share understandings of tattoos as symbols of culture, identity, and group pride.

Rubin's edited collection of essays, *Marks of Civilisation* (1988), is one of the most comprehensive treatises on tattooing within tribal cultures. Compiled during the middle of the tattoo renaissance in North America, Rubin's project has the purpose of informing Westerners about the global-historical pervasiveness of the practice. Throughout the text Rubin and his associates describe how and why tattooing has been inserted into cultural practice as a method of transforming the biological body into a social entity – or what Brain called 'putting on a new skin, a cultural, as opposed to a natural skin' (1979, 29).

According to cultural anthropologists, a tattoo becomes a signature of identity within tribal cultures, a mark representing one's lineage, social status, roles within a group, and overall exploits within the world. Tattooing is thus conceptualised as a rite of passage, revered by participants as a sacred ceremony of cultural creation and confirmation (Camphausen 1997; Mascia-Lees and Sharpe 1992). For example, the Samoan tradition of tattooing (Kaeppler 1988) is often described as a cultural ordeal. When tribal elders decide that the individual is ready, the Samoan man, like the Hawaiian, receives a full-body tattoo over several days. Men are tattooed via the traditional hand-poking or tapping method – ink made from soot and mixed with kerosene is driven into the skin with the aid of a hand-held device, resembling a long stick with a comb attached to the end, made from porcupine quills or rhinoceros horn – in a ritual test of one's commitment to one's tribe. Samoans describe the pain involved in the process as excruciating, but bear the physical trauma nonetheless. To quit in the middle of the process brings shame to the man and generations of his family. To endure the process elevates the man's status within the tribe.

Cultural anthropologists have documented the fact that similar tattooing experiences are not uncommon around the world, but rather are the norm. Tattooing is utilized to mark something uniquely human upon the skin, something not defined as the sign of the deviant, the mark of the beast, or the masochistic cry of the social misfit. Pushing fellow academics to consider how the symbolic marks etched into the skin become a vehicle for creating and confirming identity, cultural anthropologists highlight how the modified (i.e., tattooed) body is not inherently shameful for social actors. Contrarily, by underscoring the ways in which tattoos are socially constructed as normative in an abundance of cultures around the world, they give emphasis to the enduring cultural significance of tattoos.

Although research efforts on tattooing arising out of cultural anthropological studies have been incredibly insightful, aside from the rudimentary idea that tattoos create and communicate in-group affiliation, they simply do not reflect the contemporary cultural uses of tattooing in Canada. Even though it has provided some fascinating case studies on the tribal uses of tattooing as a collective body project (Camphausen 1997; Ebin 1979; Gell 1993; Rubin 1988) or on tattooing in other urban cultures (Brain 1979; Kitamura and Kitamura 2001; Martischnig 1987; Richie and Buruma 1980; Mascia-Lees and Sharpe 1992), cultural anthropological research simply does not capture either the spirit of the art form in Canada or current sensibilities about the practice. As such, case studies on tribal usage of tattooing are somewhat insufficient to serve as a directional guide for contemporary analyses of the practice.

Psychology: Marks of Atavism

The most interconnected scholarly research on tattooing is found in the literature of psychology. Hovering around organizing concepts such as personality disorder, ego identity, and stigma, psychological research on the subject postulates that individuals turn to tattooing as a method of coping with and managing psychological dilemmas. Psychological analyses of the practices have considerably advanced the study of how tattooing may be pervasive among certain criminal groups (e.g., youth gangs) or subcultures (e.g., military groups), and how tattoos have been recognized in North America as a sign of membership within disreputable communities.

The theoretical standpoint adopted by a clear majority of psychologists in studying tattooing has replicated long-standing popular cultural stereotypes about tattoo enthusiasts in North America. Almost without exception, psychological constructions of tattooing revolve around a belief in the inherent pathology or ego deficiency of the individual partaking in the practice. Psychologists have contended that a tattooed body is the manifestation of a mind fraught with disorder, and representative of an individual who cannot conform to social norms, values, and beliefs because the mind will not allow him or her to do so:

> ... [M]aladjustment is typically correlated with tattoos ... [I]t is logical to hypothesize that motivation to be tattooed is related to a paucity of inter-personal satisfactions, the need to compensate for failure by exhibitionistic display of bravado or experience, and a frustrated but strong desire to identify – even to the extent of attempting an anomic identification. (Howell et al. 1971, 33)

> ... [T]attooees experienced a flaw at some stage of their ego development and used their tattoos in a restorative manner to bolster an underdeveloped ego. The tattoo can be described as the 'personalised Rorschach of its wearer' as it reflects the deep-seated need for the individual to call attention to the body in order to assure himself that he does in fact exist. (Grumet 1983, 484).

If we are to believe researchers such as Ferguson-Rayport et al. (1955), Gittleson et al. (1969), Goldstein (1979), Measey (1972), and Pollak and McKenna (1945), predilection for tattooing is a predictor of future deviance, as individuals who cannot refrain from brutally marking their bodies in such a primitive and barbaric way cannot contain other deviant impulses (e.g., toward criminal behaviour, predatory sexual acts, homosexuality, or self-abuse):

> Many Westerners do not belong to particular groups where tattooing is expected, yet they resort to this primitive method of emotional expression. Many of these individuals congregate in institutions that cater for disordered social behaviour. This suggests that in our culture there may be a greater likelihood of tattooed persons having an abnormal personality than persons who are not tattooed. Emotional immaturity is the personality factor nominated as the primary trait associated with the urge to mutilate the body with tattoos. Tattooed men are usually of two types: the exhibitionist, and the young man seeking to compensate for inferiority feelings. (McKerracher and Watson 1969, 167–8)

Problematically, as a result of measurement and design issues plaguing the studies, psychologists fail to distinguish between cause and effect in the tattooing process. Is tattooing a product of a psychological disorder which similarly produces criminal behaviour? Inferences about this correlation are made, but never specified or empirically tested. Analyses of convict (DeMello 1993; Kent 1997) and gang tattooing (Rubin 1988) indicates that the practice becomes common among prisoners or those incarcerated in an institution of control for a host of reasons, including the search for collective identity; an affective expression of despair; a means of articulating a sense of distance from mainstream society; and as a method of exploring the self in the institutional context. In effect, by taking the inherently social and communicative aspects of tattooing out of the practice in psychological analyses, we are left with strikingly unflattering and empirically unfounded discussions of tattooing as a outward signifier of pathology.

The substantial psychological literature on the subject severely limits a broader understanding of tattooing as a culturally meaningful practice (i.e., Gittleson and Wallfn; Grumet 1983; Houghton et al. 1996; Howell et al. 1971; Lander and Kohn 1943; McKerracher and Watson 1969; Newman 1982; Verberne 1969). Psychological research casts tattooing in a pejorative light by treating the modified body as a sign of personality disorder. In this light, permanently modifying the body is natural for the maladjusted, the mentally corrupted, or the dissociated. Tattooing here loses any possibility of being considered a meaningful and communicative enterprise in favour of a position that treats the practice as biologically (i.e., genetically) or developmentally (i.e., cognitively) determined. Such perceptions have done little to produce an accurate picture of the cultural meanings associated with tattooing as a redesigning body project, and do not allow participants to explain their tattooing activities in their own terms and categories.

Sociology: Marks of Polysemic Meaning

To make a rather gross generalization, cultural anthropological and psychological research efforts portray tattooing as a uniformly decodable practice; that is, cultural anthropologists treat tattooing as a normative process of group formation, while psychologists conceptualize tattooing as a personality defect. In contrast, sociological analyses of tattooing have produced a range of theoretical interpretations and definitions of the practice. With this said, sociological accounts of tattooing may be placed into one of three main categories: studies of tattooing as a form of social deviance; analyses of tattoo artists and their everyday experiences in the business; and investigations of the tattoo as a form of political resistance.

The Tattoo and Social Deviance

Sanders's work on tattooing is the most comprehensive existing sociological analysis of tattooing as a deviant body project. His *Customizing the
Body: The Art and Culture of Tattooing* (1989) should be a starting point
for anyone seriously interested in the subject. Exploring the tattoo as
both a voluntary and involuntary mark of stigma (Goffman 1963), Sanders effectively reintroduced the topic to sociologists. Writing at the onset
of the first tattoo renaissance in North America, he provided a 'thick
description' (Geertz 1973) of the tattoo community (e.g., of key artists
in the figuration, clients' motivations for being tattooed, the actual process of being tattooed, and the phenomenological experience of being
tattooed) and alluded to its changing significance in North America.
Recognizing a turn to alternative tattoo styles, a reinvigorated youth
movement, and a boom in tattooing among females, Sanders (1989,
1991) provided important suggestions for structuring subsequent
research on tattooing.

Sanders's legacy is established by his willingness to confront exactly
what it is about tattoos that signifies deviance, and how tattoos become
defined as normative or non-normative in situated contexts of interaction. Dissecting the processes by which audiences come to interpret
social symbols as deviant or not, Sanders discredited the idea that tattoos are simply marks of 'disaffiliation' (Goffman 1963). He was one of
the first sociologists who held firm to the idea that tattooing is a practice
subject to social constructions and definitions (deviant or otherwise),
and influenced by the personal biographies of, collective world views
held by, and contextual interpretations of individuals.

Other sociologists delving into the processes by which tattoos are
defined as socially deviant take a much less culturally introspective
standpoint. Some, instance, focusing on deviant subcultural uses of
tattooing among prisoners (DeMello 1993; Kent 1997; Seaton 1987) or
ethnic youth gangs (Govenar 1988), give attention to how and why tattoos are adopted by criminals and delinquents in the process of outwardly representing disaffection with others. Furthermore, through the
rich description of how tattooing develops as a subcultural tradition
within these social settings, tattooing is shown to be a deviant way for
proving one's masculinity, commitment to a group, or desire to be different from culturally mainstream Others. Postulated to be part of what
Willis (1978) would call a 'homology' – a complex set of complementary
group practices coalescing around a shared set of ideologies, activities,

and stylistic preferences – tattooing is studied as a form of collective expression that purposefully embraces and promulgates the image of deviance denoted by tattoos in North America.

Again, while the argument that in North American and other Western figurations tattoos, deviant images, and social stigma tend to go hand in hand still has credibility, this depiction often limits the analysis of tattooing as a legitimate and respectable form of art or personal/sub-cultural expression (DeMello 1995, 2000; Friedman 1996; Gallick 1996). Debates about the changing status of tattooing have become common in North America, where tattooing and other redesigning body projects have clearly become fashionable. Vail's (1999) more recent study of tattoo art collectors made the argument that perceptions of tattooing as a legitimate art form may be changing, illustrating how North Americans are currently reconsidering the tattoo's potential as a cultural symbol. Irwin's (2000) re-visitation of Sanders's (1989) description of the negotiation process in tattooing (i.e., between artists and their clients concerning the image to be tattooed, its size, coloration, and placement on the body) similarly depicted the practice as much more culturally normative than most sociologists consider.

I commend these authors for critically re-examining the sociological construction of the practice, but simultaneously caution against eliminating tattooing from the realm of social deviance. In essence, by casting the practice of tattooing in an 'either/or' analytical framework, we ignore the possibility that tattooing is in fact both normative *and* deviant in Canada – and therefore, fail to consider how, when, where, and why tattoos are worn by Canadians, and decoded by audiences. It seems, however, that the recent trend in sociological analysis of the practice is to engage in a theoretical about-face, focusing on the trendy nature of tattoos while de-emphasizing the stigma associated with the tattooed body. In the words of John Gray, who warned against interpreting the tattoo's recent popularity as a trend toward its permanent acceptance: '[A]ccording to the media, tattooing is about to go permanently mainstream. Don't believe it. Rumours of imminent respectability have been chasing the tattoo for a century' (1994, 15).

Life in the Tattoo Studio

The second general area of investigation common in the sociological literature is the study of tattoo artists and their working environments. These are typically small-scale, idiographic analyses involving the activities of artists employed within one or a handful of tattoo studios (Burchett and Leighton 1958; J. Gray 1994; St Clair and Govenar 1981; Steward 1990; Webb 1979). They also include the study of a specific faction of the tattoo figuration such as the New York tattoo artist community (McCabe 1997) or Modern Primitive artists (Atkinson and Young 2001; Featherstone 2000; Myers 1997; Rosenblatt 1997; Vale and Juno 1989). In these studies, a cross-section of issues and concerns are addressed, including the career contingencies of becoming a tattoo artist (Sanders 1989; Steward 1990), the personal histories of some of the key people in the figuration (DeMello 2000; McCabe 1997), the tensions between competing groups of artists (Gray 1994; Steward 1990), and the contemporary organization of the business as a commercial enterprise (Sanders 1988).

Throughout these texts – Steward's autobiographical (1990) account of life as a tattoo artist and St Clair and Govenar's work (1981) are particularly illustrative – we are given first-hand accounts of life on the edge of professional respectability. As the artists' narratives interweave with sociological analysis, a sense of what it is like to be at the hub of the practice is gleaned. Readers are let into a world scarcely known but widely stereotyped, and we gain an understanding of how many tattoo artists sense that they are a conduit of social deviance. On reflecting about his experiences with tattoo enthusiasts and his role in providing the deviant service, Steward wrote:

> Two reactions seem possible in persons who see a tattoo on someone. One is complete fascination, a feeling that here is the ultimate stud, the great macho, the sexual satyr, the Marlboro man, the far travelling sailor, the incomparable sadistic master, the Genet criminal just released from prison. The other is a complete revulsion: the tattoo represents the epitome of sleaze, of low-class background, of cheap vulgarity and bad taste, everything that intelligence and sophistication have conditioned you to despise. (1990, 10)

Sociologists investigating contemporary tattooing are indebted to such studies of tattoo artists on several of theoretical and methodological levels. Through the explorations of Goffman's dramaturgical theory (1959, 1963), Lemert's labelling theory (1951, 1967), and subcultural theories (e.g., Cohen 1955; Hebdige 1979), research on the lived experiences of tattoo artists brings to light and analytically dissects the structural backbone of the figuration.

While some of these accounts read more as non-fictional narratives than in-depth analyses (e.g., Steward 1990), social researchers attending to the occupational, existential, and interpersonal experiences of tattoo artists have laid out a theoretical and conceptual map for navigating the tattoo figuration. This effort has been directly facilitated by researchers' commitment to exploring the tattoo figuration via field research, that is, by actively getting involved with artists through participant observation. These studies illustrate how first-hand research on tattooing is not only feasible but the surest way to capture the *zeitgeist* of the artists in a specific era (DeMello 2000; Sanders 1989). As a result, individuals should be encouraged to interact with tattoo artists as a means of deciphering the social dynamics of the figuration, and to pursue thick accounts of the tattoo enterprise so that members' own accounts can be presented alongside sociological understandings of the figuration.

The main advantage of in-depth, first-hand research efforts commencing in the tattoo studio is that they provide a solid basis for making *informed* (or what sociologists might call *empirical*) claims about the tattoo figuration and its participants. Studies of life in tattoo studios illustrate how first-hand knowledge paves the way for enlightened understandings of social practices and spaces. In the case of a socially marginal practice such as tattooing, or a traditionally disreputable space like a tattoo parlour, cultural stereotypes and misinformation may only be shed through informed accounts.

Tattoo This! The Politics of Identity

Recent sociological analyses of tattooing reflect prominent theoretical trends in research on body modification. Tattooing has been inserted into discussions of the ways in which bodies are essential in 'doing' identity politics. Women's experiences with tattoos and tattooing among middle class factions of the figuration such as the Neo Primitives indicate that tattoos may be utilized as an expression of social resistance. Considering the tattoo's historically non-normative status in North America (particularly as a body project for women, the middle class, and gay/lesbian groups), tattooed bodies are theorized to be political billboards of dissent. In the cliché terminology of the day, it is suggested that wilfully tattooing the body is an act of 'personal reclamation' (i.e., a statement of opposition against codes regulating acceptable gender, class, and ethnic display). Research indicates that tattooing is used as a personally therapeutic technique for coming to terms with rape experiences or gender/ethnic/sexual discrimination (Atkinson and Young 2001), as a form of resistance to capitalist ideologies of imperialism and expansion, as a collective search for spirituality and identity in an increasingly secularized and globalized world (Rosenblatt 1997), and as a way of rejecting dominant cultural constructions of art and beauty (Mifflin 1997).

Analysis offered through this line of inquiry alludes to the changing and polysemic nature of cultural understandings about tattoos in North America. Unfortunately, a much-needed sense of objectivity and detachment is typically relinquished in these discussions. Authors often become as actively involved in the resistance to culture as do the subjects. In many cases, one is led to wonder if the tattooing practices are consciously constructed by participants as resistance, or simply interpreted by researchers as such. Tattooing becomes more of a validation of strands of Marxist, cultural studies, feminist, queer, and postmodern theories than a social practice grounded in participants' (inter)subjective experiences with and definitions of tattoos. In these instances of analysis, researchers are not allowing themselves to be 'surprised' (Willis 1980) by what they find, and are missing the inherent possibilities for exploration and discovery.

A term that is apropos for categorizing extant sociological research on tattooing is diversity. Mini-traditions have developed within the small body of literature on the subject, indicating that some of us have recognized a need for 'concatenating' (Stebbins 1992) research efforts on tattooing. The overall literature taps into myriad social uses, constructions, and experiences with tattoos. Taking as their subject matter the entire range of activities within the tattoo figuration, sociological investigations of the practice are much more substantively varied, theoretically flexible, and methodologically rigorous than are their cultural anthropological and psychological counterparts.

The Sacred and Profane: Media Representations of Tattooing

A significantly different body of knowledge from which to inspect cultural perspectives on tattooing is located in the media. Although media sources do not always offer what one might call 'trustworthy' information about tattooing, the stories and commentaries gleaned from various media depictions of tattooing bear fruit nonetheless. Importantly, media accounts and reports about tattoo enthusiasts and their tastes for body modification are rising in number. As the media have begun to take notice of tattooed bodies (for a litany of reasons), tattoos have emerged out of the shadows and onto the cultural main stage. More so than in any previous era, a wide range of stories about tattooing are now being told in magazines and newspapers, in film, on television, and on the Internet. Consequently, a public forum about (and set of accompanying discourses relating to) tattooing in Canada is rapidly developing.

The stories recounted in the media about tattooed bodies are considerably more poetic, contested, stereotypical, provocative, commercialized, and emotionally stirring than are their academic counterparts. Rather than approaching the subject with the detached objectivity of a social scientist or cultural analyst (as thinly veiled as this might be at times!), media accounts of tattooing are unabashedly laden with affective viewpoints or political interests. Scanning over the images and narratives about tattooing circulated in popular media sources since 1990, one cannot help note that tattooing has spawned new debates and controversies about safe, normative, and culturally appropriate body play in Canada. To that extent, tattooing's more recent popularity, and widespread appearance in mass-media images and messages, may be a new cultural barometer by which competing attitudes about body modification may be measured.

Newspaper accounts, our most common source of media-based information related to tattooing, cover a full spectrum of tattooing issues. In most newspaper articles, a central theme or purpose generally underlies a carefully scripted story or perspective about the practice. Of late, this theme tends to revolve around the explication of the practice's new-found popularity – especially among youth. Eye-catching headlines such as 'Tattoos: No Longer' Just for Sailors' (Novak 2000), 'Tattoo Studios Make a Mark on the Mainstream' (Bourette 1998), 'The World Beats a Path to Smilin' Buddha' (Scotton 2000), 'Tattoos and Modern Britain' (Dalrymple 2000), and 'Body Art Goes Mainstream' (Aggerholm 2000), seemingly evidence the normative essence of contemporary tattooing. In drawing to the reader's attention a series of changes in the industry (e.g., new and more 'skilled' artists, increased hygiene in studios, and the opening of new studios in chic fashion districts) and the client base (i.e., its general diversification) that have apparently elevated the body project to a more socially inclusive and respectable plateau, these articles present an image of tattooing as something other than the practice of the social misfit or rebel.

Concurrently, though, other newspaper articles are more or less vehicles for the dissemination of fears and concerns about tattooing. Articles entitled 'Tattoos and Piercings: Side-effects Can Be Ugly' (MacAfee 2000) and 'Too-da-loo Tattoo: Laser Erases Skin-deep Regrets for a Price' (Connery 2001) delineate the physical and social risks of buying into the popular trend of tattooing. The characterization of tattoo clients and their body projects in such articles can be both insulting and unjustifiably naive. By portraying most clients as impetuous, unreflective, and self-mutilating risk-seekers, they perpetuate common myths about tattoo enthusiasts. Instead of promoting new discourses about the body and its modification, describing the high level of health care practised by the majority of artists and their clients, or informing potential tattoo enthusiasts about the genuine risks involved in the procedure (without engaging in exaggeration), writers prefer to shock, frighten, and alarm. In simple terms, the inflated and overstated dangers associated with tattooing practices (and supposed self-destructive nature of the average client) is clearly more marketable than is rational and informed discussion.

At the same time, tattooed bodies have become substantially more visible in print and television advertisements for commercial products. Advertisements for common commodities ranging from cellular phones to alcoholic beverages have in the past ten years deliberately included tattooed skin. Given the cultural appeal of tattooing and piercing for the 16- to- 35-year-old population in Canada and abroad, tattooing itself has been gobbled up by consumer-savvy marketers. Presenting products around hip-looking, skin-flashing people, marketers cleverly align the products with the trendiness of tattooing. Typically found in fashion or popular cultural magazines oriented toward younger readers with disposable incomes (e.g., *FHM, Loaded, Cosmopolitan, Gear, Seventeen, Maxim, Esquire, GQ*), these advertisements portray cool, tattoo-clad, young people as voracious consumers.

By relying on and reproducing traditional images of the tattoo as a marker of deviance and rebellion, these advertisements attempt to portray the products as cutting-edge, chic, or rebellious. For, after all, how uncool could a cellular phone or a photocopier be if people with tattoos used them? In 1996, for instance, a popular ad campaign (involving both print and television) for a North American car company used the slogan 'As subtle as a tattoo' to describe one of its new vehicles. In the same year, a print ad for a long-distance phone-service provider placed the phrase 'Got news?' directly under a picture of a young woman with a tattoo exposed on her back. Even less subtle was a 1998 advertisement for a cellular phone company that contained the sentence 'Extra minutes can mean a lot, when you have a lot of free time on your hands' beside a heavily tattooed prison convict shackled in handcuffs. A popular chocolate manufacturer strategically emblazoned the phrase 'Change is bad' underneath a picture of a young man (in a black shirt, with his sleeves rolled up to the tips of his shoulders) with five females' names tattooed down one arm (all of them crossed out, except the bottom name) in a 1999 ad campaign. Not only do such advertisements illustrate how tattooed skin has been commercialized in recent years, they extend our understanding of how tattooing continues to be culturally associated with danger/power, fear/freedom, deviance/ criminality, and lust/sexuality.

In stark contrast to newspaper articles and television advertisements, tattooing magazines have become the communicative beacons of the modern tattoo community (DeMello 2000). Established as the vehicles of artists and their work, resources for documenting the history of tattooing, sources for advertising and reporting about tattoo conventions around the world, and sites in which artists and their clients may share their experiences with tattoos, magazines such as *Skin and Ink*, *International Tattoo Art*, *Tattoo Flash*, and *Tattoo Savage* are mass-produced textual advocates of tattooing body projects. Artists and their clients are furnished with an outlet for disseminating their own knowledge, which thereby establishes a much-needed counter-balance in the media. For my own research purposes, tattoo magazines served as valuable references for learning about both key players in the contemporary tattoo scene (artists and clients) and current issues and controversies germane to tattooing in Canada.

Similarly contrasting with both newspaper articles and advertisements, a series of documentaries about tattooing in North America have popped up on cable channels such as *A&E*, *Discovery*, and *The Learning Channel* in the past few years. Audiences are entertained with (usually one-hour) stories about the social legacy of and cultural philosophy behind the tattooed body, along with visual depictions. Whether as an episode contained within a series of stories (e.g., about body modification among North Americans or tribal cultural practices), or as the subject of interest itself, documentary narratives about 'living in ink' have become more commonplace. Importantly, documentaries give public voices to tattoo enthusiasts; and in this process, strangers to the body project are able hear about, and gaze into, the lifestyle of a tattoo enthusiast.

Still, the appearance of documentaries about tattooing in the past five to seven years, like newspaper articles or advertisements, is by no means accidental. Coincidentally with the cultural explosion in the popularity of tattooing, cable executives and programmers have clearly recognized that stories about, and displays of, the tattooed body will attract audiences – especially young audiences. Luring crowds of young people to a learning or a 'cultural' channel might prove difficult without making the programming schedule more sexy in such ways. The tattooed body is commercialized in the process, becoming little more than the circus sideshow of channels dedicated to the exploration of high cultural pursuits. The eagerness of some tattoo artists to promote their own work or studios in these documentaries adds further fuel to the commercialization fire. By jumping onto the proverbial media bandwagon to bolster business in their studios, artists participating in televised documentaries (either as the focal subject of the program or merely as a talking head) are able to reach scores of potential clients in the increasingly competitive business world of tattooing.

While the themes underpinning newspaper articles, advertisements, and televised documentaries about tattooing are relatively straightforward to decode, World Wide Web pages devoted to the subject offer very few unifying conceptual themes. Thousands of Web pages emerging since the mid-1990s have presented on-line audiences with a cornucopia of insight and (mis)information about tattoos and their wearers. Ranging in focus from the business of tattooing to the cultural understandings underlying this body project, these Web pages defy simplistic categorization. With growing numbers of artists taking this opportunity to showcase their artistic talents and knowledge about the practice, and clients selecting the Web medium as an avenue for sharing personal experiences with tattoos, current movements and events in the ongoing history of tattooing are being electronically documented on-line.

Although I would not encourage individuals to form their opinions about tattooing, or develop their entire stock of knowledge about the practice, solely from the information gathered on Web pages, Internet sites are the most encompassing of all media sources for several reasons. With a multitude of pages intended to disturb, educate, advertise, offend, promote, shock, and enlighten audiences about the practice, tattooed bodies are firmly cemented in virtual space. DeMello (2000) might well be correct in suggesting that the flow of information over the Web engenders a stronger, and more noticeable, tattoo community in this way. Whether one is examining one of the hundreds of 'studio' sites devoted to the current business of tattooing, any of the FAQ (frequently asked question) dedicated Web pages on the subject, one of the sites devoted to 'bizarre' tattoos, or the thousands of personal Web pages constructed by devoted clients, tattoos have found a permanent home on the Internet. Ironically, it seems that the 'best' media-based knowledge about the tattooed body is found in the virtual/simulated world.

The new media coverage of tattooing could be bracketed into a few major categories – based on the form and content of the information provided. The first, and certainly most common in the past few years, theme in media accounts of the practice is underpinned by the social and physical downside of the growing popularity of tattooing. By citing the spike in the membership base of the tattoo community as a indicator of evolving (i.e., more relaxed) codes about the body and its alteration, critics issue their concerns, fears, and alarms. Indeed, much has been done in this respect to encourage a 'moral panic' (Cohen 1973) about tattooing in Canada. Reports about the health risks associated with tattooing, the unsavoury characters involved in the business, and the shame/stigma classically associated with tattooing are equally documented and hyperbolized. Journal articles written by doctors, nurses, and dentists (Armstrong 1991, 1994a, 1994b, 1995; Armstrong and McConnell 1994; Gurke and Armstrong 1997; Kom 1996) warn about the perils of manipulating the natural body in such a hazardous way. Stern warnings about the risks of transmitting AIDS (without case evidence), Hepatitis C, and other viral diseases are aimed at teenagers and their parents. Dramatizations of the tattoo-removal procedure, the loss of employment from being tattooed, and the trauma to the body are highlighted in an effort to point out the sadistic nature of the practice.

Second, the boom in media interest about tattooing has resulted in a partial caricaturing of this redesigning body project. In contending that Canadians' interest in tattooing is nothing more than cultural whimsy, a passing fancy of a lost generation of youth, media critics summarily dismiss the ideological potential of the body project (i.e., as a powerful form of group expression and cultural commentary). The use of words like 'fad,' 'trend,' and 'popular style' in articles about tattooing strikes at the heart of the practice's 'ideological form' (Cohen 1972). Trivializing tattooing as a consumer trend of contemporary pop culture dismisses the multitude of ways in which people construct their tattoos as deeply meaningful ideological expressions. Furthermore, by drawing upon the contemporary sex appeal of tattoos in print and television, advertisers of commercial products treat the tattooed body as carnival. When the practice is downplayed as an uninspired group phenomenon, the symbolic cultural gestures made through tattooed skin are reduced to rubble. Ignoring the voices of individuals who actually wear tattoos, while advancing their own maps of meaning for interpreting them, critics discount the communicative nature of this body play.

Third, media outlets are now used by tattoo enthusiasts as a way of (re)presenting alternative ways of seeing/knowing tattoos. Adopting a range of standpoints and roles (from the cultural rebel to the empathic educator), tattoo artists and their clients (and curious writers, producers, and commentators) are painting the mediascape with their own interpretations of the tattooed body. A distinctively human picture of tattooing, relying heavily on personal biographies and narratives about living in tattooed skin, is offered. In utilizing the media (magazines, newspaper articles, televised programs, and Web pages) to promote the business of tattooing, artists have found a valuable tool for marketing their artwork in the information era. However, members of the tattoo figuration also find it beneficial to use the media's appetite for tattooing as an avenue for dispelling long-standing myths about tattooing, circulating proper health-care techniques to clients, and disseminating the artistic styles common in contemporary tattooing.

The media provides some fascinating information about the popularity, form, and expression of tattooing among Canadians. With increased media exposure, the contested cultural status of tattooing is plainly in evidence. To be sure, there is no single use, definition, preference, or understanding of tattooing that all (or even most) Canadians share. Furthermore, with the increased appearance of tattoos in print, film, and on-line, Canadians can witness how prevalent tattooed skin is in our society. Treated with all degrees of seriousness and (dis)respect, the subject is a hot topic for media producers. Whether the display of a tattooed leg, or a story about one's first tattooing experience, is intended to titillate, raise contempt for tattoo enthusiasts, or facilitate an informed cultural dialogue about tattooing, the media appears to be hooked. Instead of ignoring the media as a wasteland devoid of meaningful cultural substance, we must grasp the opportunity to learn from these accounts and portrayals about the conflicting sentiments about tattooing. While inferences and suppositions about exactly what we may draw from such accounts must be tentative, the writing about, photographing, and representing of tattoos in the popular media are vital resources for chronicling the evolving status of tattoos in Canada.

Using Our Knowledge about Tattooing

After I had examined what we know, and don't know, about tattooing in Canada, I found that several main problems guided my sociological foray into the world of tattoo enthusiasm. First, a recurrent theme in the literature on tattooing is the notion that a distinct tattoo subculture exists – including tattoo artists, their clients, equipment suppliers, business owners, and so-called hangers-on. While it has been widely documented that particular subcultures employ tattooing as a means of fostering group cohesion, it is similarly suggested that a larger 'community' of tattoo enthusiasts exists (DeMello 2000). *However, we must ask if there is a distinct tattooing subculture or community of tattoo enthusiasts, as many authors have previously suggested.* If group boundaries are fuzzy and easily transgressed by members and non-members – a fact compounded by the widespread commodification of tattooing as a redesigning body project – how might we begin to categorize tattoo enthusiasts conceptually (if this group can be classified as a cohesive collectivity at all)?

Second, from the beginning of my investigation I was strongly committed to a general belief that in order to understand fully the recent proliferation of tattooing body projects in Canada, we must contextualize the motivations for modifying the body against long-term sociogenic trends in Canada. For instance, what 'outside' cultural/structural factors influence the (trans)formation of the group of tattoo enthusiasts? In this respect, sociologists must be attentive to *the ways in which tattooing (as a redesigning body project) can be understood over time; in particular, how the popularity of tattooing is affected by figurational body habits during specific historical moments.*

Third, in an era in which we are increasingly redesigning our bodies through projects of corporeal alteration, we need to ascertain why we choose to alter our bodies permanently through tattooing. While sociologists have acquired a preliminary understanding of tattooing, we need to revisit motivations toward and accounts of tattooing in light of the current popularity of the practice. Even the most descriptive and comprehensive accounts of tattooing in the literature to date fail to address *why individuals choose to participate in this body project over others, or why they engage in tattooing alongside other forms of corporeal manipulation.*

Fourth, and flowing from the previous problems, we must include *as a central part of the investigation an analysis of how tattoos are lived and experienced in everyday life*. Finally, based on the study of tattooing practices in Canada, *what might an integrated sociological model of habitus formation look like, and how might it be utilized by sociologists to analyse a full spectrum of body-modification projects?*

CHAPTER FOUR

Meeting Tattoo Enthusiasts

I became interested in tattooing as a sociological subject about seven years ago. I knew a handful of tattoo artists in the city of Toronto, and had spent several months hanging out with, interviewing, and observing them as part of a qualitative research assignment I was conducting for a graduate course in research methods. Comparing data collected in Toronto to empirical observations made in tattoo studios in the city of Hamilton, I produced a narrowly focused study of the 'career contingencies' (Prus 1987) of tattoo artists. Following this project, I spent more time hanging around with tattoo artists in Toronto, and was tattooed several more times myself. I came to view the subject as well worth pursuing in an extended way – to the degree that I decided to study and write a monograph about tattooing in Canada.

In this chapter, the method of participant observation (Blumer 1969; Dewalt and Dewalt 1998; Fine 1999; Gans 1999; Prus 1996, 1997) is outlined as a well-suited approach for exploring tattooing as a lived experience. Broadly speaking, participant observation is a method for studying social phenomena that places the researcher in the centre of what is being studied – by literally hanging out with, or living among, people doing certain social activities. Taking the primacy of engaging with the social world as the methodological pillar of my investigation of tattooing, then, I wanted to learn about tattoo artists' and clients' experiences, constructions, and interpretations with tattoos on a first-hand basis.

Where We Live and Breathe

The cities of Calgary and Toronto seemed like ideal sites for me to commence my sociological venture into tattooing. I was living in Calgary at the time, and knew several artists in the area – so I had an important series of contacts to help me along with the study. Furthermore, the city is a diverse and growing social environment, with a quickly evolving body-modification scene. My initial thoughts were that the residents of Calgary, and their apparent newfound hunger for tattooing, might be indicative of more sweeping trends in tattooing evidenced across the country (i.e., the number of people involved, their background characteristics, and the prevalence of tattoo studios in Canadian cities). By contrast, the tattoo scene in Toronto is an established one, with its heroes, icons, antagonists, and traditions. I frequented Toronto on a regular basis, knew several artists there, and had many tattooed friends in the city. Thus, tattoo studios in Toronto provided an easily accessible and conceptually different set of locations for the research.

Before the mid-1990s, only a few well-known tattoo studios existed in the city of Calgary. One studio in particular, established near the local military base, was the supplier of quality tattoos in Calgary. While novice or professionally unconnected tattoo artists operated out of basements, apartments, or other dwellings, the only well-established studio in the city was Paul Jefferies's shop, Smilin' Buddha. By 2001, there were eleven commercial tattoo studios in the city, varying in their location across the area, the number of artists employed in the studios, and the clientele sought after or serviced by the artists.

For the most part, the 'old-school' tattoo studios in Calgary are located near industrial or traditionally working-class areas (e.g., the northeast sector, the Bowness area, or along the segment of 16th Avenue splicing the north section of the city). Situated beside or near liquor stores, pool halls, pawn shops, convenience stores, garages, or fast-food restaurants, these tattoo studios resemble the classic American tattoo parlours of the 1950s and 1960s. Relatively inexpensive rental rates make these districts attractive for shop owners, but this is offset by the low flow of pedestrian traffic in the areas, limiting the amount of walkins entering the shop on a daily basis. In contrast, the newest studios in Calgary are located in the city's core – particularly in the fashion and entertainment districts (e.g., Kensington Road, 17th Avenue, and MacLeod Trail South). In conformity with more recent trends in the history of tattooing (Cohen 2000), these studios are cropping up where young, urban, middle-class groups congregate. Situated beside clothing boutiques, upscale restaurants, snowboard and skateboard shops, hair salons, bookstores, and martini bars, the most sought-after locations for tattoo studios are those that afford a high degree of visibility, a high level of pedestrian traffic, and close proximity to hoards of middle-class urbanites.

Tattoo studios in Calgary employ anywhere from one to seven artists (including some piercing artists). The average number of artists employed in tattoo studios in Calgary is two. Generally, one artist owns and operates the studio, hiring others to handle the smaller and less-complicated work. Keeping the numbers low within the tattoo studio creates a scenario in which one or two artists become associated with the studio, and allows for a substantial amount of administrative and creative freedom. However, since tattoo shops in Calgary service an average of eight to twelve clients per day, having two or three artists work in tandem proves to be an efficient and effective way of maintaining and managing a stable client flow.

In each of the studios, tattoo artists encounter a mix of individuals, ranging from ex-convicts to doctors. However, certain types of tattoo studios in Calgary tend to be frequented by particular clienteles. For example, some shops attract working-class men, motorcyclists, and those involved in nefarious enterprises. In these shops artists generally tattoo most images asked for by a client, and will tattoo almost any location on the body. Accordingly, some of these shops carry a local stereotype of a tough shop or a biker outfit. Artists employed by these shops specialize in tattoo styles and motifs (e.g., navy/carnival, death/demonic, fantasy, and fine-line), especially those associated with the more traditional tattooing themes. These shops are deliberately avoided by the middle-class clients I ended up meeting in Calgary, as their atmosphere (created by the setting, the artists, and the clients) is deemed unsavoury.

On the other hand, tattoo studios near the downtown core attract more middle-class clients. Charging slightly higher prices ($100–200 per hour), the studios within the urban core are often presented as more upscale, refined, and artistically inclined establishments that specialize in a number of tattoo styles or custom techniques. Clients frequenting the more 'middle-class' studios in Calgary range in age from eighteen to sixty-five, and include more female than male clients in ratios exceeding 3:1 in some cases. With an emphasis on mutual respect, creative exploration, and artistic integrity, these studios are the more 'friendly' alternatives in the business. For those new to the tattooing process, they appear as unthreatening environments in which to be tattooed.

The business of tattooing in Calgary has blossomed from an industry dominated by one (and then a handful) of tattoo studios into an open, diverse, and booming market. Tattoo studios in Calgary are more numerous, visible, and specialized than ever before. As the demand for tattoos has increased, the division of labour within the business has become more complex. There is room (in both economic and spatial terms) for many tattoo artists in the city. A practice previously kept on the margins of the metropolitan area, tattooing has now infiltrated its way into the popular culture of the city.

Tattoo studios in Toronto are considerably more established and diverse than their Calgary counterparts. Of the studios (varying in size, reputation, and level of professionalization) within metropolitan Toronto, many have been in operation for more than ten years. The studios are spread out across the sprawling metro area, located in the downtown fashion and consumer districts, alternative-lifestyle districts, or a handful of semi-industrial areas. In recent years, more studios have sprung up in the downtown core close to others with well-established reputations and clienteles. Moving to affluent neighbourhoods outside of the immediate central business district, other studios are pursuing what DeMello (2000) refers to as the 'middle-class client.'

Tattoo studios in Toronto are incredibly eclectic. There are several classically styled 'tattoo parlours' in the downtown area, and many of the enthusiasts frequenting these shops are attracted to these settings precisely because they emit an aura of non-conventionality. They are hidden from plain view in some cases, and laden with exterior and interior decorations that connote aggression and hyper-masculinity (e.g., skulls and daggers, motorcycle-club insignias, and specific sets of 'Traditional' tattoo flash). These shops, however, seem to be the last of an old breed in Toronto – the few remaining classic parlours from the golden era of tattooing in North America. The niche these shops have carved out seems to remain intact nonetheless. Holding firm to the idea that the tattoo parlour is a setting where like-minded people may congregate and revel in their dislocation from mainstream culture, these remaining shops maintain a loyal and steady clientele.

The more modern studios are stark contrasts to the old-school parlours in Toronto. Situated next to or near haute-couture salons and boutiques, second-hand clothing stores, exclusive restaurants, grocery stores, music stores, and laundromats, the clear majority of Toronto's tattoo studios are positioned in the heart of the downtown scene. Cleverly placed in high-traffic areas of popular downtown shopping districts, these studios are everyday institutions in Toronto's urban culture, and are frequented by a mix of individuals, from homeless street youth to corporate executives. The artistic nature of tattooing is almost universally stressed by the artists in these shops, as is the importance of quality tattoo art. The interiors of the shops are designed using a multitude of decorative styles, but most studios try to tap into and reinvigorate the feel of the classic parlours in (post)modern ways. Hot-rod flames painted on the studio's outside and inside, checkerboard tiling on the floors, pictures of pin-up girls on the walls, pool tables in the lobby, and other rockabilly motifs are juxtaposed against contemporary techno or heavy-metal music played over loudspeakers, high-tech equipment in the front areas (fax machines, copying equipment, and sterilization technologies), and post/modern furniture made from chrome/steel, leather, or Rubbermaid plastic. The outsider-hip traditions of tattooing in North America are cleverly drawn upon through physical props, but this is carefully managed and muted so that clients do not entirely associate the studio with a stereotypical tattoo parlour.

An even smaller category of tattoo studios in Toronto includes the most exclusive and esoteric shops in the metropolitan area. Located in alternative-lifestyle (gay and lesbian) districts in Toronto, these studios are marketed toward such specific tattoo enthusiasts as the Modern Primitives (Atkinson and Young 2001; Rosenblatt 1997; Vale and Juno 1989). For the most part, these studios service the 'high end' tattoo client – the individual unimpressed by and uncomfortable with the downtown tattoo parlours. To this end, these studios resemble a cross between a fine art gallery, museum, and physician's office. Walls are often covered with black-and-white still photographs or other pieces of art, plush furniture fills the waiting rooms, classical or New Age music is often played on expensive sound systems, and receptionists greet prospective clients.

The underlying ideology in the current era of tattooing in both Calgary and Toronto seems to be inclusiveness rather than exclusiveness. In competitive markets, tattoo artists cannot afford to dismiss particular clients or their tattooing interests. Finding a niche or narrow client base may prove profitable for some outfits (i.e., the old-school parlours or high-end studios), but the majority of tattoo studios in the city stress that 'if you can think it up, we can do it.' The market is ultimately consumer-driven, and tattooing practices are largely influenced (and in some cases, dictated) by clients' tastes and preferences. Each studio wields considerable agency in constructing its unique identity (i.e., the layout, artists employed, predominant tattoo styles, and dominant philosophies underlying the studio's tattooing), but this identity is negotiated and altered through interaction with clients. The prosperous tattoo studios

in Toronto are those that change with the times, interpreting and in-
corporating clients' tastes and preferences into their daily tattooing
practices.

In sum, I frequented for the most part the newer studios in each of
the cities. There are several old-school studios there, but most of the
emergent shops are categorically new school, serving clientele with a
range of tattooing tastes and preferences. Since the bulk of the existing
ethnographic-based literature on tattooing focuses on old-school tattoo
parlours, an emphasis on them in Calgary and Toronto would have
mainly replicated previous findings on tattoo enthusiasm. Instead, I
wanted to explore the tattooing practices of those who account for the
ongoing boom in tattooing in Canada and understand how the newer
studios cater to their needs.

Becoming a Participant in Tattooing

On a cold Wednesday afternoon in January of 1998, I made my way to a
small tattoo shop in Calgary. I was acquainted with several tattoo artists
in Calgary, and had been tattooed on two different occasions by artists
in the city – so, I was not exactly a complete newcomer in the community. I had ventured to a handful of the shops in Calgary on different
occasions, casing them out and speaking to tattoo artists about my own
interests in tattooing. On this day, however, I entered the shop to meet
an artist in the hope of securing him as a potential sponsor for my
research.

Aside from the loud music, images on the walls, or clients patiently
waiting in anticipation in the lobby, the first thing I am always struck
with when walking into a tattoo studio is the smell. It's a subtle yet over-
powering blend of ink, antiseptic, and latex – and it is unmistakable. I
remember walking into the Endurance studio (a pseudonym) on that
January day and being hit with the smell like a slap to the face. On a previous visit there I had briefly spoken with a tattoo artist named Jack. I
knew that Wednesday was often a slow workday for tattoo artists in Calgary at the time, and thought it would be an ideal time to re-introduce
myself to him (business would be slow and having someone to talk to
might after a refreshing break). With some nervousness I approached
Jack, who was seated behind the reception desk, and asked him if he
remembered me from my previous visits. He nodded in the affirmative
and asked, 'You wanted some of your family stuff [crest] done on your
arms, right?' I confirmed the accuracy of his memory, and we began to

talk about tattooing, his shop, and the tattooing scene in Calgary. I showed him some of my existing tattoo work, my own flesh-based business card. Showing your tattoo work to others (as I had learned from tattooed friends of mine in Toronto) can be a means of immediately displaying your interest in the practice. In essence, it buys an individual a certain amount of street credibility or cultural capital among tattoo enthusiasts. Jack admired some of my work, and asked who had drawn the tattoos for me. I told him about each of the artists, and after a brief period of small talk eventually divulged my research interests to him.

Jack immediately responded to my research program with enthusiasm. He could not believe that someone would want to (or would be given money to!) conduct research on tattooing for a doctoral dissertation. He rushed to the back room, then brought back an armful of articles, books, and historical pieces on tattooing in North America – some very obscure, old, and invaluable. It was a veritable treasure-trove of information on the practice, and for about an hour and a half we pored through the texts, discussing what each of us knew about the subject. We refrained from entering into much personal disclosure in our discussion, but covered a long list of subjects related to tattooing. The conversation broke when a client came in for a tattoo, but I told Jack I would bring some of the academic materials on tattooing I had collected over the past five years, and he seemed eager to delve into what I had found. I left the studio feeling that if I had found a potential site to begin my venture into tattooing in Calgary. Given Jack's apparent interest about my research project, I immediately felt that Endurance would be an ideal setting to launch my investigation.

In the research process, a participant observer regularly makes personal, ethical, practical, and strategic methodological choices. These choices begin with the selection of where and among whom the research is to be initiated. I chose Endurance because the shop was relatively small (employing three tattoo artists and one piercing artist), but well known within the city. During my previous visits to the studio the artists seemed quite amiable and accommodating – answering questions and readily engaging with others. It was owned and partially funded by an individual who is not a tattoo artist (as is common in the current era), located in a fashion district in Calgary, and had a strong and stable client base of young urbanites. It was also one of the newer studios in the city, with a sizable lobby in which individuals could hang out in before their appointments. Although I continued to cultivate contacts in other studios in Calgary and other urban areas, Endurance became one of the principal settings for the early stages of my participant observation.

This first day in the field had a profound impact on the role I adopted in the research process. I could have entered and left tattoo studios as a regular client, amassing a sizable number of tattoos as a way of studying the everyday practices of tattooing closely (which I eventually did anyway). Sitting or lying in a tattoo chair for hours on end could have been used as a means of interviewing tattoo artists, or serve as the basis of an extensive auto-ethnography of my own involvement in tattooing. But I sought a different role among the tattoo enthusiasts, one that would facilitate an analysis of tattooing as a form of interpersonal interaction. The search for my role (along with the description of every minute detail of the studio) would become, during the first few weeks at the studio, the subject matter of the majority of my field notes – analysing how I fitted into the scene and how I might secure an ongoing role there. After each day of interaction, I spent from three to six hours writing field notes, as fervently advocated by such champions of participant observation as Becker (1970), Blumer (1969), and Prus (1996, 1997).

Reflecting on my field notes, I noted the zealousness that Jack showed toward reading academic research on tattooing. I thought this might be an ideal way to justify my presence in a studio, as a provider of outside material or references on the practice. In combining this role with another I brought to the research process (that of a tattoo enthusiast), I gained a relatively unproblematic entrée into the setting. By making (at first) weekly visits to the shop to speak with Jack about the history of tattooing, I became somewhat of a regular at Endurance. Encouraging Jack to be a verifier and critic of academic knowledge on tattooing, I was able to establish my presence as relatively normal (or at least unobtrusive) within the shop. After a couple of months had passed, Jack and the other artists at Endurance collectively came to know me as Mike, 'the guy who teaches up at the university.'

By April of 1999 I was travelling to the studio on a regular basis. In watching clients get tattooed, talking with the artists about the business of tattooing, and discussing how cultural anthropologists, psychologists, and other sociologists have studied tattooing, I spent hours in situ studying everyday life in the studio. Essentially, I was doing what the literature on participant observation suggests is a rudimentary technique for gaining an understanding of a social setting – simply 'hanging around' (Shaffir 1999; Willis 1978, 1980) and talking with people.

I used my experiences at Endurance to gain a sense of how the business of tattooing operates in Calgary. When I started to compare the emerging information with what I knew about the scene in Toronto, I began to ask Jack about other studios in the area, and the famous (and about more infamous) artists at other studios across Canada. During this period I met scores of clients who had been tattooed across the city. I met some on site at Endurance, and others through friends and acquaintances in Calgary. The time I spent at Endurance proved invaluable to my own understanding of what it means to be involved in a tattoo studio on a daily basis, and I deeply appreciated being allowed to participate there. However, after a period of turmoil and dissent within the shop Jack left Endurance, and as a result I no longer felt comfortable there. I spent less time in the studio as the weeks passed, and began to travel and to hang out in other studios in Calgary.

A friend of mine had been tattooed at a studio in Calgary called Sacred Art, and wanted to introduce me to the artist who had performed the work (named Patrick). Sacred Art is a relatively new studio in Calgary, specializing in custom tattoo work. Taking this opportunity to foster another contact in the area, I met with Patrick and discussed my research. By using the technique I found helpful at Endurance, I slipped into the same role I had previously with Jack – a provider of academic information on tattooing and avid tattoo client. Over the course of the next twelve months I developed a friendship with Patrick, and found myself going to his studio to receive several tattoos. I visited his studio on a regular basis, hanging out and discussing the practice of tattooing with Patrick and some of his clients.

I was very lucky in the early stages of my investigation, as the processes of gaining access and securing a role in the tattoo scene proved neither arduous nor harrowing. I encountered few roadblocks in the process of gaining entry, partly (I believe) because I am an avid collector of tattoos and therefore have experience with the practice. I was able to speak with artists about the history of, current trends in, and my own experiences with tattooing. To some of the artists, my sociological interest in the subject seemed to be complemented, if not wholly justified, by my personal fascination with tattoo art and culture. I believe that I mainly escaped being categorized as a troublemaker or a bothersome client who needed to be managed and dissuaded from returning.

Over the better part of the next two years, I hung out in several tattoo studios across Canada, and travelled to the United Sates to visit some of the more famous and infamous American tattoo studios. By interacting with artists and their clients I have gleaned a deeper understanding of tattooing. As I watched, listened to, and participated with tattoo enthusiasts, I learned a great deal about how interaction unfolds among the group. Rather than strictly relying on the description of daily experiences from insiders, hanging around with tattoo enthusiasts allowed me to observe closely the here-and-now of everyday life as a member. I learned the proverbial ropes of tattoo enthusiasm, became privy to insider information regarding business practices, witnessed some of the most banal and exciting moments in the lives of individuals involved in studios, and was trusted with some very intimate stories about tattoo enthusiasts' lives. In this book, all the names of the people involved have been changed to protect their identities and respect their privacy.

Casting Out Nets: Interviews and Strategies

Early on in the course of the participant observation, I began to conduct interviews with tattoo artists and clients. To augment, expand, and inspect the information I accumulated by hanging around with tattoo enthusiasts, I actively pursued some of them for interview purposes. The interviews were intended to elicit narratives about tattooing experiences from individuals, in the quest of exploring a figurational understanding of how and why individuals select tattooing as a body project. Using data from conversations and observations made in the studios as a template for constructing 'loose' interview schedules and guides for directed conversation, I solicited both artists and clients for interviews. Almost without exception, individuals were surprised, willing, and eager to be included in an academic study of the practice.

The term 'interview' is rather subjective, and quite open for interpretation. An interview may refer to any number of interactive contexts in which one person asks another questions and then represents the question-answer process through some form of aural, visual, or performance-based text. The interview strategy I adopted closely followed the prescriptions for interviewing outlined by Glaser (1992, 1995), Glaser and Strauss (1967), Lofland and Lofland (1995), and Prus (1996) – yet simultaneously incorporated Gubrium and Holstein's suggestions (1997) for exploring and dissecting narratives through the active interviewing process. Since little is known about the actual forms and practices (i.e., meanings and styles) of tattooing in Canada, I required an interview strategy that would elicit free-ranging and highly descriptive responses from individuals about their experiences with tattooing. I needed an interview approach that would allow for a considerable amount of empirical exploration into how individuals decide to become tattooed, experience tattooing, and draw upon a series of interpretive resources (or simply perspectives) when creating narratives about their tattooing body projects.

My task became one of developing a target sample of respondents for the interviews. Given the recent diversification of the population of tattoo enthusiasts in Canada (Atkinson and Young 2001), I was faced with making another series of decisions in the data collection process. By the time I was ready to conduct interviews (i.e., after gaining somewhat of a grounded understanding of tattoo studios and reformulating my interview schedules), I was aware that tattoo enthusiasts are a relatively heterogeneous group. Possessing, in many cases, nothing in common other than an interest in modifying the body through tattooing, the individuals I encountered in the early stages of the research at the tattoo studios exhibited few biographical similarities – save for the fact that the overwhelming majority were younger (19–24), white women with little previous experience in tattooing. The selection process would have been significantly more efficient and expeditious if some form of list containing the entire population of tattoo enthusiasts existed from which a sample could have been drawn.

Purposive or theoretical sampling (Lofland and Lofland 1995), then, was the most appropriate sampling strategy for the research. The sample of interviewees initially grew in the form of a convenience sample, and I eventually targeted several core categories of tattoo enthusiasts for interview purposes. I wanted to include a balance of men and women in the theoretical sampling frame, individuals with different socioeconomic characteristics, and individuals possessing diverse sexual or lifestyle preferences. Furthermore, I sought tattoo enthusiasts with assorted levels of involvement in the practice; in reference to how long (in years) the person had been tattooed, how many tattoos (in total number) the person had acquired, how many times the person had been tattooed (number of sittings or total number of hours), and how extensively the person had been tattooed (amount of skin covered by tattoos and locations of tattoos on the body).

I met the interviewees in several different locations. The majority of interviewees (n=82) were gained through friendship networks I made during the research process in Calgary and southern Ontario. Some of the clients were regulars within the studios, while others were entirely new to the tattooing process. The rejection rate was modest (approximately one in every seven persons was unwilling to be interviewed), with most artists and clients being overtly receptive toward the prospect of being interviewed about their tattoos – even though most had no prior experience with interviewing for any purposes other than employment. To date, I have met several hundred tattoo enthusiasts in Canada, and thus I had access to a sizable pool of tattoo enthusiasts. A smaller number of interviewees (n=10) were met through acquaintances or as students at the University of Calgary.

Background Characteristics of Tattoo Enthusiasts

The number of interviews conducted for this research totalled 92, including 27 tattoo artists and 65 clients. (Some of the following information is summarized in table 4.1.) The average age of the artists interviewed was 25, with an overall range in age from 20 to 55. While men and women are more or less equally represented among tattoo enthusiasts in Canada (Atkinson and Young 2001), only four (15%) of the artists I interviewed in this study were women (to date, I have only met ten female tattoo artists in Canada). Eighteen (67%) of the artists had working-class family backgrounds and nine (33%) had middle-class backgrounds as measured by Blishen's socio-economic index (1967) for occupations in Canada. Twenty of the artists had completed a high school degree (74%), and four (15%) had received either a university degree or at least one year of university education. All the artists interviewed were white, with the exception of one Asian-Canadian artist.

Twenty of the artists (74%) were single at the time of the study, while three were married (11%) and four divorced (15%). Two (7%) of the artists had one child, and three (11%) had two children. Although extant research indicates that the income derived from the tattooing business has been modest in previous eras (Cohen 2000; McCabe 1997; Sanders 1989; Steward 1990), the income of the artists interviewed in this study averaged from $500 to $3000 per week (with charges anywhere from $75 to $300 per hour for their tattoo work). Artists ranged in their professional experience/employment in the business of tattooing from eight months to thirty-five years, with an average of six years. Each of the artists interviewed had tattoos – varying in size, location, and amount of the body covered by the work.

The majority of the artists at the time of the interview (23, 85%) had apprenticed in another tattoo studio or were then apprenticing in a studio. While DeMello (2000) argued that the apprenticeship system in North American tattooing is fracturing, the information I collected sug-

TABLE 4.1   Selected background characteristics of tattoo enthusiasts*

Background	Artists	Clients
Total interviewed	27	65
Average age	25	24
Age range	20–55	18–50
Gender		
Male	21	25
Female	4	40
Social class (Blishen index)		
Upper or middle	9	49
Working	18	16
Education level		
High school or less	21	23
More than high school	4	42
Ethnicity		
White	24	53
Asian	1	8
Afro-Canadian	N/A	4
Marital status		
Single	20	49
Married	3	13
Divorced	4	3
Average income	$500–3000 /week	$24,000 /year
Employment status		
Employed (part- or full-time)	27	51
Unemployed	N/A	14

* At the time of interview

gested the opposite (at least in Calgary and Toronto). Apprenticing at a studio under a more experienced, skilled, and savvy artist remains an integral factor in becoming a professional tattoo artist in Canada. One significant difference, however, is that the artists typically no longer remain strictly loyal to or employed by the studio at which they apprenticed. Of the artists with apprenticeship experience, twenty-one (91%) worked at more than one tattoo studio in their careers as artists.

The average age of the clients interviewed was 24, with an overall range in age from 18 to 50. Forty of the clients (62%) were women and 25 (38%) were men. Despite the long-standing association between tattooing and the working class, only 16 (25%) of the clients I interviewed had working-class backgrounds – with 41 (63%) located in the middle class and eight in the upper class (12%). All of the female clients except four had middle- or upper-class backgrounds. Based on my field research in Calgary, Toronto, and elsewhere, these proportions roughly represent the class distribution in contemporary tattooing in Canada. Thus, as other, more contemporary analyses (Atkinson and Young 2001; DeMello 2000; Mifflin 1997; Vail 1999) indicate, there is a noticeable shift in the class composition of Canadian tattoo enthusiasts. Of all the clients interviewed, 51 (78%) were employed at the time of the study, with an average group income of approximately Cdn$24,000. Considering that 21 (32%) of the 65 clients interviewed were students at the time of the study – most with little or no yearly income – this figure appears to be a rather conservative estimation of income for the group. Clients were also slightly more educated than the artists. Forty-two (64%) of the clients had a university degree or at least one year of university education. Fifty-three (82%) of the clients interviewed were white, eight (12%) were Asian-Canadian, and four (6%) were Afro-Canadian. Of all the clients interviewed, 49 (75%) were single at the time of the study, 13 (20%) were married, and three (5%) were divorced. Twelve (18%) of the clients had children – five had one child, three had two children, and four had three or more children.

A majority of the clients, 41 (63%), had one tattoo at the time of the research. Within this group, 35 (85%) were women, with an average age of 23. Seven (11%) clients had two tattoos, two (3%) had three tattoos, and 15 clients (23%) had three or more tattoos. Clients' backgrounds in tattooing varied, with the age of entry into the practice ranging from 14 to 48 (with a mean of 22). Fifty-six (86%) of the clients were tattooed in either Calgary or Toronto (including nine different studios in Calgary, and six in Toronto). Other Canadian cities in which individuals were tattooed included Vancouver, Victoria, Kelowna, Edmonton, Lethbridge, Regina, Winnipeg, Windsor, Kitchener-Waterloo, London, Montreal, Quebec City, Moncton, Charlottetown, Halifax, and St John's.

Let's Talk about Tattooing

One of the most important methodological lessons gleaned from current debates on reflexivity and representation in qualitative research is the extent to which sociologists actively create textual realities in conjunction with individuals interviewed in the research process. When the analysis of narratives becomes a primary task in the interview process, attention is directed toward the ways in which personal stories are interpretively constructed by people. In this research on tattooing, I adopted a style of active interviewing in order to examine artists' and clients' tattooing narratives.

In basic terms, an active interview is *one in which both the interviewer and the interviewee play interdependent and equally complicit roles in the construction of narratives.* In an active interview, researchers use specific rhetorical techniques including semi-directed (i.e., open-ended) questioning to tap into a range of individuals' narrative resources – or, simply, their different ways of perceiving and describing personal experiences based on the statuses and associated roles they possess (Gubrium and Holstein 1997). For instance, by asking a woman how she feels about her involvement on a recreational sports team, one might attempt to ascertain how she constructs and attributes meaning to her experiences through perceptual standpoints grounded in her ascribed/achieved statuses and roles – a mother, sister, Liberal, lawyer, or Christian. In this pursuit, the interview becomes more of an informal discussion or interpersonal brainstorming session than a one-way, formal, or otherwise closed interrogation.

I began each interview in a relatively uniform way. After I approached each enthusiast to inquire about the possibility conducting an interview (explaining what the interview would entail and explaining that the project had received ethics approval from the University of Calgary), dates, locations, and times were suggested, negotiated, and finally agreed upon. The interviews were conducted in a variety of settings such as my office at the university, a coffee shop, a local restaurant, or a tattoo studio (typically, the interviewee would choose). In all but a few instances, I avoided using a tape-recorder or other technological device in the sessions. Instead, notes were taken both during and after the interviews. The notes were (within several hours or, at maximum, a day or two) transcribed onto computer files and filled in considerably as I conceptually analysed the texts. Interviewees were given an explanation of informed consent before and after each interview. Interviews ranged in length from forty-five minutes to, in a few rare cases, four hours.

All of the participants involved were interviewed one time, and many were shown transcripts of the interview sessions at a later date so that they might review their own narratives. I wanted to provide respondents with an opportunity to edit out any sensitive or deeply personal information that they did not wish to be included in the study. As part of the informed-consent process, I ensured them that if they were uncomfortable with an aspect of their interview, they could ask to have it excluded. In all cases, the segments of text deleted did not alter the overall analysis. For instance, one female respondent discussed an emotionally wrenching childhood experience in her interview. While the event had no direct bearing on her decision to become tattooed, she discussed it nonetheless in the emergent conversation. As an afterthought, about a week later, she asked me to expunge the story from her interview transcript because she did not want to share it with others, nor did she feel that it helped to explain the character of her tattooing experiences. As another example, three tattoo artists spent small portions of time in their interviews criticizing the artwork of several of their peers. After the interviews, some remorse (and I suspect a bit of fear in one case!) set in, and they asked to have those comments excluded.

The structure of each interview would best be described as flexible. Beforehand I reviewed a schedule of approximately forty questions I wished to explore with participants. However, the questions were treated as guides for the discussions, and were not utilized as a definitive framework for the conversations. Instead, I started the interviews (following a few minutes of small talk and an explanation of informed consent) with a basic statement: 'So, tell me about your tattoo(s).' This request was intentionally vague and open for considerable interpretation. I wanted the respondents to begin their narratives where they wished – from starting points they found to be sensible. I was interested in how each participant would choose to commence the narrative. Some would stare at me puzzlingly, attempting to decipher the nature of my question. Others began by recounting why or when they first started to think about tattoos, describing or showing me their tattoos, or initiating the conversation from some other (significant to them) point of departure.

From there, the conversation would shift, venture down unanticipated alleys, and eventually travel across a field of topics. While participants were given considerable latitude in directing the course of the conversation, there were certain questions I would routinely pose if they were not addressed. Given the research questions stimulating the data-collection process, I inquired about the processes involved in being a tattoo enthusiast, and about how tattooing figures into an individual's portfolio of corporeal modification practices. 'Confronting' individuals

(Baker 1998) about how interpretations of tattoos are influenced by personal biographies, interpersonal relationships, ascribed/achieved roles, and life aspirations, I sought to understand if and how tattoos become signifiers of social identity.

Large portions of the interviews also focused on how reactions from others (whether positive, negative, or ambivalent) influenced the ways in which tattoo enthusiasts interpreted their tattoos. Some participants immediately discussed the negative reactions they had experienced, while others would testify about the scores of accolades they had received about their tattoos. However, the participants typically began their stories by discussing the negative or positive reactions received from significant others. I heard stories about how fathers, sisters, partners, or close co-workers reacted to tattoos, and how such reactions were reflected upon over time. Reactions from others (and the underlying relationships producing them) became interpretive resources in creating tattooing narratives, as participants expressed personal understandings about their tattoos as sons, daughters, partners, and fellow workers.

To facilitate an atmosphere of openness and mutual exchange, I regularly discussed my own experiences in tattooing with the participants. Being careful not to dominate the conversations, I discussed my own personal thoughts, interpretations, and feelings about tattooing as a method of encouraging participants to share the more intimate details of their personal narratives. By presenting my tattooing narratives as part of the discussion, I endeavoured to establish a context in which participants could freely ask questions and investigate my tattooing experiences – a key element in the active interviewing process (Gubrium and Holstein 1997, 1999). Similarly, I displayed my tattoo work to many of the participants – encouraging them to do so only if their tattoos were located on highly visible or non-private parts of the body (particularly in the case of female participants). In drawing upon a series of discursive and interactive techniques, I wanted the conversations to scarcely resemble a formal interview.

Rather than viewing the natural interchange and interpersonal discussion (i.e., my participation in the conversations) that occurred in the active interviews as a threat to the validity of the data, I believe it fostered a *far greater* degree of candour, confession, and narrative exploration than would a more detached or impersonal approach. Most of the research participants knew of my status as a tattoo enthusiast, had viewed my tattoos, or had spent time discussing tattooing with me prior to our interview sessions. In this way, I had developed a sense of rapport with the majority of respondents. To refrain from discussing my own thoughts, feelings, and interpretations about tattooing in the interviews, then, might not only have disrupted the processual development of our friendships, but might have inhibited the free exchange of memories, ideas, and interpretive constructions of tattooing within the interviews. The sociologist who explores participant observation and then later utilizes interviewing to expand the scope of data risks appearing phoney to participants if he or she assumes a more objective style of talk in interviews. In not one instance did I feel, as a sociologist or fellow tattoo enthusiast, that the participants bended their answers to curry favour or carefully manage an inauthentic presentation of self. Nor did I decode any of their responses as disingenuous representations of their thoughts and feelings. By interviewing the majority of respondents on more than one occasion, and developing a personal familiarity with them over time, I reaffirmed my opinions on this matter.

The mutual disclosure characterizing many of the interviews equally heightened the trust between myself and research participants. Given the way in which tattooing is a deeply personal and meaningful body project, I believe that not recounting some of my experiences would have been suspicious to them. Countless times in interview sessions respondents indicated that they appreciated speaking with someone possessing an experiential familiarity with tattooing, who could converse with them in their own (body) language. Switching gears within an interview and avoiding (some of) my personal thoughts and experiences might have discouraged enthusiasts from revealing more private portions of their tattoo narratives. I did not offer my biography to the participants during the preliminary stages of the interviews, but rather waited for key points to introduce my experiences as a means of *maintaining* an atmosphere of friendly interchange. I also steered away from overly judgmental talk when recounting my experiences in order to avoid leading respondents.

We may be hasty sometimes in assuming that people will alter their narratives when confronted with another's experiences, or change the basis of their interpretations of tattooing to appear more respectable to others. This scepticism not only paints interviewees as exceedingly pliable and subject to simple manipulation, but also articulates a distrust in the sociologist's ability to recognize when and how interviewees' narratives might be unduly affected by an interviewing style. In groundbreaking ethnographic research on tattooing (e.g., DeMello 2000; Sanders 1989; Steward 1990), the type of interactive discussion I employed with respondents is advocated as a method of achieving a sense of intimate familiarity with them. These texts (and definitely my own research) shows how tattoo enthusiasts are committed to particular ideologies and rather resistant to pressure from others who seek to impose inaccurate meanings upon their practices or experiences. Indeed, the main criticism of sharing personal information in interviews should concern whether or not active interview techniques can become standardized tools applied with equal effectiveness in all interview situations within a single study. If this is the case, the central issue is not the threat to validity created by active interviewing, but the reasons why certain active interviews do not, as they are intended, provide full accounts of lived experience in all situations and contexts.

Rather than taking an interactive approach in interviews, social researchers typically adopt a more artificial and conciliatory style of questioning in the spirit of maintaining rapport with informants. While many have laboured to eliminate response bias from their work, with reference to the dreaded desirability effect, very few have acknowledged that sociologists are guilty of asking safe questions to appear more desirable to respondents. This benignly compliant approach to data collection is interactively unnatural (especially for the participant observer), and poses serious problems for the validity of the data gathered by interviewers who believe establishing rapport with individuals is best achieved by discussing the weather, their favourite restaurants, or current events before the real questioning commences. Rather than researchers steering away from open lines of inquiry, they should extend everyday talk and mutual exchange into the data collection process.

Amidst the torrential flood of research papers, book chapters, and journal articles on the importance of reflexivity in field research, it would be irresponsible to ignore how my personal involvement in tattooing figured into the data collection and analysis during the interview phases of the research. To be sure, from the first moment I walked into a studio in Toronto or Calgary as a budding participant observer of the scene, to the very last interview conducted, my participation in tattooing has afforded me a substantial amount of credibility among tattoo enthusiasts. Artists seemed more willing and eager to speak with someone who could understand the process on a first-hand basis. Tattoo sessions would also become key in establishing my seriousness about the practice – not, in this case, as a researcher, but as an individual who shares a strong personal interest in tattooing. Similarly, many clients expressed a sense of ease in speaking with someone who was tattooed. Viewing me as one of their 'own' (Goffman 1959) – an individual with the ability to share intersubjectively an understanding of what it is like to be tattooed – clients seemed to genuinely appreciate my involvement in the practice. I frequently felt that this comfort level translated into a high degree of openness and disclosure in both the participant-observation and interview stages of the research.

While participant observers are frequently warned against the professional and personal dangers associated with 'going native,' a fine line between uncritical involvement and absolute detachment may be walked (Elias 1987). Becoming a part of the action in the pursuit of conceptual understandings about social interchange within a particular setting (i.e., in the desire to demystify the world by smashing stereotypes and clarifying social processes) does not automatically lead researchers into becoming confused, biased, intoxicated, or seduced by the life-worlds they study. I did become more heavily tattooed through the research process, and my interest in tattooing grew immeasurably throughout the research. This does not automatically spawn a virus of non-objectivity in the research, nor does it suggest that one should forsake the pursuit of social-scientific accounts of the world and embrace a highly political standpoint so that personal biases might be transformed into a provocative social text. Both of these polar extremes produce highly distorted accounts of social interaction, since unwavering objectivity or extreme subjectivity generates a text underpinned by either overly positivistic or stubbornly political constructions of social interaction.

Toward an Intimate Understanding of Tattooing in Canada

Participant observation or interviewing are not ideal methodologies for every sociological investigation. Depending upon the questions driving the inquiry, such qualitative research strategies may very well be ill suited as a tactical approach to social observation. However, in the case of tattooing in Canada, a participant observation–based approach offers a window into a social practice scarcely examined by Canadian sociologists to date. Given the lack of knowledge we possess concerning contemporary sensibilities toward tattooing in Canada, how tattooing is intersubjectively understood, and how tattooed bodies are phenomenologically experienced, a participant observation–based, exploratory methodology is clearly required at this juncture. Conceptual and theoretical innovation on the subject of tattooing is desperately needed. Extant analyses of the practice (save for a handful of ethnographies) are either outdated or wholly unreflective of contemporary tattoo enthusiasts and their practices.

For sociologists, or anyone else, committed to 'up close and personal' analyses of the social world, participant observation situates the researcher in the middle of lived experience. I believe that if sociologists are to espouse an interest in identifying, understanding, and dissecting the multiple realities of social life, we must select methodological approaches that allow for the inspection of the processes by which realities are constructed, learned, and negotiated. Participating with and interviewing individuals from a range of social backgrounds with diverse experiences in tattooing allows for a fresh exploration of the cultural significance of tattooing in Canada. Since tattoo enthusiasts are not confined to military barracks, motorcycle clubhouses, dockyards, or prisons, this research locates tattooed bodies as 'everyday' fixtures in 'everyday' social contexts.

Equally, by exploring a new sample of tattoo enthusiasts, we can question long-standing cultural interpretations, and explore untapped sociological understandings, of tattooing. I am fully aware that, as in other qualitative work, my interpretation of the information I collected on tattoo enthusiasm is ultimately only one reading. As I have noted, in order to check my own understandings of the data, I routinely discussed my interpretations and sociological analysis with artists and clients – directly assisted by hanging around with them on a regular basis and actively interviewing the participants. For the most part, I received considerable affirmation from the participants regarding my conclusions. Therefore, while I feel confident about my own decoding of the stories and life experiences presented in this book, I acknowledge and welcome alternative interpretations and insights.

CHAPTER FIVE

Subculture or Figuration?

The first time I walked into a classroom to lecture without a long-sleeve shirt (exposing my full-tattoo sleeves on each arm), I experienced the saliency of dominant interpretations of tattooing in Canadian culture. University students are a relatively well-tattooed group, accounting for a significant portion of tattoo enthusiasts in North America. I thought the students would react favourably to my tattooed arms. With some trepidation, I walked down the steps leading to the front of the lecture hall. What was typically a boisterous and energetic group of two hundred students turned into a congregation of silent spectators. I heard whispers and gasps throughout the class, and peered around to see wide-eyed students with their mouths agape. Their collective reaction was a mix of disbelief, confusion, and fascination. I am not sure the students heard anything I said that day, as their attention appeared to be focused on my arms and not my words. In sociological terms, this event was a classic breeching situation, wherein my appearance as a tattoo enthusiast violated the conservative norms and standards of physical display expected of a teacher in the classroom.

Following the lecture, a few students approached me as I had expected. Some wanted a closer inspection of my tattoos, some inquired about where I had been tattooed, while others simply wanted to ask if the tattoos were real. Following this brief question-and-answer period, I immediately reflected on the participant observation and interview information I had gathered on tattooing in Canada. Among other ponderings, I started to reconsider whether or not an actual subculture or community of tattoo enthusiasts exists in Canada. For example, all the students who approached me were tattooed themselves, and posed questions relating to my involvement in the practice or my personal connections with tattoo artists. They spoke to me as fellow tattoo enthusiasts, drawing on several common terms and expressions familiar to any individual who has participated in the practice. Even though I had been wrestling with the idea of a tattooing subculture before this day, I started to question seriously whether or not individuals who participate in this body project share certain subcultural activities, ideologies, identities, and relationships as a group. So I also asked myself, Is there such a thing as a tattooing subculture, at least in the way that sociologists have classically conceived what a 'subculture' means?

Based on the knowledge I have gained of tattoo enthusiasm in Canada, I believe that sociologists should reconfigure our theoretical understanding of them around Elias's (1978, 1983, 1991a, 1994, 1996) conceptualization of social 'figurations.' Rather than conceiving of tattoo enthusiasts as a cohesive subculture, life-world, or scene of interacting individuals, I believe that a more empirically accurate depiction of tattoo enthusiasts is formed by employing the concept of figuration. While extant sociological constructions of the practice (e.g., Cohen 2000; DeMello 2000; Irwin 2000; Rosenblatt 1997; Sanders 1989) tend to portray tattoo enthusiasts as a distinct culture, subculture, or community, such depictions are found to be misleading when we examine enthusiasts' narratives about their tattooing experiences.

The Analysis of Subculture: (North) American Influences

The concept of subculture continues to be widely used within sociology, despite suggestions (Crosset and Beal 1995; Muggleton 2000) that the concept no longer has empirical validity. Atkinson and Wilson (2001) have pointed out that rather than abandoning the concept outright, sociologists are reformulating understandings of the concept in myriad ways. To be sure, through a series of attempts to define subculture – starting with those such as McLung Lee (1945), Gordon (1947), Matza (1961), and Irwin (1977) – the concept has undergone significant development in the past seven decades. In any discussion of subculture, it is important to recognize that while the term is granted a sociologically relevant status, there continues to be no generally accepted definition of subculture or standard analytical criteria for applying the concept (Donnelly 2000).

In any comprehensive examination of the concept of subculture, the contributions of American sociologists should figure prominently in the analysis. Beginning with the pioneering work conducted at the University of Chicago in the 1920s, American sociologists produced a key series of statements on how the social disorganization of growing urban communities essentially produced delinquent youth subcultures. Thrasher (1927), Park and Burgess (1925), Shaw and McKay (1927), Sutherland (1937), and Whyte (1943) all stressed the need to study how delinquent individuals coalesce in response to weak community integration. Studying juvenile delinquents in their own contexts of group interaction, early social-disorganization and cultural-conflict theorists illustrated how, as socially structured means of achieving culturally defined goals (particularly those related to economic success) are blocked or insufficiently developed, individuals may fashion deviant subcultural solutions to their social and material problems. As Thrasher noted, '[Y]outh gangs represent the spontaneous effort of boys to create a society for themselves where none exists for their needs' (1927, 32).

The later work of strain theorists took the analysis of subculture to a different level by utilizing Durkheim's conception of anomie (1951). According to Merton (1938), for instance, anomie results when individuals are collectively unable to access legitimate opportunity structures for success in a given society (1938, 678). Like Thrasher (1927), Merton stated that one of the overriding cultural goals in North America is the acquisition of material goods, but that this goal is promulgated within a social structure that invariably prohibits equal opportunity to economic success (Agnew 1992; Cloward 1980; Cloward and Ohlin 1986). Specific subcultural formations arise as vehicles for coping with problems of material acquisition, and provide social contexts in which deviant methods of achieving material success are invented, normalized, and justified.

Albert Cohen (1955), perhaps the most influential of the early American subculture theorists, reconceptualized Merton's basic strain model and suggested that subcultural activities are generally oriented toward alleviating youth's status or identity frustration. Because status criteria or the means of achieving social status are defined and protected by middle-class standards, working-class youth are often excluded from legitimate opportunity structures for achieving social status. The delinquent subculture serves as a collective solution for working-class youth, as goals, standards, and identities are established in the subculture that can be achieved through the local means available. Most importantly, Cohen (1955, 28) wrote that since subcultural formations are derivations of parent cultures (i.e., mainly social-class factions), they express a symbolic resistance or opposition toward the dominant culture. The irony of their collective activities of resistance is that deviant subcultures often reproduce or reaffirm core values of the dominant culture, and thereby exacerbate and justify existing social and material relations.

Later American research on subculture adopted a decisively different approach toward the study of how and why individuals come together in social subunits (Arnold 1970). Undoubtedly influenced by the pioneering works of Becker (1963) and Goffman (1959, 1963), sociologists turned toward the analysis of more common, mundane, or everyday subcultures. While the study of deviant subcultures continued to flourish, Becker's pivotal concept of careers encouraged sociologists to examine a multitude of subcultures. Thus, besides studying street hustlers (Prus and Sharper 1991), gamblers (Lesieur 1977; Polsky 1967), prostitutes (Prus and Irini 1980), illegal drug users (Boyd 1991; Hathaway 1997a, 1997b), and 'mental patients' (Scheff 1966), sociologists applied the concept of career to a list subcultural formations including Little League softball teams (Fine 1987), construction workers (Haas 1972), hockey teams (Faulkner 1975; Ingham 1975), occupational settings (Fine 1996; Trice 1993; Haas and Shaffir 1987), and political parties (Grills 1994). By focusing mainly on the ways in which individuals are drawn into, experience, and exit subcultures, researchers increasingly attended to the social processes involved in becoming a member of a group of individuals who share central life perspectives, social backgrounds, work or leisure activities, and master self-conceptualizations.

The concept of career continues to orient sociologists toward the study of the micro-processes involved in becoming a member of a group of people, and explains how such membership may figure centrally into one's overall lifestyle (Stebbins 1997) and corresponding self-image. More so than previous sociological constructions of subculture, which tended to stress the importance of environmental (i.e., socio-structural) influences on group behaviour, the seminal work of Becker (1963) and others provided a useful stepping-stone for researchers interested in how individuals come to intersubjectively (sub-culturally) understand the world and develop lines of collective behaviour around such understandings.

Becker's work also paved the way for later symbolic interactionist deliberations on the concept of subculture. Resonating with ideas put forward by members of the Chicago school, truncheon-bearing symbolic interactionists of the 1980s and 1990s continued to pursue understandings of situated group behaviour through the lens of subculture theories. Breaking down and rebuilding Merton's (1938), Cohen's

(1955), Becker's (1963), Lofland's (1966), and Fine and Kleinman's (1979) thoughts on subculture, symbolic interactionists of the past twenty years have attended to the processes by which actors form social groupings around shared perspectives, activities, identities, relationships, and commitments (Prus 1996). Referring to a subculture via several related terms such as sub-world (Crosset and Beal 1995) or social setting (Lofland and Lofland 1995), interactionists have shared a general perspective that subcultures are small pockets of social membership and interaction within broader cultural matrices.

Prus's work on subcultural mosaics (1997) stands as perhaps the most theoretically advanced interactionist statement on subculture. Conjoining the study of micro-level subculture involvement with macro-level social organization, Prus posits that a society is best conceived as a patterned conglomerate of subcultures. In this way, he reconciles the culturally disjointed approach to subcultures taken by many symbolic interactionists with broader understandings of culture. In particular, he attends to how subcultures are organized and experienced in the here-and-now of everyday life, while simultaneously illustrating how social structures and cultures are formed as complex arrangements of a vast array of subcultures: '[T]he subcultural mosaic refers to the multiplicity of subcultures, life-worlds, or affiliations, that constitute people's involvements in societies or communities at any point in time ... [A]ny society or community consists of people acting in a mosaic (or set, configuration, amalgamation, matrix, or collage) of diverse subcultures or life-worlds that exist in temporal, dialectic (and in many cases only indirectly connected) relationships to each other' (1997, 36–7). Prus shows a keen appreciation for the idea that individuals are members of many sub-groups as part of their subcultural portfolio. Rejecting the notion that individuals are only ever members of one central subculture during specific trajectories over the life course, Prus contends that people's lives are replete with diverse and fleeting subcultural involvements. Splintering the study of subcultures into local, embedded, trans-locational, totalizing, focused, inter-fused, cyclical, occasional, and supportive subcultures, Prus outlines how people become involved in subcultures in practically every facet of social life.

Still, the tattooing stories I have heard do not indicate that mainstream theoretical constructions of subcultures (as produced by North American sociologists) readily apply to the group of tattoo enthusiasts in Canada. Despite the popular application of the term subculture to the collective of tattoo enthusiasts in North America, such depictions of the group are empirically fallacious. Although tattoo enthusiasts each engage in the corporeal act of tattooing, the meanings attributed to tattooing are incredibly diverse. Tattoo enthusiasts do share common understandings of tattoos, but not to the extent that one could decipher a specific subcultural perspective about the practice. Furthermore, participants' lives are not organized around the activity (perhaps with the exception of professional tattoo artists), nor does a central ideology or motivation drive enthusiasts to participate in the practice. The tattoo enthusiast Mary (22) suggested:

> I wouldn't say that I feel like the reasons why I was tattooed are like everybody else's. I have friends who are tattooed, but we never really talk to each other about our tattoos, and we don't drive up and down the street like a gang of tattooed chicks. I mean, if people ask, I might tell them a bit about my tattoos, but they're private, they're for me and that's that ... My life doesn't revolve around tattooing, it's just something I've done before.

Similarly, individuals tend not to consider their main identity to be that of a tattoo enthusiast:

> People ask me all the time how my life has been changed by my tattoo. Of course, I felt like a whole different person the first few days after I was tattooed. I stared at it everyday, and when I walked out of my apartment, even though it was covered up by my shirt, I thought people could see it. Now, I never think about it ... it's just become a part of me. It doesn't define me, I define my tattoo. It's like looking at my hair or my abs, you know? (Theo, 29)

Even though enthusiasts may share a common fascination with tattooing (i.e., as a redesigning body project), it is difficult to consider those involved in the practice as a communicative, close-knit, and tightly guarded subculture. As the tattoo artist Phil (24) commented:

> When people try to pigeon-hole everyone who is tattooed into a single group, they miss the point of tattooing. Like, bikers, gangs, and the lot of those guys still use it as part of their colours [gang insignias], but the run of the mill young guy who comes into my shop to be tattooed isn't a part of any of that. He's the guy who really digs the way tattoos make his body look, and he's a fan of other people who do it too. You know, he won't go to a club where everyone who is tattooed hangs out ... but somewhere,

some time he saw someone else with a tattoo and thought, 'That's for me.'

Without reverting into an overly individualist portrait of tattooing practices, then, one can say that North American analyses of subculture (while illustrative to an extent) are not immediately reflective of contemporary tattooing practices in Canada. While core concepts such as career or subcultural mosaic are useful in analysing elements of contemporary tattooing practices, North American constructions of subculture do not offer a sufficient theoretical structure for studying tattoo enthusiasts as interactive and culturally bound agents. The portrait of tattoo enthusiasts as constituting a unique and esoteric subculture of 'deviants' has equally served to (at least historically) sever the group analytically from mainstream cultures. In effect, by treating tattoo enthusiasts in this way, academics have unwittingly replicated stereotypical ideas about the social practice of tattooing.

Here Comes the CCCS

Established in 1964, the Centre for Contemporary Cultural Studies (CCCS) in Birmingham, England, was a nexus for the discussion of cultures and subcultures. Drawing on Ford's definition of culture (1942) as a 'traditional way of solving problems,' and Cohen's belief (1955) that culture develops in response to the material and social problems people encounter in everyday life, CCCS researchers collectively envisioned culture as a 'collective way of life' of a group of people. Much of the early subculture research conducted at the CCCS (Hall and Jefferson 1976; Hoggart 1958; Hebdige 1979; Williams 1963, 1976, 1977) held that any given social structure does not simply contain one monolithic culture, but rather several main (class) cultures, with one holding authority as the dominant or ruling culture. Since early CCCS theorists claimed that class relations are the chief determinant of one's location in a social structure, and thus in its cultural ways of life, key texts including Hall and Jefferson's *Resistance through Rituals* outlined how subcultures arise in response to socially structured class relations: '[R]elative to these cultural-class configurations, *sub*-cultures are sub-sets – smaller, more localised and differentiated structures, within one or other larger cultural networks' (1976, 13).

The main thrust behind Hall and Jefferson's text is that youth subcultures are born out of a parent class culture. In order to understand the 'structure of feeling' (Williams 1977) in any given subculture, we must first analyse its multi-layered or doubly articulated nature – locating the subculture in relation to its original parent culture (e.g., working-class), and referencing the parent culture within larger social relations: 'We must move at once to the determining relationships of domination and subordination in which these configurations [cultures] stand; to the processes of incorporation and resistance which define the cultural dialectic between them; and, to the institutions which transmit and reproduce "the culture" in its dominant or hegemonic form' (Hall and Jefferson 1976, 13). In CCCS research, this meant that studies were anchored by the analysis of how working-class subcultures engaged in social resistance against the dominant middle-class culture.

CCCS researchers believed that one of the most visible and spectacular forms of subcultural resistance is the use of provocative and morally challenging styles (Clarke 1976; Hebdige 1979). The early work at the CCCS provided key theoretical insight into understanding why youth subcultures adopted flamboyant styles to represent their ideological positions. There is perhaps no better text (aside from Hall and Jefferson's) on how subcultures utilize style as a form of resistance than Hebdige's *Subculture: The Meaning of Style*:

> Subcultures are therefore expressive forms but what they express is, in the last instance, a fundamental tension between those in power and those condemned to subordinate positions and second-class lives. This tension is figuratively expressed in the form of subcultural style and it is appropriate that we should turn here to a metaphor for a final definition of subculture ... I have interpreted subculture as a form of resistance in which experienced contradictions and objections to this ruling ideology are obliquely represented in style. (1979, 132–3)

Directly influenced by early American youth subculture analysis, Hebdige's work is also a complex pastiche of Gramsci's Marxism (1971) and Barthes's semiology (1972). Focusing on the study of how British youth subcultures such as the Teddy Boys, Mods, and Rockers were products of social construction, Hebdige provided insight into the processes involved in creating unique forms of (subversive) ideological representation through style. In so doing, Hebdige unpacked the working definitions of subculture and popular culture developed in the CCCS.

According to Hebdige, style is intentionally fabricated to signify symbolically both in-group cohesiveness and disassociation from the dominant culture. To this end, style is constructed from a range of available cultural commodities that have pre-existing (i.e., dominant or preferred) meanings. These objects are transformed through a process of bricolage that seeks a societal recognition that the subculture supports a socially challenging ideology (ibid., 101). As bricoleurs, subcultural members steal cultural objects and use them in their ideologically altered forms to win back cultural space. The Italian theorist Umberto Eco (1972) called this process 'semiotic guerrilla warfare.' As Clarke wrote: 'Together, object and meaning constitute a sign, and within any one culture, such signs are assembled, repeatedly into characteristic forms of discourse. However, when the bricoleur re-locates the significant object in a different position within the discourse, using the same overall repertoire of signs, or when that object is placed within a different total ensemble a new discourse is constituted, a different message conveyed' (1976, 104).

Over the course of my data-collection process, I encountered members of several indigenous North American subcultures that actively utilize tattooing as part of their resistant (or socially disaffiliative) styles. Hebdige (1979) contends that we can decode and interpret the constitutive elements of style utilized by individuals because the objects hang together as part of a homology. (Inter)subjective group experience is represented through the homology and 'each part [of style] is organically related to the other parts and it is through the fit between them that the subcultural member makes sense of the world' (Hebdige 1979, 113). For example, subcultural members from groups such as Gothics, Straightedgers, Psychobillies, Riot Grrrls, and Ravers all employ tattooing in their homologies of style as a means of intextuating oppositional cultural ideologies onto their bodies. These subcultures, mostly consisting of lower-middle-class or working-class individuals, express a collective distaste with and dislocation from mainstream culture. Resisting what they perceive to be conservative culture, jock culture, misogynist culture, or square culture, these subcultures respectively use tattooing as part of their alternative body styles. A Goth girl I interviewed named Jane (21) stated:

> My tattoos tell everybody I meet that I'm not like them. You know, I dance to my own beat, and if people get me confused with Satanists or whatever fucked up group of kids that are getting tattooed, then I can't help that ... For me, a tattoo is way of expressing who I am in a society that pushes

everybody to look the same way. My hair is blue, my music is different, and I like that. The Goth kids I hang around ... we all believe that ... to be different is alright.

Similarly, a Straightedge named Carl (26) described his tattooing practices in the following way:

If I'm out at a club listening to a band or doing my own thing downtown, people can see that I'm not some jackass drug-taking, beer guzzling jock. I mean, I like to work out, but a lot of us [Straightedge] are sick of those guys who torture everybody. Straightedge is about not taking drugs and trying to live a clean, poison-free life; not acting like the guys who picked on us when we were kids ... and my tattoos tell people that right away. It's an in-your-face thing.

In some cases, while it is difficult to understand exactly what group members are resisting, their involvement in tattooing is predicated upon waging various cultural wars through their bodies.

Other subcultures such as the Neo Primitives (Atkinson and Young 2001; Rosenblatt 1997; Vale and Juno 1989) have pushed forward an interpretation that encourages us to look at the use of tattooing as cultural protest. Including tattooing as part of a homology of style, these individuals (with a core membership in the sixteen- to thirty-year-old age range) ask to be treated as modern tribalists of the urban jungle. Rejecting both the traditional Western image of the marked individual as deviant and the often dehumanizing way in which individuals are treated in modern urban life, they intend to capture the spirit of acceptance that tribal cultures exhibit toward tattooing. Acknowledging that the group is by no means completely homogeneous, Atkinson and Young (2001) maintain that the Neo Primitive use of body modification is directly opposed to Christian-based codes of bodily display that are a part of the hegemony in Western culture. As the self-proclaimed Neo Primitive tattoo artist Cliff (32) stated:

I got into the NP scene about ten years ago because I was tired of looking like everyone else, and walking around like a zombie in my own body. Ripping up your body with tattoos is a way of getting in touch with yourself and others who are tired of being spiritually beaten down by our culture ... With so many people getting tribal tattoos, though, it's hard to tell a tribalist from a poser, you know? Someone who likes the art or finds it 'safe' [in comparison to other tattoo styles], but has no idea what any of it means.

Cliff's comments demonstrate how complicated classic American conceptions of subculture become when applied to tattoo enthusiasm. I did not meet any tattoo enthusiasts, Neo Primitive or other, who considered themselves to be posers in any way, but I did meet many who viewed the tattoos of others to be less meaningful than most. Quite simply, everyone who is tattooed will have opinions about others' tattoo projects. Being deemed a poser, as Cliff might suggest, is a question of situated audience response – anyone could potentially be considered a poser by another, as not all enthusiasts fully understand the motivations underpinning others' projects and may come to judge them critically. The difficulty in being able to tell who, exactly, is a tribalist poser illustrates that there is no core group of enthusiasts (in any context) who share identical perspectives, lines of communication, lifestyles, or understandings about tattooing.

As another case example (while not based on the act of social resistance), tattooing has become increasingly popular among members of athletic teams since the late 1980s. Athletes frequently use tattooing as a method of creating in-group cohesion, displaying loyalty to fellow teammates, and commemorating participation in specific athletic competitions such as the Olympics. Rejecting the tattoo as a symbol of deviance or social protest, athletes often modify their bodies through tattooing in the process of representing the athletic component of their self:

> I was tattooed when I heard I made the Olympic team. I dreamed about going to the Olympics all my life and being a member of a legacy in this country. I know so many other athletes with the Olympic rings tattooed on their body ... It's not about being bad, or rebelling against my parents. I wanted to capture the joy and pride I felt about my accomplishments by becoming tattooed ... My memories might fade, but I will always have this tattoo to remind me how I felt when I walked into the stadium during the opening ceremonies, or when I competed for my country ... Knowing a lot of other Canadian athletes have the same tattoo is really cool too, it makes me feel like we're together, we're one as a country. (Emily, 25)

> I never questioned it. I knew that if I made the university [hockey] team I would get our logo tattooed on my right shoulder. The rookies all do it, it's

an honour to be allowed to ... I worked all my life to get here, and this is a badge for me. These guys are my brothers and we share this. (Kurt 22)

Tattooing is utilized as a ceremonial rite of passage in such subcultures. The tattoo is incorporated into the group's homology of style as a way of consolidating team and individual identity. For athletes – who undergo body modification on a daily basis and are thus highly attuned to bodily performance and representation – tattooing is a way of outwardly confirming and expressing membership in a unique group of individuals. This uniqueness is not as much an expression of athletes' distance from mainstream culture as it is a corporeal articulation of their sense of in-group cohesion – or, in other terms, their sense of interdependency.

Hebdige (1979) and other CCCS theorists argued, though, that socially alternative subcultural styles are ultimately stolen within a dominant culture (see Brake 1985). Poaching the clothing, language, or music of subcultures becomes fashionable in the larger culture, and the widespread distribution of style as a commodity minimizes its resistant or subculturally authentic nature via mass incorporation. Simmel (1957) argued that this process of hegemonic negotiation is inevitable in the fashion or style industry. In the case of tattooing, co-opting the symbols and images commonly used by individuals in alternative or esoteric subcultures becomes trendy. Thus, wearing the symbols of bikers, Skinheads, Punks, or Olympic athletes becomes chic:

I was walking down the street the other day and I saw this kid get out of a brand new Honda, and he had Harley-Davidson tattoos all over his arms. I mean, c'mon man, I drive a Harley and hang out with guys who take that seriously. This little puke probably lives down in the south east [of Calgary] with mom and dad, and he's trying to act like a hardcore rebel. It makes me sick ... If you're gonna get tattooed, don't take someone else's property ... think of something original. (Dan, 34)

I remember when no one was getting tattooed. That was only about ten years ago. Nowadays, it doesn't matter what you do, who you know, or what your life is like, people pick anything and everything for their tattoos. Ravers get Skater tattoos, hippies get tribal tattoos, chicks get pin-up girls, white guys get Malcolm X tattoos, conservatives get Punk tattoos, you name it. No one owns anything anymore, and looking like someone you're not is 'in.' (Jack, 25)

Subcultural style becomes incorporated into and saturates the market-place as popular culture, and clear lines of distinction, experience, ideology, and lifestyle are lost in the mass usage of style. Subcultural boundaries become increasingly hazy and authentic membership in subcultures more difficult to discern. Those consuming the styles typically find little importance in being considered a genuine member of the group. Instead, imitation becomes more important than wearing an original style or interacting with subcultural members. As the tattoo artist Ray (31) told me:

> So many people come into my shop with the attitude that if they're going to put money down for a tattoo, they can get anything they want. In today's tattooing, if you can draw it, it can be tattooed, and if it can be tattooed it can be bought and sold. It's no different than going to a hair studio or buying a new pair of earrings ... it's all about having the money and the demand for something ... So when a White guy comes in and asks for a black panther, I just laugh ... it's all I can do to keep me sane.

Furthermore, with the recent attention tattooing has received in popular sources (newspapers, magazines, television, advertising), an argument could be made that deviant or oppositional expressions of it may be decaying throughout North America. As tattooed bodies are used to sell sports cars, cell phones, CDs, and other mainstream cultural commodities, the modified body may have become a true floating signifier of the twenty-first century. A tattoo enthusiast named Robin (30) commented: 'I see tattoos everywhere. You can't turn on a TV without seeing someone who is tattooed. I know that not everyone is doing it, but I can't help feeling more like everyone else now when I see everyone who has a tattoo.' Paradoxically, the media refer to the increase in tattooing as a reflection of the subterranean, profane, or hedonistic values of modern youth that arise in the face of moral, family, and spiritual decay (Bourette 1998; Connery 2001; McGill 1998; Novak 2000):

> I saw this article in the paper a couple of weeks ago about the health risks involved in tattooing, and its popularity among criminals in the States. What a fucking joke. These guys have no idea how safe tattooing is, and as for the immorality of it ... they obviously don't know that the person working at the desk beside them, the lawyer handling their divorces, or the women working at their favourite restaurants are all probably tattooed. (Earl, 26)

While it might be tempting to apply the CCCS model of subculture to contemporary tattooing practices given some of the conceptual and theoretical linkages noted above, the CCCS understanding suffers from several core deficiencies. First, with such overemphasis on social class as the chief determinant of cultural interpretation and intersubjective understanding, other subcultural formations (i.e., non-class-based) tend to fall into the background. While the CCCS model of subcultural development is directly informed by Gramscian Marxism and recognizes the plurality of sites of power and authority within a culture, theorists undertaking subcultural research within the CCCS exhibit an unwavering commitment to social class as the aetiological origin of subcultures and subcultural styles. Second, the CCCS description of subculture, much like American theoretical and empirical descriptions, defines a subculture in rather tidy conceptual terms; that is, subcultures (until the process of co-option and incorporation occurs) are identifiable, distinguishable, and authentic social conglomerations. Expressing disaffiliation with the mainstream, subcultures are tightly bound subsets of broader parent cultures. Since they are invariably engaged in social resistance during their genesis, subcultures are easily located and perceivable social groupings until their styles are co-opted, and members move onto something more 'meaningful.' Unless we focus on specific subcultural uses of tattooing and not on tattoo enthusiasts as a particular subculture, the CCCS theoretical understanding only loosely applies to the study of tattooing.

Third, and perhaps most significantly, CCCS researchers hinge a significant portion of their conceptualization of subculture on semiotic readings of subcultural style. By treating style as text that can be read and deconstructed, CCCS researchers ventured away from empirically studying the material and social conditions that members encountered and found problematic in everyday life. Readings of fashion replaced ethnographic research, deconstructions of music stood in place of empirical description, and theories about the authenticity and co-option of style overtook theoretical development. In moving away from the phenomenological experience of social inequality, or intersubjective understandings of the world, researchers come to view subcultures as a collection of mannequins upon which resistant styles are worn. Social interaction and the processes of constructing meanings in everyday life fade into the background, as subcultures are nothing more than arrangements of signs.

Postmodern Fragmentation and Fuzziness

If the CCCS preoccupation with subcultural style limits the application of the bulk of the research produced there, then recent postmodernist research efforts on subculture are even less applicable – despite their growing popularity in the social sciences. In taking the study of signs, signification, and textual deconstruction to the extreme, varying postmodernist positions on the nature of subculture (Beezer 1992; Chambers 1990; Evans 1997; Jameson 1991; Kotarba 1991; Kratz and Reimer 1998; Lash 1990; McRobbie 1994; Redhead 1993, 1997, 1998) uphold a central belief that within commodity-obsessed Western cultures, subcultures are nothing more than consumer markets oriented toward the ongoing circulation of styles.

In postmodernist research, the term subculture has supposedly been updated and revised to account more adequately for the socio-cultural and socio-historical conditions of the current era. For example, Muggleton (1998, 2000) has argued that with the development of more eclectic and fragmented styles, it has become difficult to resist symbolically, since the distinction between alternative and mainstream symbols has become blurred. For example, shaved heads, dyed hair, ripped clothes, or tattoos, once considered political symbols of resistance, have become ideologically diluted fixtures in popular styles. Consequently, Muggleton, Redhead, Polhemus (1994, 1996), and others argue that the postmodern period is characterized by a loss of cultural meaning, a heightened sense of nostalgia, and a decline in personal authenticity. Thus, Redhead (1993, 1997) has suggested that earlier American or CCCS models of subculture are no longer appropriate for analysing subcultural expressions because they overstate the extent to which subcultures are able to (or even attempt to) effectively create authentic expressions of resistance or other in-group beliefs.

Since bricolage occurs so often within Canadian culture – as a result of our integrative sensibilities toward cultural artefacts – resistance or any other subcultural concern can no longer be encoded into homological styles. What a specific style communicates may be impossible to ascertain, as there is not one truly dominant interpretation of the style either inside or outside of a subculture. If, as Polhemus (1994) suggested, there is a current gathering of the subcultural tribes and stylistic exchange between groups, then authenticity is engulfed by a sea of mass-marketed commodities and images. In this supermarket of style, individuals are free to select from a flood of products to pastiche together hybrid styles. No longer does adorning oneself with a particular look signify membership within a subculture, as mixed and ideologically neutralized versions of subcultural styles become co-opted as public property (Fiske 1989a, 1989b). As Muggleton described, '[T]he logical consequence of this postmodern predilection to mix, match, and plunder is to create greater scope for the construction of individually unique looks' (1998, 77). The only matters worth studying are the processes by which styles are arranged on individual bodies, and the reasons why isolated individuals deliberately choose commodities in the construction of personal styles over time (Fiske 1992; Widdcombe and Wooffitt 1995). What subcultural style signifies is subject not only to multi-interpretation but also to multi-use.

The widespread borrowing and 're-mixing' of style has raised the question of whether the measures (if any) that subcultures invent to police internally the styles they fabricate are effective in retaining their style's authenticity in a commodity-based culture. Thornton's (1995) and Sardiello's (1998) statements on the complex processes by which members of subcultures are able to assess the authenticity behind mass-marketed style aside, many postmodernists refute any sense of subcultural integrity given the increasing interest in physical styles (Andes 1998). Subcultural boundaries are now fuzzy, permeated by anyone able to draw upon a series of physical props, language, and body movement to emulate an 'original' subculture's style (Kratz and Reimer 1998; Muggleton 2000). Since identity in the postmodern era is defined by purchasing power, the consumption of signs, and imitation without understanding, being a genuine or authentic member of a subculture is not as important as looking like a subcultural member or symbolically aligning oneself with the expressed ideologies of a subculture. As individuals are able to drop in and out of subcultures on a regular basis by purchasing their styles, subcultures themselves are open for mass bricolage.

The ramifications of postmodernist lines of inquiry on the study of subculture are unambiguous. First, for postmodernists (like those at the CCCS), style is the dominant focus of investigation in subcultural research. Unlike the CCCS researchers, however, postmodernists have become overwhelmingly concerned with individual style. Given this approach, we need to investigate not the ways in which style becomes intersubjectively defined as meaningful, but rather the importance of style for isolated individuals living within broader consumer webs. As sociologists attend to the free-floating nature of the self in Western cultures, emphasis is given to the ways in which individuals define (on a moment-by-moment basis) identity through readily purchasable and discarded styles (Evans 1997; Jameson 1991; Lash and Urry 1994; Miles et al. 1998). Again, understanding why and how individuals adopt styles (or, for that matter, homologies of style) is secondary. With such an approach would be led to ignore the words of tattoo enthusiasts like Marc (32), who described his tattoo experience in the following way:

> I spent about three years trying to decide what I was going to be tattooed with. I have so many friends with tattoos and they all advised me to put a lot of time and effort into making the decision. So I went down to a couple of places [studios] in Calgary, talked to a couple of the guys to see what their artwork was like, and really thought about what captured my spirit ... After narrowing down my choices to three I spent two months weighing the pros and cons of each and chose one. I knew I would have the tattoo for the rest of my life, and I wanted something I wouldn't get tired with ... It had to be something I could look at everyday and be comfortable with this being part of me. That's why I chose to have the maple leaf tattooed ... I'm always going to be Canadian and it's something I'm proud of.

In postmodernist research on style, semiotic understandings of how individuals experience postmodern schizophrenia – the transitory, conflicting, and confused self (Jameson 1991; Kellner 1992; MacCannell 1992) – are preferred. Postmodernist positions on the nature of subculture may well sound a death knell for the concept within sociology.

Second, when attention is turned toward collective lines of behaviour within the cultural sub-groups, postmodernists seem to be more interested in the effects of style on larger cultures than on the interaction among subcultural participants (Muggleton 2000). The sociological relevance of any collectivity appears to be derived from the style(s) they generate and offer to others. Any phenomenological consideration of subculture is overlooked in favour of the social process of co-option occurring around their styles. Third, if we eschew the need to locate interacting individuals within contexts of group activity, individuals become nothing more than consumers weaving their way through advertisements, television programs, movies, and malls. Joined by little other than the activity of buying and circulating hollow images via commodity consumption, social formations (however small or large) are not culturally meaningful for people but are simply conduits for creating and displaying postmodern realities. Again, the sentiments of tattoo enthusiasts such as Lucy (23) are unimportant:

> I've learned a lot about my tattoos by discussing them with other people. You know, from the very first time I started to think about being tattooed until today, so many other people have been involved with my tattoos ... Well, I mean that my tattoos are influenced by the Traditional tattoos my friends have. They got me thinking about Traditional as a style, and after talking about the history of Traditional in North America, I really love the tattoos, totally. So many people comment on how cool they are ... It's a wicked feeling to have your body art admired like that. And I think I look at my tattoos differently, after having lived with them for five years, because every time I speak to one of my fiends or other people who are tattooed I learn something new about me and my tattoos.

The ramifications of postmodernist lines of inquiry on the study of tattooing appear to be manifold. In line with Shilling's discussion (1993) of body projects, we are encouraged to believe that the process of modifying the body through tattooing is best conceived as a hyper-individualistic yet fluidly meaningful practice. Motivations driving an individual to become tattooed, and the social relevance of the tattooing body project, are located in the individual's quest to purchase specific images pre-signified by their tattoos. Second, an immediately relevant area of investigation becomes the ways in which tattoo styles or images are poached and endlessly reconfigured. The fodder of much recent debate among tattoo enthusiasts (Atkinson and Young 2001; Cohen 2000; DeMello 2000), this subject is, in fact, provocative and explosive. However, the subject is more appropriately subsumed under a more encompassing investigation of how specific tattoo styles retain identifiable meaning structures in Western cultures. I am particularly wary of reducing the socio-cultural significance of tattoo styles to the ways in which they are endlessly borrowed or stolen by enthusiasts in the contemporary era.

Fourth, based on my own involvement in tattooing as a client and a client-researcher, postmodernist theoretical understandings of identity creation and image exchange through subcultural style simply do not resonate in the tattooing stories I have heard from fellow enthusiasts. Canadian tattoo enthusiasts articulate their experiences with narratives that indicate a much deeper and interpersonal understanding of the tattooing process. Rejecting the idea that tattooing is merely a body project of fragmented individualism, tattoo enthusiasts describe their tattoos in ways that exude alternative and highly interdependent understandings:

I wouldn't say we [tattoo enthusiasts] are this one big happy family of people getting tatts [tattoos], but from all my years in the business I can tell you this. When someone meets another person with tattoos they have common ground. They can talk about their experiences and get together immediately ... It could be an ice-breaker at a party or might be a way of meeting a guy at a club. But it's all about feeding off of one another and meeting people who you feel safe around ... They're not going to judge you or nothing like that. (Miles, 25)

I didn't get tattooed for 'just' me at all. When I got tattooed, I was with three of my closest friends, right, and we had the same flowers tattooed on our bodies. We grew up in [town] together, and these flowers [points to tattoo] were painted all over the gym in our elementary school. It's reminds me of being a kid, and it being the happiest time of my life ... I got it here [points to left ankle], Betty had it tattooed on her right ankle, Cynthia had it done on her hip, and Kim got it on her shoulder. I love knowing my girls and I will always be together like that. (Susan, 22)

While such constructions are not created or confirmed on a subcultural level between all tattoo enthusiasts, we should not limit our sociological understanding of tattooing to hyper-individualism. Instead, tattooing is more accurately perceived as a process involving interdependencies between individuals. By reconceptualizing tattoo enthusiasts as a figuration rather than a subculture one can direct attention toward the ways in which individuals experience tattooing in highly interdependent ways.

Tattoo Figurations

In developing a preliminary case for considering how and why tattoo enthusiasts constitute a figuration of interrelated social actors instead of a community or subculture, we must bracket the nature of enthusiasts' interdependencies into two major components: becoming tattooed as a process and developing of relationship chains in tattooing. In the following, an analytical overview of these components is offered as a means of initiating a larger discussion of how sociogenic transformations both inside and outside of the Canadian tattoo figuration play roles in alter-

ing enthusiasts' tattooing habits, how individuals actively choose tattooing as a redesigning body project, and how individuals construct narratives about their tattooing projects over time.

1. Becoming Tattooed as an Interactive Process

Previously, I commented that, upon first inspection, the tattoo enthusiasts I encountered over the course of my investigation appeared to share
little in common other than the actual physical process of being tattooed. Still, this is the basic chain of interdependency forming the first
fragments of the figuration. We could not commence an analysis of contemporary tattooing practices in Canada without this recognition – as
trivial or taken-for-granted as it may seem.

The actual process of tattooing has changed only minimally over the
last one hundred and twelve years. The electric tattoo machine invented
by Samuel O'Reilly in 1891 has been modified only marginally, and the
inks used in the process slightly diversified (i.e., range and quality of
colours). For the most part, though, the ways in which tattoos are
administered in Canada are barely different than in previous eras. Let's
focus, as an example, on the tattoo machine, which operates roughly
like a sewing machine. A needle, or a combination of needles, are sol-
dered onto a bar that is encased in a steel tube. The tube is attached to a
bar running underneath the transistors of the tattoo machine that regulate the current supplied by the external power source.

When electric current is sent into the machine, the needles rapidly
move up and down through the tube, slightly poking out of its tip. The
tattoo machine is held in the hand, the artist dips the tips of the needles
into colours stored in small ink caps, and the machine is moved across
the skin to perform the tattooing. The needles penetrate the skin (anywhere from 50 to 3000 times per minute), and ink seeps into the subcu-
taneous holes created by the needles. Perforating the skin to about $\frac{1}{8}$ of
an inch, the needles are pushed deep enough into the skin to prevent
the ink from bleeding out, but not so deep as to mulch the skin or mute
the ink's appearance through layers of thick skin. With the exception
of individuals who choose tribal methods of tattooing (i.e., hand-poking
or tapping, where larger needles are inserted into the skin manually) or
are tattooed in some prison contexts (i.e., using a crude variation of
hand-poking or a makeshift electric 'tattoo gun'), the vast majority
of Canadians are tattooed via the standard electric method administered by a professional artist. Only two of the tattoo enthusiasts I inter-

viewed had experience with hand-poking or another method of tattooing. Furthermore, only a handful of the group were tattooed by a non-professional artist. Thus, enthusiasts share the electric experience as perhaps the most elementary tie binding them together.

However, by exploring how enthusiasts begin to interact with others who are tattooed (particularly during the initial stages of the process), we can see how they venture down a series of common interactive pathways that go beyond the simple application technique. For instance, before participating in the act of tattooing, individuals generally undertake a several-pronged fact-finding mission about the process. Most people know little about the physical process of being tattooed before they participate in the body project for the first time. Contrary to cosmetic-surgery body projects (Davis 1994, 1997a; Dull and West 1991; Gillespie 1996), people do not extensively consult with the individual administering the tattoo in order to review the process in detail. Instead, clients may sporadically pose random questions about the process to close friends (or, in some cases, artists):

I knew a bit about tattooing but couldn't tell you how it was actually done, and that worried me a bit. Truly, it did. Three of my friends have tattoos so I asked each of them about how it feels and all that stuff about healing. They couldn't tell me much. I guess it's something you have to learn as you go through it, but I just wanted to have my mind put at ease ... especially about how much it hurt and how to take care of it [afterward]. (Susan, 21)

The first question people who are new to this ask, and I'm sure you've heard this before, is, 'how much does it hurt?' – usually right before I'm going to hit them with the needle. I get sick of answering that question, but you have to be patient with people because you understand that they're scared about needles and the pain and all that. They don't know what it feels like to be tattooed ... They may want a tattoo but have no idea what to expect. It's not like going to get your hair cut. People know there's blood involved, so they want to know about the pain. I tell them it's not bad, and people handle it with no major convulsions. (Jimmy, 24)

Sometimes, travelling to a tattoo studio with a friend and sitting in while they are tattooed provides a prospective client with some preliminary knowledge about the practice:

I went down with my best friend Carmen when she had the band [barbed

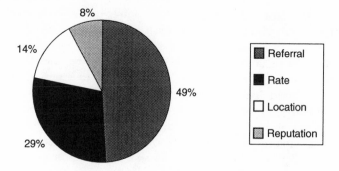

Figure 5.1   Selecting a Tattoo Artist

wire] done around her arm, and that calmed me down. I got to talk with the artist for a while and I saw what he was doing ... a lot better than even Carmen got to see! He went through the procedure, so I knew what to expect when I was going to go in. (Rosalyn, 22)

Almost universally, individuals commencing their quests into tattooing search for some cursory knowledge about the physical process.

Another central feature in the fact-finding mission involves locating a suitable tattoo artist. The individuals I interviewed indicated four main ways in which an artist is located and then selected (see figure 5.1).

The most common method of acquiring knowledge about a specific tattoo artist and selecting them for the project (49% of the clients interviewed) is through a referral from a tattooed friend: 'I knew about Sean [tattoo artist] because four of my friends were tattooed by him. They raved about his work and how nice he was, and I've seen their tattoos, and they're done well. There's a whole whack of shops in town, but I figured since he was highly recommended by my friends, that's good enough for me' (Kurt, 22) The second most common reason for selecting a particular artist is the rate they charge for the service. Nineteen of the clients (29%) stated that the tattoo's price, as quoted by an artist, was the determining factor. As artists vary in the amounts they charge (by the hour or the size of the tattoo), some clients engage in a considerable amount of price-shopping. This practice continues to be frowned upon by many tattoo artists, but price is a key consideration for neophyte enthusiasts nonetheless. The tattoo artist Jimmy (24) commented:

Well, if I had five bucks for every person who went down the wall of flash [in his studio] and asked, 'how much is this ... well, how much is this one ...

okay, what about this one?' I get pissed by that, but people try to negotiate and haggle prices all the time. It's mostly people who don't know shit about tattooing, and don't realize that a thirty dollar tattoo looks like a thirty dollar tattoo ... You get all kinds [of customers]. From teenage girls who come in with three of their friends asking if they could get a discount if they were all tattooed, or a guy who tells you one of your competitors said he'd do the same tattoo for fifty bucks less. Whatever the case, I tell them to beat it ... I will never figure out why people try to find the best price when they're going to have their tattoos for the rest of their lives.

Compare these sentiments to Clarice's (26) words:

Why should I pay the most for the same tattoo? ... I mean the one I have isn't complicated. I really don't care how famous the artist is or anything like that. I thought I shouldn't be paying more than a hundred dollars for it, and I searched around town until a found a guy who would do it for under that.

The third most common route to finding an artist involves the location of the artist's studio. Nine of the clients I interviewed (14%) chose to be tattooed in studios that were close to their respective places of residence. Sanders (1989) suggested some time ago that individuals will likely select a tattoo artist who operates out of a studio in or near their neighbourhoods. Being able to learn about the studio by walking or driving past becomes the only criterion for selection – perhaps strictly for convenience:

I walked past Sacred Art about five times a day, on the way in and out of my apartment. I live right down the block and I've looked into the studio hundreds of times ... When I committed myself to tattooing, I just walked down the street and starting talking to the artist there. It was really simple and hassle free. (Yvonne, 26)

The fourth most common method of learning about and then selecting a particular artist is a personal inspection of the artist's work. Five of the tattoo enthusiasts I interviewed suggested that the reputation (i.e., for high-quality art) of the tattoo artist dictated their selection. Again, informal friendship networks are vital sources of information here. More frequently, however, people will examine artists' portfolios (readily available in the lobbies of tattoo studios) as a means of assessing their abilities. Assessing the quality of the artwork generally involves looking to see if the colours used in the tattoos displayed are vibrant, the designs are complex and creative, and the lines clear and smooth:

> I know these guys [artists] probably put their absolute best work in the albums up front, but there's no better way to see what a guy can do. I wouldn't have done it any other way ... I wanted to have some northwest Native Indian work on my back, and searched around until I found Kris. He's a master in that style, and you could tell right away from the pictures of his tattoos. I didn't care how much he charged, I just wanted my tattoos to be as good as that. (Sandra, 34)

While individuals typically participate in one of the above methods of locating and selecting an artist, they similarly pass through *common* processes and figurational patterns in scheduling and experiencing a tattoo appointment. For instance, while some studios allow for 'walk-ins,' most require that clients schedule appointments (usually one to five weeks in advance) and provide down-payments to secure their appointment (typically 10% of the total cost of the tattoo). Clients are also regularly asked to arrive anywhere from thirty minutes to one hour before their appointments, and are asked to sign a consent waiver before the process commences:

> I ask people to sign a waiver just because you have to cover your ass ... in case someone is allergic and doesn't know it, if they have some medical condition, or like, if their body is going to react weirdly to the ink. Also, it's about making them declare that they are over the age of eighteen ... All the consent form is really about is just a way of making them sign a sheet saying they're aware of the dangers and that they're doing this under their own free will. (Jones, 27)

The bulk of in-depth ethnographic research on tattooing (e.g., Sanders 1989; St Clair and Govenar 1981; Steward 1990) details along these and similar lines some of the minute processes involved in securing and initially experiencing an appointment. Describing the everyday interactions unfolding in tattooing studios, the research furnishes a thick account of how individuals become first involved in the physical practice.

In the participant-observation phases of this investigation, I also noted that artist fabricate standard 'routines' for tattooing their clients. When I asked tattoo artists about the rituals involved in tattooing their clients, they agreed that standard ways of interacting with clients become conscious and unconscious habit. For instance, clients are told to sit in tattoo chairs in particular ways (depending upon what segment of the body is being tattooed), given a briefing about the technical aspects of the procedure (e.g., sterilization procedures), and provided with detailed instructions for after-care (a daily regimen to maximize the skin's retention of ink and minimize the possibility of infection). Moreover, they are spoken to frequently during the process (small talk and humour to reduce clients' nervousness), encouraged to vocalize their pain (i.e., as a means of helping clients manage their identities), advised to maintain steady and deep breaths (to avoid fainting), and given opportunities throughout the procedure to stop for a brief period (e.g., three to five minutes to rest and recoup). As a way of bolstering client's feelings of accomplishment and pride after the process, one tattoo artist I met recited the same humorous speech to his clients: 'Congratulations, and welcome to the club. We have meetings every Tuesday night at Desperado's nightclub. Knock three times at the back door, and flash them your tattoo to get in. Just tell them shaky Pete the tattoo artist sent you' (Doug, 26). Routinely drawing upon what works well, artists create and adjust their scripts for interaction. They forge routine verbal and physical scripts, resembling what Schutz (1967) might call 'typifications' or what Garfinkel (1967) might refer to as 'objectifications,' to lead their clients through the process. Clients, therefore, experience various segments of the actual tattooing process in very similar ways. The fact that artists have concocted standard or typical ways of interacting with clients based on their cumulative past encounters illustrates the ways in which clients are connected to one another through chains of interdependency. As Atkinson (2000) noted through research on the ticket-scalping community in Canada, formulating categorical understandings of clients is a mainstay aspect of conducting any commercial business. Each client unknowingly (and sometimes knowingly) enters into a set of pre-established interdependencies and scenarios of interaction that pre-dates their involvement in the practice.

Finally, clients also experience a common process of physical pain and healing in tattooing. While felt and expressed in varying degrees (depending on one's overall health, threshold for pain, and previous experience with tattooing – as well as the portion of the body being tattooed, size of the tattoo, number of needles used in the process, speed of the tattoo machine, and audience witnessing the event), physical discomfort is relatively inescapable in the procedure. Described by clients through terms such as 'burning,' 'irritating,' 'scraping,' 'pinching,' or 'cutting,' pain is an ongoing concern for tattoo enthusiasts. While pain is a factor preventing some individuals from dabbling in the body project, once it is met and managed in the process, clients seem to be more comfortable with the practice. As a tattoo enthusiast named Jill (34) stated:

> I don't think of myself as a wimp or anything like that, but I was nervous about how much I thought tattooing was going to hurt ... The first few lines, and maybe the first half-hour kind of smarted a bit, but after that it was pretty easy to sit through ... Now, I don't consider the pain at all ... That's not going to stop me from covering my body.

Artists will not mislead their clients about the pain involved in tattooing, neither downplaying nor exaggerating the physical trauma involved. Viewed as a sacred part of being tattooed and as a mark of one's commitment, the ability to endure pain is lauded by many enthusiasts: 'Tattooing is not for everybody, and probably too good for most people, and how someone deals with pain is a good indicator of how deep they will become involved. It's not too painful to sit through, so people will do it, but painful enough that a lot of people are scared away ... It's like a Zen balancing act' (Ed, 29).

After the process is complete, and the person has managed the physical pain involved in being tattooed, a healing period (between seven and twelve days) is endured. The abrasions, cuts, scabs, and bruises quickly fade away and the skin heals. Following only the most rudimentary restrictions (e.g., no swimming, no direct exposure to the sun, washing once per day with mild soap, and applying aloe or a salve to the skin three times per day), the tattoo will heal in most cases without complication:

> Some people freak out when they start to see their skin flaking off and think their bodies are rejecting the ink or they're having an allergic reaction. Even though we go through the procedure for after-care with everyone, and they all receive our sheet of instructions, about three out of every ten calls that come into the shop everyday [not appointment-related] are about healing ... whether that's a general question by someone who is thinking about being tattooed or someone who is healing and some condition they are experiencing isn't listed on the sheet I gave them ... It's usually nothing, right. Like a pimple from all the cream, or an area where you went too deep and it's scarred up a bit. (Phil, 24)

After-care is nothing. I was all worried after my first tattoo, and treated it like I'd been shot or something. It's so stupid, your body is so much tougher than that. If you just use your common sense, your skin is really resilient, so, no problems. I've been tattooed four times now, and I'm learning what works best. A tattoo artist or one of your buddies just can't tell you that. (Kevin, 25)

Thus, clients commonly experience several pathways or trajectories in the processes of arranging to be, and becoming, tattooed. Through the experience of similar corporeal and interactive practices, preliminary links between individuals' body-modification practices are formed. Just as individuals who participate in cosmetic surgery are collectively tied to one another in the reproduction and reaffirmation of class- or gender-based codes about sexuality and corporeal aesthetics (Dull and West 1991; Gillespie 1996), tattoo enthusiasts are linked by their common experiences in this form of body redesign. As a series of interdependencies between artists an their clients is created, the first strands of the figuration are forged.

2. Relationship Chains

The loose chains formed between artists and clients through the processes noted above are welded into tighter interpersonal bonds as relationships begin to take shape around, or are affected by, tattooing body projects. Preliminary relationships between artists and clients are based on the physical act of tattooing (one takes the role of the artist and the other the role of the client). Tattoo artists and clients are mutually dependent upon one another, since artists cannot parlay their flair for tattooing into a profession unless clients can be secured on an ongoing basis, and clients may not fulfil their desires to modify their flesh (in most cases) without the expertise of a tattoo artist. Personal involvement in the practice tends to have a ripple effect in one's relationships both inside and outside of the tattoo figuration. Involvement in tattooing alters one's interdependencies among tattoo enthusiasts and non-enthusiasts alike.

When an individual participates more extensively in tattooing, he or she can become immediately recognizable to others as an enthusiast. To this end, some of the individuals I encountered deliberately wear tank-top shirts, shorts, or other revealing articles of clothing to show off their tattoos. Clients that I interviewed often spoke of such display as a means of sending out a communicative beacon to like-minded others:

When I'm out and about and people roll up on me and comment on my tattoos I like it. I wouldn't wear sleeveless shirts if I didn't. Seeing someone else with heavy coverage is always cool for me. I go right up to people who are showing off their tattoos and ask them about where they were inked and who did them ... I kind of think about it like a port in a storm. You're weaving your way through life and every once in a while you meet somebody by accident and you hook up with them immediately because you feel comfortable with how they look. After you get inside their heads, you find out they're a lot like you, they've been through the same stuff and can relate to you. (Stu, 27)

Similarly, hanging out in tattoo studios and displaying one's 'work' to heavily tattooed others is utilized as a method of meeting fellow enthusiasts:

Sometimes I just want to talk to somebody who likes tattoos as much as me. So I go down and talk to some of the guys who go to Sacred Art. We just lean on the counter for a while and flip through tattoo magazines or something ... Some days I really miss hanging out with the guys there, and can't wait until Saturday when I have a day off from work. (Pete, 23)

As this process occurs, studios often become known locally for the specific types of patrons serviced, and can transform into informal hang-outs for some of these patrons. For example, one tattoo studio in Toronto is an informal meeting place for Skaters and Ravers, who share common interests in tattooing and broader world views as well:

Whenever a rave is coming to town, you can be sure that there will be ads posted [at the studio] or some kind of pamphlets or something. Most of my good friends will meet there before a rave too, and organize how we are going to get there and sort out who brings what [drugs] ... It's a friendly place, a place where no one will judge us or hassle us for hanging around and talking about rave. Plus, like twenty of us have been tattooed there, and know the guys [artists] really well, so whenever we go in, it's like, one of us is getting tattooed. (Davey, 22)

In this case, the tattoo studio is utilized as an interactive context in which social relationships are cultivated over time. However, not many people hang around in tattoo studios for extended periods. While some people do return on occasion to speak with artists for one reason or another, most are not regulars in the shops.

A significant portion of the contemporary groundswell in tattooing practices may also be explained through the formation of relationships inside the figuration. As enthusiasts become more deeply involved in tattooing and incorporate their corporeal transformations more centrally in their respective self-conceptualizations, they typically depend upon fellow enthusiasts for positive affirmation. Existing in a state of mutual dependency, enthusiasts turn into advocates of tattooing – not as fanatics who exhibit prejudices toward non-tattooed others, but as lobbyists for increased cultural acceptance of and respect for the body project. Encouraging others to be more tolerant of tattooing, attempting to dispel long-standing cultural stereotypes about tattoo enthusiasts, and promoting future participation among current enthusiasts, tattoo enthusiasts often become lobbyists of the body project:

> I don't hesitate to encourage other people to do it. I think it's the most beautiful thing you can do with your body. It's a way of making your skin into artwork that reflects your very soul ... I never thought about it that way until a close friend of mine went through a long battle with cancer and was tattooed to reclaim her body's aesthetic spirit. I started to reflect about her and found myself fascinated with some of the art the artists are capable of now. It's amazing, it really is ... and I tell everybody that. (June, 45)

The increased participation of one individual (and their advocacy efforts) creates a domino effect inside and outside of the figuration. Thirty-two (49%) of the clients I ended up interviewing stated that they first began to ponder the viability of being tattooed following a discussion about tattooing with one of their tattooed friends, co-workers, or family members. These individuals did not articulate their initial contemplations about tattooing as the product of being passionately recruited by others, but instead expressed a sense of influence from others who possessed favourable definitions of tattooing. Sutherland's landmark analysis (1937) showed how favourable definitions of behaviour are disseminated through social interaction. Similarly, exposure to pro-tattooing definitions can be key in stimulating an individual to consider the body project of tattooing: 'I don't think I would have any tattoos at all unless my friends did. They were responsible for my first thoughts about tattoo art, and were my role models, really. It's not like I followed them blindly. I mean, I am my own person, but when the people all around you are tattooed, you can't help think about it all the time' (Erin, 27). The relevancy of the informal advocacy process appears in the ways in which individuals are linked together through relationship chains and networks. Thus, the number of tattoo enthusiasts in Canada may be growing as a result of the sheer number of people routinely exposed to pro-tattooing definitions of the body – with the pool of enthusiasts in Canada multiplying exponentially over time. Contrary to Shilling's (1993), Kleese's (1999), or Sweetman's (1999) understanding of body projects such as tattooing as highly individualistic and isolated practices, enthusiasts involved in this study suggested that their involvement in tattooing is highly linked to significant others' involvement in the practice. As further evidence, seventy-six (82%) of the enthusiasts interviewed were tattooed with a close friend, partner, or fellow enthusiast present in the studio – indicating that enthusiasts tend to include other enthusiasts in their experiences with tattooing.

We may also explain the heightened interest in tattooing experiences by attending to the interpersonal relationships formed between artists in the figuration. A core subject in much of the extant sociological literature on the practice, relationships between artists are pivotal in creating a sense of community within the figuration. While DeMello (2000), Rubin (1988), and Sanders (1989) provided arguments as to how the figuration is splintered by social class, stylistic preferences, territorial competition, and artistic envy, Canadian artists seem to be a 'friendlier' and more encouraging lot. Some artists in Canada actively circulate one another's business cards to clients, post stickers in their studios advertising others' business, refer clients to one another, and find jobs for their apprentices in other studios. They also teach one another about specific techniques, exchange 'secrets' for shading or other colouring techniques, and provide tips on how to set up shop and manage clients:

> My best friends in the entire world are other tattoo artists. I'd do anything for most of them ... whatever they need in the way of promotion or anything like that. When you do this for a living, you naturally meet others in the business, and it's that much sweeter when you can get along with people who love it like you do ... I have no problem doing a solid [favour] for one of my friends. Like last week, one of the guys at Pleasure and Pain called me up to ask if he could 'borrow' some of this new ink I'd ordered and I said, sure. He's giving me a hand building a new [tattoo] machine, which is pretty cool, so it's no skin off my nose. (Harland, 26)

By linking together efforts to promote the efficient and smooth operation of the business of tattooing, artists develop working relationships with one another. On a personal level, such relationships frequently morph into close friendships outside of the studios. A tattoo artist named Phil once told me that in order to be a successful tattoo artist, 'you have to live, eat, and sleep tattooing.' Being engrossed in the practice, artists find occasional solace in hanging around with other artists who are able to share and understand their commitment to the art. In this way, the personal relationships formed between artists provide structural pillars for the figuration. With increased collegiality among artists and collective commitment to the practice, their exuberance and devotion to tattooing is transformed into chains of professional interdependencies inside the figuration. In turn, clients enter into a professional setting characterized by communication and mutual respect.

Bonds outside of the Tattoo Figuration

Participation in the activity of tattooing does not always engender favourable responses from others. Any Canadian who has ever gone 'under the needle' is aware of this simple fact. For clients, in particular, venturing into the realm of tattooing may pose a series of threats to one's statuses, roles, or relationships among individuals outside the figuration. Although tattooing has acquired a heightened respect (or indifference) from non-enthusiasts in Western cultures over the past twenty years, cultural stereotypes and distaste toward the tattooed body still prevent some (at least for a while) from participating in the body project:

> I waited a long time to be tattooed. I didn't want to walk through a mall and have people staring and pointing at me. I know it may sound foolish, but I couldn't get the idea that people would treat me like a carnival freak out of my head. My family all called me crazy, and asked me if I was dating a criminal whenever I discussed doing it ... that really dissuaded me from doing it for a long time. (Sandra, 34)

Similarly, in fearing that generalized others will interpret their interest in tattooing as sadomasochism, involvement in a criminal subculture, a sign of disrepute, a corporeal abomination, or some other fanciful deviance, enthusiasts may go to great lengths to hide their tattoos from others and 'pass' (Goffman 1963) as normal:

> I've never shown my tattoos to anyone at the office. Christ, I can't even imagine how my boss would freak out, because I work with our customers and clients on a daily basis and he would probably fire me on the spot. So

I'll never go into work, even on the hottest days, with short-sleeve shirts or shorts on ... That would be crazy. If there's even the slightest chance that the tattoos might show through my clothes, I buy this skin-coloured bandage to cover them, and no one, so far, has noticed. (Gwen, 27)

The fear of presenting one's tattoos to others is mainly fuelled by the potential deleterious reactions from three main groups: family members, close friends, and superiors at work. First and foremost, enthusiasts are concerned with negative reactions from their parents, and the potential detriment to their familial relationships. Enthusiasts often described their parents as conservative, holding values that oppose body practices that permanently alter the skin in such a manner. Twenty (31%) of the clients suggested that they refrained from being tattooed for years to avoid the potential wrath of parents – waiting to become involved in tattooing until they had moved out of their parents' houses. Thirty-two (49%) of the clients interviewed stated that they concealed their tattoos from their parents for at least one month, and twelve of these individuals have never revealed their tattoo(s) to their parents. This seemed to be more applicable to female enthusiasts, as they felt more constrained by dominant cultural expectations about tattooing and by gendered codes about corporeal alteration supported by their parents:

My dad would kill me if he ever found out. The entire time I was sitting in the chair [being tattooed] I cried because I thought my dad was going to hate me when he saw it ... To this day, I won't wear a bathing suit around him because he'd see it and probably disown me. I've always been daddy's little girl and I think he'd look at me like a prostitute. He's always told me how much he hates tattoos and associates them with the guys in pool halls he used to grow up around. (Sadie, 24)

Nine of the clients interviewed (14%) stated that their increased participation in tattooing had seriously strained relationships with one or both parents, and seven of the artists interviewed (26%) experienced the complete severance of a relationship with some family member as a result of their participation in the profession:

My mom stopped talking to me the day I told her I was quitting my job at the bank and becoming a tattoo artist. I had a couple of tattoos at the time, but she seemed to have no problems with those. To her, it's a whole other ball game now. She can't tell anybody what her son is doing for a living, because she's ashamed of me, and says I'm throwing my life away for a bunch of hoodlums. I know I'm practically dead to her. (Steven, 23)

Clients and artists equally discussed how their body markings altered relationships with close friends who have not partaken in the practice. Some friends met the tattoos with a mix of fascination and confusion, others with outright condemnation. In most cases, enthusiasts do not hide their tattoos from their friends as they do from parents, and thus open the door for myriad reactions. Negative reactions were understandable yet perplexing for the enthusiasts I met. On the one hand, negative reactions were understood if they expressed a lack of congruence between the friend's understanding of the individual (i.e., as conservative or introverted) and their tattooed body, or were encoded with an underlying jealousy:

Some of my friends kept on saying to me, 'I can't believe you, I can't believe you.' They always saw me as the timid and shy girl who would never do anything like this. But I shocked the hell out of them, by showing them exactly who I am. This is me, this is who I am, and I don't have to meet anyone's expectations about what I should or shouldn't do with my body. (Roma, 23)

My one friend Kate is so jealous, I know she is. She's always yapped and yapped about getting a tattoo but hasn't screwed up enough courage to go and do it ... So, when she saw me at the bar the first weekend after I had it done, she flipped out. I came in wearing a shirt that showed off my stomach and because the tattoo is around my belly button you could see it right there ... She hasn't spoken to me in almost a year. (Karen, 20)

On the other hand, negative reactions and the weakening of bonds between friends were confounding when an individual believed that the negative reactions had no basis or highlighted deep-seated ideological differences that could not be reconciled:

When my friend Art saw my Straightedge tattoo he looked at me a couple of times right in the eyes and didn't say anything, at first. Then he started to rip into me about being a hypocrite and all that stupidity. He doesn't know, he hasn't been there. He hangs around with a lot of the same guys as me, and knew what a Straightedge tattoo means. It means that I've cleaned

up my life and am not smoking drugs anymore, no drinking, or nothing
that will pollute my body. He's still into that scene, so I think he took my
statement [the tattoo] as an insult. (Carl, 26)

Finally, the extent of enthusiasts' participation in tattooing can be dictated by their professional aspirations or current employment situations. As tattooed bodies are not normative in most work settings, the
enthusiasts I spoke with frequently selected locations on the body to be
tattooed that are easily concealed, such as the upper arm, lower back,
thigh, chest, or abdomen. This precludes tattooing on the neck, hands,
forearms, feet, and other locations regularly exposed in the work setting. Under the fear of reprisal from superiors or outright dismissal, the
moral atmosphere at work largely influences one's involvement in the
body project:

The place where I work, we still have policies about body art. You can't
have it on your face or anywhere else that's visible with 'normal' business
attire. So, I'm filling in all the areas where you can't see a tattoo right away!
That's not going to stop me at all, but it certainly does limit my choices ...
Sometimes, I get angry because I feel like they're breaking my constitutional right to be whoever I want to be, and do what I want with my body,
but they sign my cheques so I have to dance to their tune. (Rachel, 35)

In conforming to and reproducing dominant cultural prescriptions that
outline normative standards for body alteration and corporeal display,
while underlining the importance of work relationships and material
prosperity in Western cultures, more-involved (i.e., tattooed) enthusiasts describe their work-related responsibilities as highly constraining:

I'm of the mindset now that I want a full sleeve of tattoos. I have two
already on my back, and since I've been reading tattoo magazines I can't
believe the incredible art that goes into a full sleeve, so I want one. The
possibilities are endless, and it's a way to really get into the art and create
something unique for yourself. Well, of yourself, I guess. The stuff is crazy
cool, but there's no way I can do it because it would peek out at work and I
would get in shit. Basically, I have to quit my job if I want to do it. (Ryan,
28)

In a manner reminiscent of Hathaway's research (1997a, 1997b) on
managing one's usage of marijuana while on the job, or Young and

Craig's discussion (1997) of the importance of concealing visible markers of one's membership in the Skinhead subculture at work, enthusiasts learn how and when to explore an interest in non-normative practices within occupational settings.

Clearly, then, relationships both inside and outside of the tattoo figuration are formed, cultivated, and altered through participation in tattooing. The lengthening or shortening of one's chains of interdependency with others' (individual and collective) participation in the body project over time may shift and redefine one's social relationships, identities, and responsibilities. By conceptualizing the body project of tattooing in this way, we begin to appreciate how a seemingly isolated and privatized act is firmly based on mutual dependence, orientation, and foresight.

The concept of interdependence calls for an alternative understanding of Canadian tattoo enthusiasm. Rather than hinging the analysis of tattoo enthusiasts on the conceptual linchpin of subculture, one should take direction from Elias's understanding (1978, 1991a, 1994) of figurations. Venturing away from much of the existing literature on tattooing in America, which tends to depict the collective of enthusiasts as an esoteric sub-group of intimate actors, the concept of interdependence provides fresh theoretical insight on how individuals' unconventional redesigning body projects may be aligned and intersubjectively meaningful in quite non-subcultural ways. Stressing that individuals are deeply enmeshed in matrices or chains of social interaction that we may refer to as figurations, Elias (1991a) draws our attention to the interpersonal ties that bind seemingly isolated individuals together in social interchange. Following this line of thought, our conception of the tattooing body project is reconfigured as we explore how interdependence rather than subcultural membership forms the social mortar of this redesigning body project.

CHAPTER SIX

Sociogenesis and Personality Structures

By building upon the empirical observation that tattooing is best conceptualized as an interdependent social activity, we can extend our understanding of tattoo enthusiasm in Canada by inspecting the rationalizations people offer about their tattooing body projects. As a first step in advancing our understanding of individuals' motivations to become tattooed, however, we might find it worthwhile to take a step backward and investigate some of the reasons why Canadians' attitudes about body modification (in general) are shifting at present. In principle, we should inquire about the impact of socially pervasive constructions of bodies as sites of self-exploration and display on Canadians' sensibilities about corporeal modification. By investigating narratives provided by tattoo enthusiasts, in particular, one gains a sense that the current interest in tattooing may be a product of changing cultural interpretations of appropriate body modification.

To illustrate how specific sociogenic transformations have altered cultural habituses in Canada – and opened the door to increased participation in tattooing – the following discussion is segmented into three main sections. Elias's description (1983, 1991a, 1994) of the interrelationship between sociogenesis and psychogenesis is first revisited as a means of unpacking a series of conceptual tools for deciphering how cultural habituses form. Next, tattoo enthusiasts' narratives about their perceptions of bodies and their modification are examined, followed by a discussion of how information acquisition, ownership, and exchange in Canada profoundly influences social constructions of body modification practices. Finally, cultural-diversity and globalization processes are analysed as key contributory factors influencing our willingness to redefine the boundaries of socially acceptable body manipulation.

Sociogenesis and Body-modification Habits

A dominant theme running throughout Elias's research on long-term sociogenic and psychogenic transformation in Western figurations is the idea that 'earlier' (11th century AD and prior) social conglomerates typically relied upon coercion and external force as their *main* mechanism of social control. That is to say, with competing social factions all vying for situated power, economic opportunities, and possession of material or natural resources in emerging figurations – and little fear of reprisal from a central social authority (Elias and Scotson 1965) – violence was an instrumental tactic for acquiring control over others. Individuals feared violence from a plethora of social groups and submitted to the will of those possessing a greater ability to wield power through violence. Elias (1983, 1994) argued, however, that central authorities (e.g., a court or state) eventually obtained a recognized and legitimate ownership over the means of violence within these figurations. Among its other social functions, a state (i.e., some form of secular government) became the regulatory agency of violence, administering social control through formal punishment mandated by its role as social guardian – protecting the rights and personal freedoms of all. Elias referred to this process of social pacification through the centralization of violence as the 'monopoly mechanism,' and described it as part of the 'parliamentarisation of conflict' (1994).

In this context individuals were (mostly) protected from others' random whims of violence and uncontrolled affective outbursts. Accordingly, however, all individuals were forced to curtail their own emotional outbursts to ensure their personal liberty and protection. The mechanism of social control largely remained external as individuals submitted to the will of one central authority. Although there was a general pacification of social figurations as a result of these sociogenic transformations, inclinations toward personal control were largely based on the threat of punishment from the state.

Over the course of time (i.e., as chains of interdependency expanded and were consolidated between individuals into dense webs of relationships), external control gave way to inner control as the mechanism of social order. As social functions within institutions became increasingly differentiated, and people came to rely upon others more extensively in daily life, individuals became increasingly attuned to the needs of others (Elias 1994). Predictability of action is required in such figurations, as individuals acquire more specific, extended, and interdependent social roles. Elias's comments are worth quoting at some length here:

> The closer the web of interdependencies become in which the individual is enmeshed with the advancing division of functions, the larger the social spaces over which this network extends and which become integrated into functional or institutional units – the more threatened is the social existence of the individual who gives way to spontaneous impulses and emotions, the greater is the social advantage of those able to moderate their affects, and the more strongly is each individual constrained from an early age to take account of the effects of his or others people's actions on a whole series of links in the social chain. The moderation of spontaneous emotions, the tempering of affects, the extension of mental space beyond the moment into the past and the future, the habit of connecting events in terms of chains of cause and effect – all these are different aspects of the same transformation of conduct which necessarily takes place with the monopolization of physical violence, and the lengthening of the chains of social action and interdependence. It is a 'civilising' change of behaviour. (1994, 448)

Persons choosing to act impulsively or irrationally (through uncontrolled affective outburst) jeopardize their ascribed/achieved social positions and statuses (Elias 1983). As standards of civilized behaviour are promulgated within figurations as normative (i.e., generally to buttress ideologically the actions, behaviours, and positions of the ruling elite), dominant social codes of conduct are established. Personality structures are transformed over time such that cultural habituses involving high levels of affective control and inner containment become second nature (Elias 1991a, 1994, 1996). Fearing both the formal punishments levied against affective outburst and the social stigma assigned to unbridled behaviour, individuals carefully self-regulate all facets of their public conduct.

Upon closer inspection, the position Elias developed is contingent on a central belief that human beings possess both self-protecting and personally destructive instincts, drives, libidinal impulses, or motivations that are altered through the course of long-term civilizing processes (1991a, 1994, 1996). When figurations become more functionally diverse and complex, and as inner control is increasingly demanded to maintain social cohesion, personality structures are changed in such a way that unconscious drives are significantly moulded by learned behaviours, as structured by dominant cultural habituses. While biological drives are not eradicated from personality structures entirely, individuals come to steer their actions based on *learned* impulsions rather than unlearned affect – a process that underlines the malleability of human drives and emotions (Elias 1996).

As people are expected to engage in a high degree of affective control, the individual desire for free affective expression (self-gratifying or not) is curtailed and subsequently replaced with a drive toward inner containment. Elias noted, however, that the drive toward self-regulation is not an unnatural psychic imposition created within a figuration, as human beings possess natural leanings toward behavioural control (1991a, 35–6). Still, what psychologists might refer to as 'unconscious' or 'id' drive economies are permeated by learned (i.e., social) motivations and impulses, thus is altered the personality structure of individuals. As Elias commented:

> Every investigation that considers only the consciousness of men, their reason, or ideas, while disregarding the structure of drives, the direction and form of human affects and passions, can be from the outset of only limited value ... A real understanding, even of the changes of ideas and forms of cognitions, can be gained only if one takes into account the changes of human interdependencies in conjunction with the structure of conduct and, in fact, the whole fabric of men's personality at a given stage of social development. (1994, 486)

An important aspect of this personality-(trans)formation process is the extent to which *shame* becomes a constitutive element of self-regulation (Elias 1983, 1996). An emotion elicited by actions receiving sanction or reprisal from significant or generalized others, shame is a product of external relationships or bonds with others and internalized standards of behaviour (see Elias 1994; Goffman 1959; Scheff 2001). Shame or embarrassment about one's actions represents a conflict between individual behaviour, social expectations of appropriate behaviour that define and hold together social relationships, and one's personality structure. Shame is not merely the product of negative reaction from situated audiences, but also represents an inner tension created through self-reflection on one's own action (Elias 1994). The avoidance of shame becomes a *learned habit*, a motivation perpetuating what we might call normative social behaviour – and hence is an extension of self-restraint and affective control.

In conjunction with the monopoly mechanism, the push toward self-control, and the notable impact of shame and embarrassment on personality structures in dense figurations, cultural thresholds for violent, lascivious, or otherwise disgusting behaviours are lowered (Elias 1978, 1994). When the control of affective behaviour is demanded externally and then regulated internally in a social figuration, that which is viewed to be physically or morally repugnant (as defined by culturally diffuse norms, values, and beliefs) is pushed behind the scenes of social life, or perhaps controlled through 'mimetic' social activities such as sport (Elias and Dunning 1986; Dunning 1999; Dunning and Rojek 1992; Maguire 1999; Sheard 1999). Over the course of long-term historical processes, habituses come to reflect an immediate revulsion toward overtly violent, hyper-sexual, or other uncontrolled bodily behaviours, as such behaviours are neither individually rational nor beneficial to existing chains of interdependency (Elias 1983).

Through his discussion of long-term sociogenic and psychogenic change, Elias (1994) underscored equally the importance of the body as a site of civilized display. Arguing that the body transforms into a text through which one is able to represent one's distinction, status, and affective control, Elias (1983, 1991b, 1994, 1996) pointed to the ways in which bodies become intextuated with communicative social symbols. In particular, he noted how the body turns into a primary text upon which an individual's ability to control affect and portray desirable images of the self can be gauged. This line of thought clearly interweaves the study of sociogenesis and psychogenesis, as linkages are made between chains of interdependency, personality structures, and dominant or normative forms of physical display. By once again eschewing the *homo clausus* model of personality formation and development, Elias showed a keen understanding of how specific individual body habits form within figurations.

Therefore, as the collective threshold of repugnance toward egregious affective behaviour lowers (particularly toward violent and lascivious behaviour), the body becomes a central target toward which emergent standards and conventions of internal restraint are directed and exhibited (Elias 1978, 1983, 1994). Quite some time, then, before Goffman's (1959, 1963), Foucault's (1977, 1979), or Bourdieu's (1984) expositions on the regulation of bodily shape, display, and functioning in society, Elias had clearly acknowledged the body as a dominant marker of cultural norms, values, and beliefs. His work thereby underscores the importance of modifying the body in the process of manufacturing both dominant and subordinate body styles (Elias 1994, 471). Also key to understanding Elias's analysis of corporeal performance and display is the premise that bodies become increasingly *rationalized* over the course of long-term civilizing processes (1994, 475–92). If affective containment and the exhibition of personal control largely symbolize one's cultural refinement, and are therefore crucial in maintaining one's positions, roles, and varied social statuses, the internal pacification one displays through body representation is chief in shaping one's social identity (Elias 1983, 1994). Since individuals jeopardize their social positions and (occasionally) freedom by violating norms of bodily conduct and display, corporeal representation is carefully scripted to convey socially desirable images of the self (e.g., as cultured, distinguished, or civilized).

If, in the study of tattooing, we attend to the impact of ongoing sociogenic change on dominant cultural habituses, focus may then be directed to how individual inclinations toward tattooing (or others forms of body modification) are influenced by changing relationships and interdependencies within figurations. Reciprocally, we are led to investigate whether the continued increase in tattooing practices influences cultural habits *and* social relationships inside and outside of the tattoo figuration. Furthermore, if the body is a communicative text detailing one's capacity for affect management and control, we must question whether or not tattoo enthusiasts intentionally represent affect, or a degree of affective management, through their tattooing practices. If such behaviour has culturally denoted one's inability to manage affect in self-controlled ways (Atkinson and Young 2001), then is the contemporary upsurge in the popularity of tattooing in Canada actually an indicator of the widespread inability to control affect? The increased participation in tattooing would thus be accurately viewed as a signifier of de-civilizing processes in Canada. In pursuing preliminary answers to these questions, it is appropriate, and analytically invigorating, to interweave figurational sociology with several streams of theory related to changing social environments and cultural landscapes.

Information Cultures and Body-modification Habits

Pointing to the methods by which hegemonic discourses are encoded and strategically circulated through television, news media, and other public platforms, Stuart Hall (1980) – and scores of other cultural studies theorists (e.g., Cohen 1972; Cohen and Young 1973; Fiske 1989a, 1989b; Hebdige 1979; Johnson 1983; Williams 1977) – deftly outlined how the control over information distribution is key in consolidating social leadership and ideologically supporting pervasive (e.g., class-based) social relationships. Following a trail of social investigation traversed by post-structuralists and critical theorists (Adorno 1991; Althusser 1971; Arnold 1932; Horkheimer and Adorno 1972; Marcuse 1964) and semioticians (Barthes 1972, 1975; Lacan 1977), Hall illustrated the importance of understanding how the 'ownership' of information is crucial in acquiring social power.

To a certain extent, Hall's arguments resonated with Foucault's description of the politics of social power (1977, 1979, 1980), and Baudrillard's later thoughts (1983, 1988) on the saliency of communication technologies and semiotic messages in arranging preferred ways of viewing the world. The message presented by these authors (in their own respective ways) is based on a clear assumption – that within neo-capitalist work structures control over the means of producing, assessing, and disseminating information is central in securing social leadership. Paralleling Marx's ideas (1977) about how super-structural relations are buttressed by cultural ideologies that are promulgated through state apparatuses (Williams 1977), these authors drew our attention to the ways in which battles over discourse shape social experience. This is an idea that feminist scholars (see Bartky 1988; Bordo 1990; Butler 1990; and Martin 1994), committed to the smashing of gender myths, would clench tightly in deconstructing how patriarchal structures of social domination are created and confirmed.

While sociologists have pointed to the importance of owning or controlling dominant ways of knowing in the process of securing social hegemony – part of what Haraway (1991) referred to as the 'informatics of domination' – few have attended to our insatiable appetite for *all types* of information in the cyber-culture (Balsamo 1996; Haraway 1991) or information era. In many respects, the ability to wield power in Western cultures is predicated on the control over some medium of information; not in a grand structural sense as presented by neo-Marxist or postmodernist researchers (i.e., leading to the ownership over the means of material production), but in a situated, contextual, or everyday sense.

In figurations characterized by ongoing social exploration – medical, spiritual, economic, sexual, emotional, technological, and spatial (terrestrial and even extra-terrestrial!) – information is both social currency and a source of pleasure for individuals. We live in an era in which researchers involved in the Human Genome Project purport to have discovered the 'Bible of Life' – the complete breakdown of human DNA sequencing and encryption (Critical Art Ensemble 1998). The ramifications of this discovery range from the analysis of individuals' genetic coding, as part of predicting an individual's susceptibility for certain diseases, to the ability to clone humans. We also live in an era in which snowboarders search the globe to find the most thrilling mountain trails and paths (Humphreys 1997). Referred to as 'nomadic cosmopolitans' by Maguire (1999), these individuals continually seek information about the world's best 'runs' in order to pass the details on to their peers – thereby securing bragging rights and kudos for their sporting discoveries. Similarly, we live in an era in which individuals pursue new understandings of sexual arousal through asphyxia and other radical forms of stimulation (Laumann et al. 1994), and New Age religions search for spiritual enlightenment in the face of Judeo-Christian challenges and resistance (Goode 2001).

The quest for new types and forms of information continues to be an organizing principle in the work sphere. As a product of diversification within complex divisions of labour and bureaucratic modes of organization (Durkheim 1951; Marx 1977; Weber 1930), the social importance of acquiring, disseminating, and receiving work-related information is evident. For instance, in the e-culture of today, rapid access to information has proved to be critical for surviving and succeeding in business. Those left behind in the ongoing explosion of electronic information (sources, types, and technologies) suffer, as they are literally disconnected from the flow of business. The person informed about high-speed Internet connections, Web design, tele- or Web-conferencing, e-mail, voice mail, scanners, compact-disc writers, cellular forms of communication, MP3s, graphic manipulation, and computer programming has a decisive edge in the workplace. The tattoo enthusiast Marc (32) commented:

> My whole life is about gadgets. I work in an office and fix them everyday I go to work. It's not a formal part of my position there, but I grew up tinkering with video games like Intellivision and Atari, and I can fix practically everything – so everybody pesters me to fix their monitors, faxes, or whatever. They'd probably fire me if I ever gave up doing that [laughs].

Similarly, tattoo enthusiast Gwen (27) stated:

> I'm a data processor, and five years ago I couldn't have even told you what a data processor was. But now there's like nine of us in the department. I

never thought the computer science classes I took in high school and university would pay off. I'm really into computers, though, and spend about three-quarters of my paycheque on my personal computer systems at home. I probably sound like a freak or some kind of loser, but I just have to have all the latest [computer] gear. It helps because when I go to work, I'm up on all the latest technology and don't have to have somebody holding my hand when we get in a new piece of software or have to rebuild our network.

As the division of labour in Canada is increasingly diversified and extended by information technologies, being on the cutting edge of information processing and exchange is an integral aspect of being employable and a valued link in the work chain. Yet, as noted above, the dependence on technology in the workforce also permeates personal lives.

One might say, then, that given the ongoing diversification and specialization of roles in the workforce, and the degree to which the division of labour is increasingly defined by control over (particularly electronic) information in organizational structures, individuals are now hyper-conscious about the importance of possessing specialized stocks of information (Sennett 1998). As social interdependencies in Canada are created through information ownership and control, what one knows or is capable of knowing forms the basis of extended chains or webs of relationships between people. Individuals are dependent upon one another for information in the performance of daily life (McQuail 1994), and thus are highly attuned to others who possess some specialized or beneficial stock of information. As Mannheim (1971) might argue, every successive generation of individuals brought into this web of technology experiences the need for technological knowledge in greater degrees. Equally, since we are told that the world outside of Canada is now open to be known, our desire to acquire information has (perhaps) never been greater. Cultural habituses have shifted such that the quest for information is deeply ingrained in our personality structures.

Postmodernist insights about the centrality of information in the current era would also challenge us to believe that increasing specialization in the workforce creates a detrimental sense of cultural dislocation among individuals (Dunn 1998; McRobbie 1994; Strinati 1995). Cultural fragmentation and interpersonal disjunction occur as individuals feel distanced from others in the endless pursuit of information. Furthermore, as what we know is continually redefined and updated (i.e., identities, images, and forms of knowing are constantly being questioned), there are no truly objective sources of information structuring social life (Behar 1996, 1999; Denzin 1997; Rosneau 1992; Tyler 1986). These postmodernist claims apparently dismiss (among other realizations) the possibility that individuals are bound to one another in more extended chains of interdependency by our collective quest for information exchange. While postmodernists generally acknowledge that cultural habituses have been transformed in such a way that the desire for information exchange has been stamped onto social life, their positions swirl around a basic belief that social cohesion has been splintered by the creation of new ways of seeing and knowing the world (Denzin 1997).

The issue here becomes how these ongoing and unintended sociogenic changes influence cultural habits as they relate to the body. That is, does the widespread cultural interest in information exchange alter sensibilities about body modification? Through the course of my venture into the world of tattooing, tattoo enthusiasts' narratives suggested three main ways that our collective cultural interest in information ownership and exchange has shaped their respective perceptions of bodies as sites of creation and display.

First, the cultural thirst for information and its circulation has influenced people to become preoccupied with representation (During 1999; Barthes 1972, 1975; Woodward 1997). In an age where portals to the world have opened through voyeuristic electronic media – collectively referred to as the 'information superhighway' – accessing and reassembling representations of the world is everyday practice. Alongside Elias's research (1983, 1994, 1996) on the subject, postmodernist theorizing about the image-sensitive nature of Western cultures sheds considerable light on the relevance of self-representation in social figurations. While in some ways these ideas abounded in earlier theoretical understandings of the processes by which people consciously manipulate images in everyday life (Goffman 1959, 1963), postmodernists drew our attention to how the circulation of images is a defining feature of pan-capitalist cultures (Critical Art Ensemble 1998). Simply put, in high-speed, hard-wired, digital, hooked-up, on-line figurations, visual forms of information reign supreme.

The tattoo enthusiasts I interviewed (especially the middle-class ones with considerable financial resources to access information technologies) expressed both a fascination with and concern about electronic representation, and about the extent to which Canadians appear to be evolving into an 'on-line' culture. The younger tattoo enthusiasts in this study (adolescents at some point in the 1990s) grew up as the first truly 'electronic' or 'digital' generation in Canada. These individuals have never known life without a vast array of electronic games, communication technologies, and personal computers. This 'Generation D' is highly attuned to information technologies and spends copious amounts of time each week on the Internet or exchanging e-mail. They are informed about the latest innovative technologies, and are able to access information about the world via any number of electronic sources. A tattoo enthusiast named Gill (29) stated:

> I spend about three or fours hours on the Net every day. I use it, like most of the time, for my own entertainment. But, like, I can't tell you how many times I've needed to look something up, or like wanted to know a little bit more about something and researched it on-line ... I couldn't get it out of my life if I wanted to, really ... Some people need their coffee in the morning or a smoke at lunch. I need my time in the chat room or time watching movies at the computer. It's how I relax, you know.

As the Internet has become a forum for invading all biological, social, cultural, and religious spaces, individuals participating with others on-line incorporate their tastes for textual display into every facet of their lives – including their corporeal practices. In interviews about their tattooing experiences, self-confessed 'info' or 'techno junkies' (18% of all enthusiasts interviewed) addressed the importance of visual representation in their lives:

> Even when I studied in university, I could only remember things if I came up with some kind of picture to remember them by. I'm a very visual person. I love to draw, make pictures, and take pictures of things ... but I don't have the physical skills to be good at it ... That's really come out in the last few years since I've spent a lot of time on the computer with a couple of graphics programs. One is an architectural program for designing homes and the other is this thing you can use to actually create paintings. It's totally awesome because you can create visual images in homes or on a simulated canvass that reflect who I am and what I feel. I would have never picked up a drafting tool and tried to do it that way, or stood at an easel with a pallet and painted away ... Technology has really liberated me to be so expressive ... I get ideas about how I want to look when I start working the programs and creating pictures. I see my body as a blank room that I

can fill with texture and movement by hanging things on it like clothes, or painting it with make-up. (Amy, 28)

Another tattoo enthusiast added:

I'm on-line so much that I'm used to being stimulated with cool pictures and texts. The Internet has made me more creative because of that, you know. I think about what I like in a Web site, right, what captivates me and makes me say, 'Damn, now that's a cool ass site.' I try to do that with the way I look, like the way I dress or comb my hair. I want people to look at me and see me as a cool Web site. (Aaron, 23)

Similarly, the tattoo artist Mel (22) commented:

I never thought I would have to look my best while talking to somebody on the phone, but with this new Net cam [camera] I'm using to talk with my girlfriend overseas, I have to get dressed up and comb my hair so she doesn't think I'm being a total dirtbag while she's away on a work-term for a year.

The sentiments expressed above indicate that while the preoccupation with representing the self physically is not a product of sociogenic change in the current era, sensibilities about physical representation through body modification have clearly been influenced by our collective use of electronic (information) technologies. This factor appears to be particularly germane to middle-class enthusiasts I met, whose lives are increasingly infiltrated and structured by new forms of technology and communication, and who possess the monetary resources required to purchase state-of-the-art electronic 'toys.'

However, not all tattoo enthusiasts were as flattering about information technology and our cultural fascination with information exchange. Claiming it to be an invasion of personal privacy and a dehumanizing influence on our societies, critics of the Internet and other communication platforms stress the impending need to return to our natural selves. These people read about 'wearable technology' (computer devices that are worn), cybernetics, and others forms of human-machine interfacing that facilitates information processing, and worry about the impact of this technology on our species. Particularly disgusted with the ways individuals are reduced to serial numbers, PINs, street addresses, telephone numbers, or other homogenizing forms of identification, self-proclaimed Neo Primitives charge that individuals should get more in touch with their spirits through radical body modification (Atkinson and Young 2001; Rosenblatt 1997). Their resistance to information technologies is launched through physical representation, as they believe the sacredness of the body has been lost through the seduction of electronic media and non-corporeal representation:

> All people care about is what number you are in their line, or if you're the guy sitting at home watching their commercials. It's not about the person you are, it's about your bankbook or if you're watching their shows and buying their colas. You're no different than the next guy with a fat wallet, and I can't go home at the end of the day accepting that ... I've never been more close to my body than right now. Waking up to the ways we're numbed by our culture made me explore who I am, and I started by knowing what my body is and how I am a real flesh and blood human ... So, I go to yoga class, changed my diet to promote better health, take care of my skin, and, oh god, so many other things to make sure my mind, body, and spirit are all aligned. (Ingrid, 24)

The Internet has also profoundly affected our interest in seeing others. With video cameras situated in just about every social space imaginable, and graphics or pictures of these spaces posted over millions of Web sites, browsers are virtually transported to every nook and cranny of the world. Information about this world can be accessed by many – thus, all aspects of social life are given to be read by others through communication possibilities. Once solely the subject matter of picture books or atlases, or the product of an individual's imagination, far-away places or inconceivable social occurrences are but a click of the computer mouse away. Given our ability to range the world and acquire textual information about diverse social actors and events through the Internet, individuals often feel as if their lives are open to be penetrated by others. Nineteen (21%) of the tattoo enthusiasts I interviewed suggested that they feel as if personal space is being threatened in the race to acquire more information about life. By describing this process as the erosion of borders between the private and the public, or the local and global, some enthusiasts expressed concern about the lack of privacy in their lives: 'I mean, everywhere you go, someone is watching you. You send an e-mail and it can be scanned, or you answer your cell phone and the signal can be picked up by any hacker who knows how. I go to the mall, or walk the streets and there are security cameras everywhere.

Where does it all end? So many people are setting up home cameras that it's like you're expected to be an exhibitionist. (Jack, 25)

Paradoxically, feelings of public invasion may manifest themselves in a strong embrace of personal representation through the body. Instead of lamenting the constant impositions created by prying social eyes, some enthusiasts articulated a self-confirmed need to express themselves publicly as a way of being seen and known. As the body is a directly accessible and mouldable text of representation (de Certeau 1984; Elias 1994), it is no wonder that people who wish to be seen and read by others so frequently engage in representation through physical display:

> My body is much more important than my words. Every day when I get up, I'm in a certain mood and I want people to know what I'm feeling by reading my body language. I might dress a way that tells people to piss off, or might do my hair so that I'm inviting people to talk to me ... I know people are looking at me anyway, we all do it. I mean, we used to call it 'people watching' like it was a pastime or some innocuous hobby that kept us from being rude to each other ... When I get up in the morning, I ask myself, if I saw me go by, what would I think ... and I proceed from there. (Quinn, 25)

Tattoo enthusiasts express a sense of conformity to emergent cultural habits in different ways. Some feel threatened by the public quest for information on their private lives. Others view bodies as 'natural' texts of personal representation – a slate upon which aspects of their personalities may immediately be written for others. In Foucault's terms (1977, 1979), they experience a sense of panopticism, as they are constantly monitoring their bodies and manipulating images of themselves with the idea that (to borrow and slightly alter a catchphrase of the film production company THX) 'the audience is watching.' Or, in figurational terms, sociogenic change related to information acquisition and distribution partially alters personality structures (especially regarding the body and its manipulation). The Orwellian 'Big Brother' is not simply a body of state officials, board of governors, or collective social elite – but rather one's partners, family members, neighbours, co-workers, and fellow citizens, who teach us how to use and display our bodies. The tattoo artist Archie (30) suggested:

> We live in a culture where people love to stare. It's human nature, everybody checks out everybody. We can't help do it, it's in our nature and a big part of it is looking at each other's bodies. People sit in my chair and they

go on and on about people looking at them. It's something that makes people walk through the front doors of my studio ... All that p.c. [political correctness] crap that tells you that you shouldn't look at people and size them up is nonsense. It's like, fuck off, right. It's like telling a rabbit not to hop or a monkey not to eat a banana. It's the law of our jungle.

As will be discussed in more detail in following chapters, it is clear that body modification becomes a conscious tactic in the process of 'doing individualism' (i.e., creating, negotiating, adjusting, and confirming identity). Contrary to the idea that body projects are hyper-privatized and solely individual acts, the social impetus toward information gathering on cultural habituses and body habits reveals how wide-scale sociogenic change alters sensibilities about the body as a project of identity display.

Body Perils and Physical Maintenance

Access to information sources (electronic or print) has also heightened our awareness of the biological and social perils confronting humans. For instance, we are regularly bombarded with reports and findings about the prevalence of biological diseases and epidemics such as AIDS, cancer, heart disease, Ebola, meningitis, E. coli, and other physical pathologies. Audiences are shown every detail about the 'disease process,' including microscopic pictures of viruses, charts and rates about the increasing number of individuals affected by specific diseases, and images of patients convalescing in their beds (Aggleton et al. 1989; Crawford 1994; Frank 1991b; Juengst and Koenig 1994; Sontag 1991). Focus is normally directed to the methods (biological or medical-technological) that people may adopt in protecting their bodies from disease. The underlying message is that while one may not effectively protect the body from all biological threats, increased body awareness and vigilant self-defence are still key in maintaining a healthy life. People are encouraged to be hyper-reflective about corporeal practices, and 'healthy' modification of the body (through diet and exercise) is strongly advised by medical experts. Carl (26), a tattoo client, commented:

I can't pick up a magazine anymore and not see some hideous skin disorder or a woman suffering from a disease. I'm actually terrified to read the paper anymore, I can't sleep for a week when I read the 'health' section ...

but if there's an upside to it, it's that by raising consciousness about the bad, you kick-start people into thinking about how vital our bodies are, and what we should or shouldn't be doing to ourselves.

With medical journals existing on-line, diagnostic manuals readily available to the public, and television documentaries profiling available or innovative surgical procedures, healthy body modification has become a cultural mantra for Canadians.

We are concomitantly exposed to media reports detailing the sharp rise in social problems such as crime (especially youth crime). Often the product of media dramatization and hyperbole (Bennis and Mitroff 1989; Smandych 2001a, 2001b), emergent 'folk devils' (Cohen 1973), serial killers, mass murderers, gang members, and social malcontents become points of considerable social concern – even though recent statistics indicate that rates for most categories of crime in Canada are declining (Gomme 1998; Smandych 2001a, 2001b). Through television programs such as 'To Serve and Protect,' 'Cops,' 'America's Most Wanted,' and 'The World's Most Dangerous Criminals,' the face of violence becomes domesticated. Such programs show footage of criminal behaviour taking place on street corners, in middle-class districts, and across the urban landscape. Like the stories about biological threats, reports concerning crime rates and dangerous offenders encourage citizens to protect themselves physically. As noted by Elias (1983, 1994), the body is the primary site of personal control against violence, as it is the territory over which individuals possess the greatest amount of agency and direction. A tattoo client named Clarice (26) suggested:

> If you believed everything you read, I mean, you would never leave your house. It's made people scared of their neighbours, and terrified us to be out and about in the world ... Yeah right, we naturally draw back like turtles into their shells ... So, I totally understand why people are caught up in themselves and why we think about what we can do to make ourselves feel safer. I do it all the time, and I think you're nuts if you don't prepare for the worst. Like, I won't put my neck on the line by going in certain neighbourhoods at night, or at least I won't walk around without my pepper spray and rape whistle ... I've even taken tae kwon do classes so that I can defend myself. People might look at me and see a helpless woman, but I guarantee you my body is the only weapon I really need.

According to 'opportunity' or 'routine activity' theorists (Cohen and Felson 1979; Gartner and McCarthy 1991; Liska and Warner 1991; Miethe et al. 1991), the desire to strictly monitor one's exposure to risk may be evident in individuals' daily physical practices. With the body (or material objects enhancing bodily experience) as a focal point of concern, individuals may learn to minimize the social risks posed to their bodies in the face of de-civilizing processes. In particular, women tattoo enthusiasts living in downtown areas (who are now more exposed to risks than ever before) are especially conscious about these potential bodily harms, and include such sentiments in their tattooing narratives. Here, tattooing the body (as a symbol of personal control) reflects one's involvement in environments marked by risk and personal threat.

Ultimately, it seems that bodies have become more culturally significant loci of control and communication as a result of our increased appetite for information exchange. I would never wish to reduce the interest in tattooing body projects to a single causal factor, but artists' and clients' narratives indicate that the exchange of cultural information has, in some ways, changed their understandings of and relationships with their bodies. While not to be conflated with motivating 'factors' behind the act of tattooing, sociogenic and corresponding psychogenic change along these lines has clearly shifted attitudes toward the body and our body-modification habits.

Cultural Diversity and Tolerance Thresholds

Elias (1983, 1994) outlined how cultural ways of seeing the world involve rationalized (yet not necessarily rational) standards and codes about body performance and display (i.e., in that they communicate decodable and culturally affiliative messages about individuals). While some of these standards are dominant within a given social figuration (as noted at the beginning of this chapter), competing or esoteric cultures may promulgate alternative understandings and uses for bodies (Elias and Scotson 1965). As discussed previously, the history of tattooing in North America indicates that marginalized social groups have utilized the body as a billboard of political protest through tattooing practices. By violating mainly Christian, white, middle-class standards of bodily respectability, tattooing body projects have traditionally signified the conscious intent of people to be visibly different from the cultural mainstream.

However, the boundaries between dominant and alternative constructions of the body have become significantly blurred, with definitions of normative body modification challenged or torn asunder. In many ways, this has been a product of increasing cultural diversity in Canada, cultural conflict and subsequent tolerance toward others, and ongoing globalization processes. As argued, these sociogenic transformations have a combined effect on cultural habituses – such that long-standing metanarratives demarcating the boundaries of normative body modification have been questioned.

Unfortunately, sociologists investigating the cultural significance of body projects (including tattooing) have normally adopted an ahistorical approach toward the study of body habits; that is, sensibilities about modifying the body are neatly encapsulated within period-specific time frames without referencing corporeal practices against broader historical processes. This 'retreat into the present' (Elias 1978, 1991a) by sociologists fundamentally ignores figurational trends and conditions that influence how people view their bodies as appropriate sites for modification over time. Tattoo enthusiasts I spoke with often suggested how unfolding diversities within Canadian culture and patterns of our social organization have influenced their respective perceptions of bodies and their representation. Discourses provided by artists and clients indicate how cultural diversity and the breakdown of traditional or 'established' (Elias and Scotson 1965) ways of knowing have redefined the parameters of acceptable body play in Canada. Along with changing tastes for information exchange, increased cultural diversity in Canada appears to affect how individuals perceive their bodies as open for non-traditional forms of body modification.

Cultural Diversity in Canada

Canada is recurrently referred to by sociologists as a pluralistic rather than an integrated social figuration (Driedger 1996; Isajiw 1999; Li 1999). The idea underlying this assertion – while wrapped in sociopolitical encryptions of tolerance and respect – is that Canadians are not a homogeneous cultural lot, but rather a mosaic of heterogeneous subcultures (Lian and Matthews 1998; Prus 1997). For this reason, Canada is appropriately viewed as a culturally and hierarchically segmented figuration in which groups (ethnic, class, religious, etc.) meet one another through shared institutions, rituals, and patterns of social interaction.

Rather than adhering to cultural-assimilation or melting-pot doctrines, Canadians revel in the ability to embrace (mostly symbolically) human diversity and weave it into a distinctly Canadian cultural tapestry (Kalbach 2000).

Demographic statistics for the cities of Toronto and Calgary suggest that these urban areas are more ethnically, racially, religiously, and economically diverse than ever before. When demographic data for other cities in the country (e.g., Victoria, Vancouver, Edmonton, Regina, Winnipeg, Ottawa, Montreal, and Halifax) are inspected, similar patterns emerge (Statistics Canada 2001). With growing cultural diversity evident across Canada, a concern about normative confusion and weakened cultural consensus should understandably arise. If, as social-disorganization theorists point out (Shaw and McKay 1927, 170–89), urban expansion and resulting cultural pluralism breed ineffective social communication and hamper cohesion (consistently in particular urban areas over time), then visibly alternative, or outsider, ways of living might promote widespread cultural dissensus in culturally heterogeneous communities. If individuals are overexposed to competing cultural understandings of the world, a breakdown of traditional ways of interpreting the world might follow. The dismantling of barriers against corporeal experimentation within a specific culture would be a product of confusion in the face of competing ways of using bodies.

However, conceiving the impact of pluralism on Canadians to be that of cultural dislocation and pervasive confusion downplays the ability of people to interpret, assess, negotiate, reject, or incorporate others' cultural perspectives. With increased cultural diversity, there might follow heightened cultural reflection and adaptation (Clifford 1992, 1999). When groups come into spatial contact with one another, traditions and ideologies are exposed through an ongoing process of cross-fertilization – and dominant cultural ways of viewing the world are transformed. Cross-fertilization between cultures (not to be conflated with cultural assimilation) becomes a product of socialization processes advanced through key figurational contexts of interaction, such as families, schools, the workplace, political systems, and media networks. Elias and Scotson (1965) pointed out that while established groups in a specific figuration profoundly affect the cultural ways of life of the many outsider groups, the impact is not solely one-way. The established culture is shaped and altered through the exchange process, with traditional ways of understanding life subject to redefinition.

Tattooing stories I have heard over the course of my investigation indicated that dominant body habits have been affected by cultural pluralism and diversity in Canada. In describing their attitudes toward their bodies, tattoo enthusiasts frequently discussed how exposure to others' (non-Western) traditions have altered their perceptions about bodies. Citing the fact that they go to school or work alongside individuals who dress in varied garb, have alternative preferences for body styles, possess different standards of physical attractiveness, and participate in a full gamut of non-Western body-modification practices, enthusiasts express a sense of corporeal awakening:

> If someone had told me when I was a kid that I'd be working in downtown Toronto in a cubicle right beside a Sikh on one side of me, a Muslim in front of me, and an orthodox Jew behind me I would have said you're crazy. I grew up in a small town in northern Ontario, and we just didn't see anyone different from the rest of us ... Working here for the last five years has changed my life, in so many ways. I don't have to travel all over the world to meet people from different lands, they're all here. And so I spend my lunch hours talking to people with really different ways of seeing the world, and I really enjoy that. We talk about things like what we find attractive in women, and one thing I've come to realize is that there are different sizes, shapes, and tastes for everybody. That makes me feel more self-confident and comfortable with the way I look because I've always been on the heavier side, and learned that in some cultures, my body shape is adored ... Yeah, it's really made me rethink our narrow ideals about what our bodies should look like. You realize that our standards about the body are not the only standards. (Drew, 33)

Again, while enthusiasts comment that they have been exposed to and reflective about differences in body shape, presentation, and modification, their cultural ideologies for interpreting bodies have not completely decayed, but rather been strenuously questioned and partially amended:

> I have a ton of friends who are East Indian, and when I go over to one of their houses ... well, it shocked me at first to see how different their clothes were and how people are drawn in their artwork. The women are a lot fatter, sorry to say that. And the men are often drawn wearing this thing that almost looks like a dress. It's incredibly different than what I'm used to, but it's their culture and you have to respect that ... I'm more aware of what I

find attractive, and define as 'right' for me. The more I learn about other cultures, the more I learn about mine – like what clothes I like to wear and the way I want to present myself. (Kimberly, 21)

Exposure, therefore, to growing numbers of individuals bringing varied understandings of the body to our cultural landscape creates a figurational condition in which new ways of viewing bodies are internalized as normative (or at least tolerable) over successive generations (see Mannheim 1971). As outsider groups develop more established positions (political, economic, or civic) within larger cultural webs, the willingness to accept and respect their ways of displaying body styles seems to increase. Dominant standards defining acceptable body performance are changed as individuals are exposed to a vast array of meaningful body practices and ways through which cultural expression may be intextuated on the skin. With the body inferred as a socially constructed and culturally meaningful text, experimentation with corporeal performance is accurately envisioned as a barometer by which the appreciation of cultural pluralism (as opposed to assimilation) may be read.

Tolerable Differences

We should be careful not to assume that growing cultural diversity and pluralism in Canada automatically leads to cultural exchange, acceptance, and revision; for pluralism most rapidly manifests itself in cross-cultural fertilization when a significant amount of tolerance or empathetic understanding exists in a given figuration (Kalbach and Kalbach 2000; Maguire 1999; Stebbins 1996). If, as tattoo enthusiasts indicate, cultural diversity leads to an exploration of alternative ways of inscribing culture on the body, then this process is surely enhanced by mutual consideration and tolerance.

Tolerance toward ideological, political, religious, or lifestyle differences has become a dominant trend in Canada (Hathaway and Atkinson 2001). Whether we attribute this burgeoning tolerance to liberal values, ethnic diversity, political correctness, or expanding Western market economies is subsidiary to the realization that cultural absolutes about acceptable or unacceptable behaviour are waning. As definitions of normative behaviour are shifting, sociological theories describing, explaining, and predicting deviant behaviour are concomitantly in flux. In this respect, an underused tool for theorizing abour normative behaviours –

including corporeal modification activities – is Stebbins's concept (1996) of *tolerable differences.*

While a particular activity may be designated as non-normative or deviant in reference to existing social laws, norms, conventions, or values that explicitly prohibit the behaviour, it may not be viewed collectively as an immediate threat to society. 'Tolerable' deviance therefore refers to contra-normative behaviours that individuals or larger collectivities do not interpret as warranting widespread moral condemnation and official control within a particular figuration (Stebbins 1996). Whereas sociologists, criminologists, and other students of deviance have long been attentive to the ways it is interpreted and controlled by individuals, rarely do they investigate the situations and context in which deviance is tolerated. Similarly, in sociological research on body-modification practices, rarely do researchers indicate how traditionally deviant or culturally alternative modifications of the body find tolerance over time.

Tattoo enthusiasts frequently discussed how the social expectation to be tolerant or respectful of cultural difference is apparent in most facets of everyday life – such that it becomes second nature in the course of social interchange. Individuals are primarily instructed by family members, teachers, employers, clergy persons, media personalities, and political officials to be tolerant of others' (sometimes seemingly incomprehensible) cultural practices. This includes, of course, tolerance toward what one might perceive to be a deviant use of the body:

> I was on the subway a couple of months ago and this asshole made some racist comment about an Indian woman's dot in the middle of her forehead. I don't know what it's called, but know it's a sacred cultural symbol. He called her a 'push start' or something like that, so I turned around and called him a fucking jerk, and told him to mind his own skinhead business. There's no excuse for being discriminatory against someone for marking their religious beliefs on their body. Some of us just need to wake up and realize that whatever she wants to do with her body is no one else's concern. (Amber, 27)

Amber's concern reaffirms Elias's idea (1983, 1994) that foresight and mutual orientation are essential for individuals enmeshed in extended chains of interdependence. The increasing tolerance for, or defence (in the case above), of others' differences might best be viewed as a product of such sociogenic change. As mutual orientation develops over time, cultural absolutes about what constitutes normative or non-normative body display are splintered. In the words of tattoo enthusiast Rachel (35):

> Ten years ago, if a white guy shaved his head people would think he was a Punk rocker or a neo-Nazi ... some militant guy with an axe to grind. Now it's in fashion because we have been exposed to men from all over the world who do it as part of their cultural routines ... And it's like that in respect to what people are wearing, how they dance, what music you listen to and even the way we walk. It adds so much seasoning to our cultural stew, and I'm glad it's made the last two generations of Canadians change our perceptions about what 'normal' looks like.

On the other side of the coin, other tattoo enthusiasts' narratives similarly indicate that the trend toward escalating tolerance of others' body practices is equally a product of cultural malaise and disinterest. In line with the sentiments of Generation Xers (Coupland 1991), widespread cultural tolerance is viewed as having bred a sense of present-centred fatalism and self-indulgence in some. Cynical about capitalist cultures, Judaeo-Christian ideologies delineating strict codes about right and wrong, and the promise of progress proffered by previous generations (the Baby Boomers), many tattoo enthusiasts in the 28-to-35-year age range frequently expressed the idea that cultural diversity is simply a cultural codeword for the death of tradition and normative ways of living. Whether this trend is culturally good, bad, progressive, or disintegrative is simply not a concern:

> It may sound way too cynical, but we've been talking about cultural diversity, and all I think that means is that we water all down cultures in capitalist economies because we don't want to offend anybody. So everything gets tossed out the window and traditions are replaced by fashion trends. All that matters is how much money you have and how you can spend it. (Miles, 26)

Interestingly, this age demographic of enthusiasts participated in the second renaissance of tattooing in North America. Diving skin first into tattooing during the last years of the 1980s and early 1990s, these enthusiasts paved the way for current practitioners. To that extent, their sensibilities about cultural tolerance and body-modification practices shed considerable light on current interpretations of the tattooed body:

Anything, and I mean anything, is fair game now. It's like the floodgates are open and people are getting swept away with screwing around with their bodies based on whatever mood they are in, or whatever cultural style they can appropriate. This week it's liposuction to look like a person from this country, next week it's dyeing your hair to look like you're another nationality, and who knows, next month it might be getting shark fins on your back ... I grew up in the eighties, in a real time of excess in our society. I think that really influenced how we view ourselves, like these big lumps of clay that can be added onto or ripped apart at whatever whim ... We can talk about tolerance, and all that, and I think it's true, but we're gluttonous as a culture, and it shows in how we treat our bodies in all respects. (Regina, 29)

In essence, these figurational changes in Canada have profoundly affected our attitudes about cultural tolerance. As individuals have become more tolerant of or indifferent to others' cultural practices (and explored or co-opted others' ways of life in the process), attitudes about what constitutes acceptable body practice become more elastic. While some might be hasty to categorize cultural exploration along these lines as an indicator of a permanent cultural dissolution, this trend might be more accurately depicted as sign of a figuration wrestling with unintended change.

Globalization and the Decline of Meta-narratives

It may seem ironic that given sociologists' growing interest in deconstructing individuals' narratives about lived experience, many would support the contention that master or meta-narratives in Western cultures are losing their potency. However, as a direct consequence of growing secularism, ideological pluralism, evident imperfections in scientific bodies of knowledge, and the receding of moral boundaries, individuals find very few 'Truths' in contemporary life. To be sure, young Canadians appear to be rather sceptical of master narratives that clearly delineate a world order.

Globalization processes constitute a leading set of influences that are creating a collective distrust of intolerably rigid ways of viewing the world. The subject of considerable social debate both within and outside of the academy in the past twenty years, the impacts of globalization processes on our understandings of bodies are manifold. Without adhering to singularly focused globalization theories – be they formed around the perspectives of modernization (Baker 1982), dependency (Frank 1967; Larrain 1989), imperialism (Emanuel 1992; Tomlinson 1991), world systems (Wallerstein 1974), or hegemony (Donnelly 1996) – we can loosely describe the ramifications of globalization on Canadians' sensibilities about body modification through a series of points.

Although the fact is frequently lamented by social critics as an unfortunate consequence of eroding cultural boundaries, globalization processes appear to have (like cultural-pluralism processes in Canada) exposed Canadians to a diversity of body traditions from around the world (Hill 1992; Hladki 1994; Philip 1990; Todd 1990; Trinh 1991). Globalization is often cited as a catalyst of cultural assimilation, a direct product of what Appadurai (1990) and Hannerz (1990) might term the 'cultural flow' of commodities between nations – including the international circulation of capital, technology, cultural artefacts, people, and textual images. To cite Hannerz: '[T]he world has become one network of social relationships, and between its different regions there is a flow of meanings as well as people and goods' (1990, 237). Through such cultural exchange, ways of viewing the world and creating meaning in everyday life are globally disseminated – including many divergent cultural attitudes about acceptable body modification. Approaching the global community as an immense figuration of increasingly interdependent and mutually oriented individuals, theorists (Maguire 1999) point out how cultural habituses from around the world are exposed through globalization processes. As the tattoo artist Cliff (32) suggested:

In the 1980s, I couldn't even have lasted a week in business doing only artwork from tribal cultures. No one was really interested or knowledgeable about the art from other societies. Now you go down the street and look how many stores sell artwork, clothing, or furniture from around the world. Your neighbours are from every conceivable nation, television programs contain people of all races, and you're just bombarded with the idea of global culture. People are always coming in and asking me about artwork from around the world ... And if you go to some of the more famous [tattoo] studios in Toronto, the artists there now specialize in all sorts of body-modification rituals and practices like scarring that no one was getting into even five years ago.

Through the exchange of cultural commodities ranging from movies to body lotions, Canadians have been exposed to alternative ways of culturally managing bodies through modification. In correspondence with dominant capitalist ideologies in Canada that stress the importance of treating the body as a site of commodity consumption (and the body as a commodity itself), trans-cultural body-modification practices are made readily available. Commercial products and sacred body rituals from around the world all teach Canadians how people 'cook the body' (i.e., transform it into a social text) through cultural practice (Lévi-Strauss 1966, 1969). Some of these corporeal performances might be viewed as culturally uncivilized or undesirable, as in the case of female circumcision or foot-binding (Robinson 1998), while others are seen to be stimulating or exciting, as in the case of piercing and scarification (Myers 1997). Rather than being viewed as a threat to dominant 'Canadian' ways of socially constructing and physically managing the corporeal, however, these globalization processes appear to jibe well with our existing attitudes of tolerance and cultural pluralism. As the tattoo enthusiast Heather (21) commented:

> As I see it, we've [Canadians] always been a little repressed about being super expressive with our bodies. The openness I see everyday with showing our bodies in the past little while is really good for us. Instead of hiding who we are, and celebrating how different we are from one another, we've hidden under drab and uninspired clothes ... I don't want to look completely like everyone else, and I don't want them to look like me exactly. That's not human to do that, to make everyone who comes to this country conform with the same ways of looking.

In this light, cultural exchange via flowing global economic markets and networks of ideological dissemination (although sometimes one-way and exploitive rather than mutually beneficial) is generally not perceived as a competitive form of cultural struggle. Instead, Canadians may be interpreting the opening of cultural doors (exposing alternative perspectives on body use, image, and display) as facilitating an enlightened understanding of the body as an entity that links all people together. Here, we might refer to globalization processes as a conduit for instilling a sense of 'communitas' (Turner 1969) between individuals from different nations. As the tattoo artist Jenna (24) noted:

> One of the most positive outcomes of the elimination of most of our insane hang-ups about modifying our bodies is that by encouraging everybody to do it, by letting people explore all kinds of methods for changing their looks, we are allowed to appreciate physical difference. It's funny that way,

we have this really common attitude that your body is yours, right. Saying do with it what you will makes us equal in a really bizarre way, and it brings people together on a common ground.

Contrary to previous eras in which Western exploration, colonization, and economic imperialism played a role in marginalizing body styles from around the world, current discourses appear to indicate that Canadians are meeting body difference with a curiosity tempered by tolerance.

Simultaneously, it seems that global exchange processes have encouraged Canadians to distrust Western science and its authority over corporeal matters. Even though we are ever driven by the pursuit of innovative technologies and scientific wonders (cybernetics, medical technologies, 'breakthrough' household or personal products, digital computer devices, information technologies, and weapons of mass destruction), our collective trust of scientists, biologists, and medical professionals as the sole guardians of knowledge about bodies has been breached (Featherstone 1991, 2000; Frank 1991a, 1991b; Shilling 1993; Williams and Bendelow 1998). We should not ignore the fact that today, as compared with previous eras, more individuals are willing to pursue technological and surgical procedures in the process of permanently modifying their bodies (Balsamo 1996; Haraway 1991). Moreover, we should recognize that so-called alternative (e.g., Chinese, Indian, Native Canadian, or New Age) medicines, lifestyle practices, and body regimens are now widely explored by Canadians. The avid tattoo collector Sandra (34) described her interest in alternative healing methods in the following way:

I went through a series of illnesses in my early twenties, and became very disgruntled with what my doctors were doing. After seeing a dozen or so specialists and being poked and prodded a million times they finally decided I had leukemia. I went through radiation treatment for about a year and nothing worked ... They eventually told me it wasn't cancer, and they had made a horrible mistake. Some mistake ... I don't trust doctors now, and prefer to visit an herbalist when I'm sick. A friend of mine who is a reflexologist from Russia introduced me to her. They were friends in Russia, and left to set up a medical practice in Canada ... At first, my attitude was that it couldn't hurt and it might help, right, like it couldn't get any worse than it was, but I'd never go back to a regular doctor now. The herbal treatments I take are so much more pleasurable, and my herbalist and I have a very special relationship. She helps me treat my body and my mind as a single unit.

Tattoo enthusiasts in this study suggested that the distrust of Western scientific methods of treating the body is part of a contemporary expedition to discover alternative ways of experiencing corporeality. To that extent, enthusiasts implied, Western discourses detailing appropriate body practice (including sound body modification) no longer dictate how individuals should relate to their bodies.

> I was always taught to run to the doctor when anything went wrong with my health. That's the way most people grew up. You listen to your doctor and he tells you what to do with your body and how to keep it running in tip-top shape. I grew out of that a long time ago, and I've realized that my doctor doesn't always know what's best for me. At the very least I see my spiritual healer, my homeopathic doctor, and my acupuncturist when I'm under the weather ... It's like going to buy a car, you have to shop around and find which one feels the most comfortable to drive. (Trevor, 28)

The net impact of globalization on Canadians' body-modification habits (although complex and not reducible to a solitary outcome) can be succinctly summarized by using Maguire's idea of 'diminishing contrasts and increasing varieties' (1999, 41–6). Through increased exposure to an assortment of cultural ideologies about bodies, ritual body practices, products to enhance bodily function and display, and homologies of body style, Canadians feel encouraged to be more tolerant of and willing to experiment with a full range of corporeal experiences. As more people participate in diverse body rituals and learn to share common perspectives about bodies (e.g., the benefits of experimentation), the uniqueness (occasionally referred to as the 'authenticity') of such rituals may be lost – or, in Maguire's terminology (1999), contrasts between distinct cultural patterns of behaviour are diminished. Yet when cultural borders are opened and individuals feel free to pursue a plethora of corporeal practices – thus rearranging meanings about bodies and their social representation – increasing varieties of corporeal styles and performances are created. As noted by Polhemus in his description of the gathering of cultural style tribes (1994, 1996), globalization processes promote social interest in bodies as communicative texts of cultural exchange.

As we transform into a more visually stimulated, information-oriented, biologically threatened, ethnically diverse, and global figuration, one could argue that representation through highly visible body modification is becoming more deeply ingrained in collective habituses. In empirical examinations of body-modification processes, then, emphasis should be given to the ways in which sociogenic transformation effectively alters social constructions of bodies. Previous sociological analyses of tattooing – and the bulk of extant research on body projects – have largely ignored the need to contextualize body projects within ongoing and unintended social processes. As we investigate why scores of Canadians are participating in tattooing body projects and how such projects are intersubjectively understood by enthusiasts, however, a preliminary assessment of their understandings of bodies as sites of socio-cultural excavation and display should be advanced. *At the same time, however, we must strive to understand why individuals deliberately choose to redesign their bodies through tattooing amidst a full range of body-modification possibilities.*

CHAPTER SEVEN

Life-course Transition and Representation: The Deviance Tightrope

There is perhaps no other topic related to the practice of tattooing that has been more scrutinized than enthusiasts' motivations for going 'under the needle.' In past twenty years, sociologists have built a considerable understanding of why individuals choose to tattoo their bodies. Although most empirical or non-empirical investigations of tattooing include a typology of enthusiasts' motivations, the works of Sanders (1989), Steward (1990), Camphausen (1997), DeMello (2000), and Atkinson and Young (2001) arguably provide the most interconnected expositions on the subject.

Sanders's pioneering work (1989) on tattooing highlights how a series of emergent interdependencies may stimulate one's interest in tattooing. Claiming that individuals chiefly mark the body through tattooing as a mechanism for indicating social affiliation and fostering mutual identification, Sanders pointed out how interpersonal attachments are intentionally created or affirmed through the process. He equally noted that individuals often 'drift' (Matza 1964; Prus 1996, 1997) into tattooing with no other motivation than to alleviate personal boredom. Moreover, he suggested that others may choose to be tattooed as a means of shocking audiences, since the tattoo is an immediate marker of social difference. Other motivations Sanders describes include the use of tattooing to symbolically chronicle life transitions or status passages on the skin, and as a technique for doing gender – namely, in the social construction of 'hegemonic' masculinity (Donaldson 1993).

Steward's reflections (1990) on his own career as a tattoo artist yield the most extensive list of client motivations compiled to date. In a rather massive overview of enthusiasts' motivations, Steward outlined some twenty-eight different reasons why individuals purport to redesign their bodies through tattooing. The list Steward offered is comprehensive in this respect, but is replete with unnecessary overlap. In paring down his cumbersome list, Steward identified three basic groupings of motivations. Like Sanders, Steward emphasized the importance of tattooing as a conduit of cohesion among small groups (e.g., gangs or subcultures). Tattoos are sought after because they immediately build bridges between an individual and a set of mutually identified others.

Second, Steward concurred with Sanders's assessment that tattooing may play a central role in ritually transforming the self. In this case, tattoos symbolically mark the passage from one self to another. The attraction of the tattoo is in its lasting reminder of the transition, and the manner in which the transition may be publicly communicated to others through body display. Third – perhaps the most eclectic of his categories – Steward assembled a veritable shopping list of psychological reasons why people are tattooed. He noted that individuals are drawn to this deviant social practice as a way of expressing what we might consider to be potentially destructive (emotional, physical, social) tendencies. For Steward, these pathologies include homosexuality, rebellion, narcissism, sadomasochism, fetishism, and excessive ego compensation. Reverberating with themes proffered in the psychological literature (e.g., Grumet 1983; Houghton et al. 1996; Howell et al. 1971; Lander and Kohn 1943; McKerracher and Watson 1969; Newman 1982; Verberne 1969), Steward's analysis hinged on the idea that motivations toward this redesigning body project may be largely unconscious and symptomatic of an individual's incapacity to manage id drives effectively. The motivations are interpreted as unlearned psychic mechanisms of defence through which an individual's libidinal impulses are transferred into socially marginal body practices.

Camphausen's more recent (1997) cultural analysis of global tattooing practices provides a slightly different perspective on enthusiasts' motivations. Highlighting the role of tattooing in solidifying group identity, Camphausen detailed the ways in which tattoos are pursued as a normative cultural ritual. One's motivations in cooking the body with cultural icons are structured by a desire to be a valued (and visibly recognized) member of a 'WE' (Elias 1978, 1991a) group. By conjoining these motivations with the use of tattooing to invoke spiritual energies, heighten one's sexual attractiveness, or transform the body into an intimidating entity, Camphausen drew attention to the idea that participation in tattooing practices can be underpinned by the desire to conform with prevailing in-group habituses and corporeal rituals.

DeMello's ethnographic investigation (2000) of the post-1980s middle-class movement into tattooing produced a new conceptual map for interpreting enthusiasts' motivations. She astutely constructed an understanding of enthusiasts' motivations around the axial idea that cultural deconstructions of tattooing in North America are fluctuating. DeMello argued that classic motivations for being tattooed remain popular in North America (e.g., deviant affiliation, ideological rebellion, or a challenge to the prevailing socio-structural order), and simultaneously inspected the more socially congenial reasons regularly offered by Americans for tattooing body projects (i.e., as a way of stimulating personal growth, exploring alternative or New Age forms of spirituality, and pursuing alternative cultural body rituals). However, DeMello placed undue emphasis on the extent to which involvement in tattooing is motivated by the desire to be an 'individual.' Even though a close inspection of her subjects' narratives clearly indicates otherwise, DeMello often portrayed tattooing body projects as the isolated search for unique identity (2000, 161–2): 'Most of my informants emphasized in their narratives the individuality of their tattoos and how this was connected to their own personal uniqueness ... Having a tattoo should be, according to many in the community, linked to something personal and special about the person. The tattoo should indicate what is on the inside of the wearer.' While DeMello supplied one of the most empirically informed and substantively rich descriptions of tattooing practices in America, her conceptualization of the quest for individuality through tattooing is unfortunately plagued by an assumption that individuality is only achieved in a *homo clausus* fashion. That is, she reproduced the idea that a tattoo is a manifestation of one's private search for identity (despite championing the idea that a tattoo community exists), a component of the self that is deliberately hidden from, or unknowable by, others. The sociality – as is evident in much of the extant literature on body-modification practices – is either overlooked or underplayed through this analysis.

In Atkinson and Young's research (2001) on Neo Primitives in Canada, the authors took into account and questioned the motivations of a relatively small faction of tattoo enthusiasts. By focusing on the ways in which the body is a text of political resistance and cultural commentary, they contextualized motivations for choosing tattooing as a body practice (including resistance, status passage, physical endurance, beauty and art, and spirituality) against dominant social codes about bodies and their representation. The list of enthusiasts' motivations presented was informed by first-hand narratives provided by Neo Primitives and by existing research on other enthusiasts' narratives. As part of their conclusions, the authors contended that previous research fails to explore adequately how motivations to become involved in tattooing are historically, culturally, and contextually specific – and thus should be understood as learned and commonly circulated rationalizations.

If one reviews the existing literature on tattooing, the two most salient motivations seem to be the confirmation of identity within a group of individuals and the use of the body as an outward signifier of some form of cultural commentary. The literature on such body-modification practices as cosmetic surgery (Davis 1997a, 1997b; Gillespie 1996), cross-dressing (Garber 1992, 1997; Segal 1994), physical exercise (Klein 1993; Loland 2000; Maguire and Mansfield 1998; White et al. 1995), and dieting (Lupton 1996; MacSween 1993) resound with similar themes. Motivations for modifying the body, principally under the influence of cultural body-modification habits, are structured by the wish to communicate symbolically with others through the flesh (i.e., through specific body shapes, sizes, or contours). Communication is based on socially diffuse cultural norms that help orient individuals to the symbolic gestures made through the body in everyday life (Labarre 1947).

Extant research efforts on enthusiasts' motivations are incredibly useful for sketching a cursory understanding of how enthusiasts describe their motivations for being tattooed, but almost uniformly fail to fully discuss *why* individuals *specifically* choose tattooing in the process of communicating with others; that is, why participate in tattooing and not cosmetic surgery, colouring one's hair, or an aerobics class? Similarly, the research tends to reduce individual tattooing projects to a single motivating factor, instead of considering the projects as multiply motivated. Furthermore, rarely are seemingly dissonant motivations conceptually compared in a coherent manner. Lastly, researchers have failed to address how motivations are learned over time and incorporated into one's body-modification habits.

To pursue a more empirically based answer to these neglected areas of investigation, we must take a another step backward and re-address the question why and how tattooing has historically breached dominant social codes delineating acceptable bodily use and display. If social marginality actually attracts many enthusiasts to the practice, it poses an interesting paradox in relation to dominant cultural body habits – in that while we are strongly encouraged to modify our bodies through a range of normative techniques, many feel encouraged to pursue alternative body projects that remain on the periphery of social respectability.

Of equal interest is the fact that tattooing may now be a quasi-normative body ritual among legions of social actors. By invoking the study of life-course transitions (Elias 1994; Sampson and Laub 1993), sociologists may direct their focus to those life events and interactive occurrences that alter personal life trajectories – subsequently transforming one's body modification tastes and preferences. In this pursuit, a deeper investigation of Elias and Scotson's understanding (1965) of 'established' versus 'outsider' codes about the body and its representation is worthwhile.

Dominant Body Codes: Established and Outsider

Norbert Elias and John Scotson's *The Established and The Outsiders* (1965) is a historical analysis of a small British community in the English midlands given the pseudonym Winston Parva. Principally, Elias and Scotson analysed how community life is moulded around relationships between established and outsider social groups. Rather than hinge the experience of social life on a hierarchy of socio-economic class factions, Elias and Scotson inferred a model of figurational relationships that takes into account the distribution of power chances between groups. Established or outsider factions in a figuration include racial groups, ethnic communities, religious sects, or social classes. Although Elias and Scotson did not reject the significance of class dynamics in society, class position does not supersede all other sources of social power, nor does it provide the sole means by which individuals mutually identify with one another.

Established social groups are more deeply embedded in both the base and superstructural segments of a figuration – typically because they have a longer history in the figuration – and thus control many ideological state apparatuses. Established groups have greater access to, but not outright ownership of, economic, political, moral, and cultural power chances (Elias and Scotson 1965). They also have a considerable ability to influence the construction of social laws, promulgate cultural norms, and promote collective ways of viewing the world. Outsider groups are the more marginal members of a figuration; they are less embedded in power positions and are dominated on the basis of their limited statuses. Outsiders are excluded from participation in a figuration's socially influential power structures, and their cultural ways of life (although not entirely dissimilar to established ways of life) are often deemed inappropriate or uncivilized. Members of outsider groups constitute key links in the vast chains of interdependency within a figuration, yet their interdependencies are not as extensive or as deeply enmeshed as those of their established counterparts.

As is reflected in some of the more central principles of Elias's work (1983, 1991a, 1994, 1996) on civilizing processes in Western cultures, Elias and Scotson (1965) revealed how social standards (including norms detailing acceptable bodily display) protect the vested interests of established groups. Pursuing the idea that social groups are mutually oriented and interdependent, they articulated how both established and outsider groups coalesce around shared WE images of identification (Elias 1978, 1991a). WE images are partly formed in relation to common social positions, roles, attributes, and intersubjectively held belief systems, but also include shared tastes or preferences for specific outward forms of collective representation such as bodily comportment and style (Elias and Scotson 1965).

Mutually identified collectivities exhibit clear preferences toward particular styles of bodily display, and define differences in such preferences as a sign of membership in a THEY group (Elias 1987, 1991, 1994). As Polhemus (1996) and Muggleton (2000) have confirmed, members of THEY groups tend almost uniformly to be defined by members of a WE group as identical (e.g., their biographies, personal characteristics, physical capabilities, and cultural practices). THEY groups are accordingly deemed to be homogeneous collections of actors. Not only do established groups crystallize a collective sense of community around shared understandings of appropriate behaviour, cohesion is also fostered through the process of collectively condemning the attributes of outsider THEY groups – or, more simply, by perjoratively labelling the WE images and attributes supposedly shared between outsiders (Elias and Scotson 1965).

In brief, established groups are mainly the social leaders in a figuration and develop into its legitimate or recognized social authority (dominant racial groups, patriarchies, and ruling classes). Since established groups wield greater power chances in the figuration and manage to finagle higher levels of social status than outsider groups over long-term historical processes, they are able to translate their ideologies and value systems into social conventions while discrediting the attributes of outsider groups – whose identities are often made to represent human inferiority and barbarism (Elias and Scotson 1965, 152). Included within these ideologies and value systems are social codes regulating bodily comportment and style – what Goffman (1959, 1963) might refer to as dominant codes of body idiom. Importantly, established groups are able to virtually dictate how norms about bodily appearance and conduct are codified into social norms and conventions.

As I spoke and interacted with tattoo enthusiasts over the course of my time among them, it became evident that while enthusiasts were typically aware of the marginality of tattooing in respect to the established lexicon of standard body practices (cultural pluralism and tolerance in Canada aside), they nonetheless expressed a sense of being drawn to tattooing. The question becomes, then, why would an individual align one's identity with outsider codes or body practices at particular points in the life course? In particular, what is it about tattooing that motivates an individual to perhaps risk social respect, status, or identity to be associated with a discreditable THEY group?

Walking the Deviance Tightrope: Motivations and Rationalizations

One might conclude, from an analysis of enthusiasts' *self-described* motivations for their participation in tattooing body projects, that established associations between tattooing and social deviance remain in tact. For instance, what we might refer to as rebel or outsider participation in tattooing continues to flourish. DeMello's study of tattooing in America (1993, 2000) indicates that while there has been a bourgeoisification of the tattoo community in recent years, a loyal client base remains in the working and criminal classes and among social malcontents. Given such continuance, linkages between tattooing and those existing on the fringe of society are still made in popular culture (Carter 2000; Connery 2001). Even though Canadians appear to be more tolerant of a melange of corporeal experimentations and cultural preferences about the body, the dubious shadow of deviance lurking over the practice prevents its widespread acceptance (Gray 1994).

The information I collected on tattoo enthusiasm in Canada indicates that most enthusiasts are not ambivalent about the tattoo's long-standing status as a symbol of disrepute. Interestingly enough, many enthusiasts *actively* employ tattooing body projects as purposive violations of established body codes and sensibilities – mainly in the process of representing social difference or challenging established figurational relationships and ideologies. One of the most consistent themes in the stories I heard about tattooing centred around tattooing's relationship with social 'difference.' Most of the people I interviewed described themselves as some kind of outsider (i.e., a person qualitatively different from some group of others) and suggested that their tattoos represented this feeling of difference. For people who feel that they stand out from the crowd (through some positive or dubious distinction), tattoos come to symbolize their self-perceived sense of difference. Drawing upon the immediate outsider image of Otherness that the tattooed body conjures in Canada, individuals actively 'walk the tightrope' between deviance and social respectability. Canadians seem to be willing to participate in this historically outsider form of corporeal manipulation, but cleverly negotiate and co-opt the deviant status of tattoos – to assert their feelings of Otherness – in the process of conforming with specific cultural norms about the body.

Embracing Deviance: Marks of Disaffiliation

The analysis of enthusiasts' motivations should commence with an acknowledgment that tattooing continues to be sought out actively as a method of aligning one's identity with non-normative behaviours or ideologies. A process dialogical with existing established codes of body idiom, tattooing the body with images and icons can be an irreverent gesture to prevailing cultural body-modification standards. Given the extent to which we are encouraged to modify our bodies as part of doing identity, those wishing to assert some form of social or cultural difference find in tattooing a ready-made technique for creating and consolidating personal difference.

1. Deviant Affiliations
Stories and comments presented in previous chapters have suggested that social outsiders often collectively employ tattooing as a technique of mutual identification. In conformity with the outsider traditions of tattooing in other Western cultures, Canadians' tattoos in the current era often signify affiliation with a group of deviant actors – such as style-oriented youth subcultures, street gangs, or prisoners. In these contexts, the tattoo is offered as a public badge symbolizing the interdependencies forged between individuals and to indicate a sense of disaffiliation with more established others (e.g., dominant social classes, a dominant gender, or racial majorities).

Motivations to participate in tattooing along these lines are easily decoded. Tattooing the body immediately indicates one's membership in a select, albeit outsider, social group. Indelibly marking the body with a tattoo denotes that the individual wishes to identify permanently with the group. In this process, common symbols, icons, or images are utilized by outsiders as insignias of the collective:

> About seven years ago, my brother convinced me to join the gang he and his friends had formed. It wasn't really much of a tough gang, these guys liked to pretend like they were all hard, and walk around school intimidating people. I thought, he was my brother, right, and of course, if he's asking me to join the gang what am I gonna do, not join? I got jumped in, the guys took turns for about half an hour beatin' the shit out of me. I came away with a broken arm, twenty stitches in my head, and bunch of bruises over my body ... It hurt like hell, but you have to do it, cause everyone else did. Just when I thought everything was done, and I'd go home and sleep it off, they dragged me to this guy downtown for a tattoo. I totally forgot about that. I knew they all had tattoos, and I wanted one too [shows the tattoo]. See, it's a sign of the cross with a crown on top and flames rising behind it – we're kings of hell ... The whole gang thing got really stupid after a couple of the guys were arrested and sent to jail, so we just quit that business. I still have the tattoo, and when I look at it, I don't regret anything about it. I'm still good friends with most of the guys, it's just that now we go out and drink or chase chicks instead of finding people to beat up. (Quentin, 23)

Similarly, a self-proclaimed Raver named Rhonda (20) stated:

> I have the word 'PLUR' tattooed across my back. It stands for 'Peace, Love, Unity, and Respect,' which is a motto a lot of Ravers really believe in. I shouldn't call it a motto, because it's really a way of life. Six or seven friends of mine have the same tattoo. Don't tell them, but I really ripped their style off! ... The whole rave culture is about making connections with different kinds of people, but I really think it's about meeting people who are depressed or picked on at school or by their parents. They come to raves to feel like somebody. Despite all the bullshit you read about raves in the paper, they're really places for people who feel like they don't fit in anywhere else. I started going to raves for exactly that reason. People are so open and respectful here that I thought I would tattoo the rave philosophy on my body as a symbol of devotion really.

The tattooing process, because it is defined by group members as a violation of established middle-class standards of bodily performance, fits into the homological practices of outsider groups. It therefore meshes well with the alternative fashion styles, music, political ideologies, and overall lifestyles (Stebbins 1997) of group members:

> Tattooing is just a natural offshoot of my interest in Goth style and music. When I first started wearing Goth clothes, people freaked out on me and it was like my parents were going to have a major coronary or something. Then, when I started exploring my darker thoughts through poetry and dance, they thought I was getting ready to kill myself. Just because I like something that most people are afraid of, that shouldn't make people scared ... Goth is about looking different because you feel different than everyone else ... I can't look around and be all smiley. I feel depressed, and I want everyone to know that I am sick of being told what to do and how to look. That's what [pulls up shirt sleeves] these tattoos are about. (Christine, 24)

In the current shopping mall that is popular culture, however, looking like an outsider is commonly fashionable. Appearing like a member of a deviant THEY group, or aligning one's identity with subversive ideologies, may actually be more important than authentic membership in the outsider group (Muggleton 2000; Thornton 1995). In explaining the heightened interest in tribal tattooing styles, for instance, the tattoo artist Earl (26) commented:

> When someone comes into the shop and asks for a tribal tattoo, you can almost guarantee that they live in Mount Royal or somewhere in the southwest [of Calgary], and are getting tribal work because they want to look like a Modern Primitive. They can't tell you where [country] the design has come from, or what it means, but they've seen them on other people and think they're cool. A lot of people are still getting caught up in that whole primitive thing, and from my experience, it's the rich kids and the women who are doing it just to wig out their husbands. It's the hip thing in tattooing right now, but as more people get them, it will die off.

Hence, some enthusiasts described their interests in tattooing as solely motivated by the 'coolness' of the practice.

The deconstruction of the term 'cool' in this context is rather elementary if we first acknowledge that the 'coolness' of a tattoo is largely derived from its traditional outsider status. Just as British and North American middle-class youth adorned themselves with fashion symbols worn by resistant working-class Punks in the 1970s and 1980s (Baron 1989, 1997; Hebdige 1979; Young and Craig 1997), established individuals in Canada incorporate tattooing into their physical representation practices as a method of exploring social deviance while retaining the bulk of their social respectability. Through the course of the research's interview phase, the term 'cool' was used by thirty-seven (40%) of the participants to describe their tattoos. For some, 'cool' denoted that tattoos transform the body into something devilishly unique in reference to pervasive body norms:

> I never thought I would feel this way after getting tattooed, but when I go to the gym and see myself in the mirrors standing beside other people, and our skin is all showing, I see how *cool* I look now. People stop and sometimes stare at me, and I like that. I like looking different and knowing that not everyone will do this to their bodies. (Stu, 27)

For others, 'cool' indicated that the body transformed into an intimidating text:

> When I go to the park on a Saturday afternoon and play Ultimate [Frisbee] with my friends I always take my shirt off so people can see my tattoos. It sounds like I'm a narcissist or something but I'm not. I just like to go out and flash what I think is a symbol of my power. Just watch the guys in the NBA, athletes do it all the time. Showing off a tattooed body is a *cool* way of getting an edge in competition. (Brian, 26)

'Cool' is also used by some enthusiasts to describe their symbolic association with social deviants – a means of closely but not completely identifying with a THEY group of outsiders:

> I don't know, I guess I have always liked the style of the Harley-Davidson logo, and think the guys who drive Harleys are pretty *cool*. They are the last real social rebels, the only ones who really tell everyone just to fuck off ... My mother never let me have a motorcycle growing up, so I never got into it. But I love the design, and couldn't wait until I was old enough to get a tattoo. (Kelly, 26)

But for groups of WE-identified outsiders, the tattoo is not just symbolically or aesthetically cool. Tattooing remains an essential marker of commitment to a specific lifestyle, a series of interactive practices, and a set of supporting ideologies that signify one's difference (real or perceived) from the homogeneous THEY of the cultural mainstream. It is sought out as a signifying practice of outsider groups, with the pain involved and permanence of the tattoo understood as a stark illustration of one's commitment to socially alternative norms, practices, ideologies, or identities:

> People always asked me if it hurt, and I say, hell yeah it did. If it didn't hurt like a bitch everyone would go out and get one! But the guys [Skins] I hang with, we don't give a fuck about how much it hurts. In fact, we probably wouldn't do it if it didn't hurt. I'm hardcore about my beliefs, and if it means sitting through misery to prove it, that's just that then. (Colin, 21)

> If one more person asks me, 'What are you going to do when you are ninety,' I'm gonna smash somebody in the teeth. I'm not worried that my tattoos aren't going to wash off in the shower. I wouldn't have even considered it if it wasn't a forever thing. I'm what you might call a radical for animal rights, and for most people, that makes me a weirdo. But I'm committed to saving or bettering the lives of animals, and I'm never going to give that up for any reason. I'll fight for animals until the day I die, and the tattoos of animals I have on my body tell you that I am a true believer. (Paula, 28)

One's motivation to be tattooed, then, is reflective of interdependencies (real or perceived) between members of a social group. The tattoo can be a physical statement made to others that one has assumed membership in an outsider group. This sense of belonging may be confirmed by established others, who react negatively to tattooed individuals based on their culturally profane body practices. As individuals are labelled members of outsider THEY groups by conforming peers – and are encouraged to feel shame about their outsider body modifications – the process of secondary deviance (Lemert 1967) unfolds. In this process the deviant identity is solidified in one's self-conception, and tattoos become outward manifestations of a deep commitment to an outsider lifestyle. Permanently marking the body through tattooing is therefore part of what Amanda (22) expressed as 'looking what people expect me to look like because I am different [a Punk rocker]. That's the way I feel, so that's the way I should look.'

2. Cultural Resistance

The symbolic expression of affiliation with deviant others through tattooing need not be as esoteric or subculturally based as in the above cases. For some Canadian enthusiasts, tattooing body projects are motivated by a nagging sense of malaise or ennui. In these instances, the tattooed body represents cultural dislocation and social resistance. Somewhat in the way the CCCS understands flamboyant or spectacular body styles as signifiers of social protest, tattooing projects among Canadians may be motivated by a desire to wage cultural dissent through the skin. Once more, key is the idea that participation in tattooing is an immediate violation of established cultural standards about the body and its modification – and, as such, carries preferred cultural connotations of deviance.

Disenchantment with established Canadian culture may be a product of one's social location (class position) and a lack of social mobility. As Merton (1938) and Agnew (1992) stated more generally, participation in such forms of deviance might be adaptations to the strain an individual experiences when avenues for success are blocked by structured inequality. In figurational terms, strain is produced by a lack of figurational embeddedness, or a deficiency in one's economic interdependencies. For four (25%) of the working-class participants involved in this study, motivations to become tattooed reflected a present-centred fatalism and feelings of social impotence:

> I never got the impression that people really cared about how I look. They see the dirty work pants and the hard hat and ignore you, or turn and look away. No one is watching me, and in some ways I don't think I count that much in the grand scheme of things. I mean, my job sucks. I know that, but hey, it's a living. I've been working construction since I was fifteen, and I probably won't ever do anything else ... Yeah it's frustrating sometimes, but you find ways of getting by, you know, umm, you do things that make you feel good. Like I don't feel I have to live up to looking like somebody 'respectable' so if I want to get more tattoos I can. It's one of those things that I do for myself, that makes me feel like I have some control in my life. (Arn, 30)

For some (and indeed, surprizingly few) members of the Canadian working class, involvement in tattooing may be described as a 'magical solution' (Cohen 1955) to common class-based problems of status adjustment – since tattooing allows for individuals to express a certain degree of anger through the body (and thus produces a degree of personal empowerment), but does little to actually alleviate the material and social concerns of wearers. While tattooing the skin may engender feelings of pride, self-control, and satisfaction, it simply cannot remedy the very real conditions of poverty, status discrimination, and social marginalization experienced by many members of the working class. In many ways, this may account for the relatively low percentage of working-class youth in Canada who choose to describe their tattoos as symbols of class resistance.

In reference to the sociogenic changes noted in the previous chapter, cultural resistance through tattooing may occur on a purely symbolic level for many Canadians. While not wishing to be a full-fledged member of a truly outsider social group, some may align their body practices with those of social outsiders in the process of waging a particular brand of middle-class resistance. Among individuals who feel entrenched within and ultimately oppressed by dominant capitalist philosophies, tattooing can be a method of expressing an affect-based resistance to consumerism. By arguing that individualism is ritually dismantled through purchasing practices and the accumulation of popular commodities (from video-game systems to automobiles to sports drinks), some Canadian enthusiasts talk of how they were motivated to become involved in tattooing as part of, in Sanders's (1989) words, 'customizing the body' in an increasingly bland and sterile world:

> There aren't too many ways you can make yourself look different anymore. Fashions are shoved down our throats. People are walking down the street all looking the same, and we call that 'our' culture. We're humans though, and a big part about being human is the struggle to make ourselves look different from each other. Just think about how exciting it is to see someone different in a crowd of walking replicants. The main reason why that's true is because we are told early on in life that being different is bad ... For me, marking my body with tattoos is all about difference, it's my cosmic way of leaving my body and then getting back into it when the lines of my skin are redrawn. I evolve each time I am tattooed, because no one else in this universe look likes me. (Claire, 27)

These enthusiasts confirmed the idea that capitalist ideologies emphasizing consumption, and not simply the existing relations of production within capitalist economies, disintegrate personal uniqueness among Canadians:

A lot of people are caught up in buying what our neighbours have or what we are sold over the television. Not as people who choose to buy, but as people who are forced to buy to fit in ... So, tattooing my body is a way of not fitting in all the way. How many times have you seen a tattoo shop advertised during the five o'clock news, or seen some fancy print ad for tattoo artists? You're not going to, most people don't want you to buy those services. (Jack, 25)

Interestingly, such enthusiasts rejected the idea that their tattooing practices were acts of conformity in relation to the cultural pressure to consume – particularly, to consume products related to the body and its alteration (Featherstone 1991, 2000; Maguire 1999; Williams and Bendelow 1998; Woodward 1997). The fact that one purchases the services of an artist (and in fact buys, or trades something for, a tattoo) is inconsequential to most enthusiasts. The avid client Evan (26) suggested, 'It isn't that I paid for the tattoos that makes them important, I don't really care how much it cost, and I don't ever tell anyone how much I paid. You can't ask these guys [artists] to do it for free. The cost is a necessary evil.' These enthusiasts fervently argue that they are not engaging in such body-modification projects in the process of conforming with established cultural expectations to improve, redesign, and beautify the body:

It's not like buying a greeting card or choosing a new blender. You have to carefully think about your tattoo and sculpt it with an artist so it reflects your inner spirit. You know, so it's not like going to get your haircut because all the cool kids are getting it done this way, and if you don't like it you don't care since it will grow back ... We are image conscious, but tattooing is nothing like the other common ways of changing the way you look. A tattoo is a permanent pact, and you sign on the dotted line the minute the ink hits you skin for the first time. There's no going back after you start, and that's really different than the disposable products we use to change our outer facades. (Harland, 26)

To enthusiasts like Harland, the integrity of outsiders' social commentary is maintained since they construct understandings of their tattoos as symbolic gestures of resistance to consumer ideologies. Simply, most tattoo enthusiasts do not view their purchasing practices as a subversion of their philosophies of resistance.

Other enthusiasts were motivated to tattoo their bodies to oppose symbolically the ways in which capitalist social structures produce differences between people. Five (12%) of the middle-class clients interviewed in this study discussed how social difference is produced by the stratification of social classes, and the extent to which such stratification creates false cultural barriers. Like members of the white middle class wearing Malcolm X T-shirts or emblems of Africa on their clothing as a cultural statement denouncing racism (Hebdige 1979; Polhemus 1994, 1996), a small segment of middle-class Canadian enthusiasts utilize tattooing as cultural protest. Ironically criticizing their own WE positions of privilege in Canada (while not being willing to give up their own privileged positions in the middle class!), these enthusiasts express a distaste for the systematic ways the working class is marginalized as an outsider THEY group. Tattooing the body with THEY symbols of Otherness is a type of in-group criticism among the established:

> I look around and see homeless people walking the streets and massive poverty in a city that is supposed to be rich. I feel guilty driving my expensive car sometimes, and hate the way our classes are divided into the haves and have-nots. We shouldn't have social classes in Canada, and we're told that all the time, but no one takes any steps to bridge the gaps. We might not be able to eliminate differences between people's incomes, but we can get involved in one another's traditions ... I read this book about tattooing once, and learned about the traditions of tattooing among the working class in the United States. So, part of me thought this might be a way understanding how the 'other half' lives. (Joyce, 29)

Here, enthusiasts further articulate how the tightrope of bodily deviance is walked. These middle-class enthusiasts engage in ideological resistance to protest the material and cultural impacts of class-based social relationships – yet they do not wish to lose the tangible social benefits associated with being a member of an established WE group. This is revealed by the images they choose (which tend, in what they describe, to be artistic or aesthetically striking), the locations on their bodies which are tattooed (those that are typically concealed in everyday life), and the sizes of their tattoos (ten to thirty centimetres wide or under on average). Ray (31), a tattoo artist, said: 'You can always tell someone who has a lot at stake in keeping their tattoos private. They get tattooed on their backs or around the waist because you can't see that in a business suit ... They want to feel hip, but they don't want anyone to know it unless they are trusted and won't judge them.'

To extend some of these ideas about cultural protest even further, resistance to the technological nature of Canadian culture was also noted by eight (9%) of the middle-class tattoo enthusiasts I interviewed. Advances of techno-culture may increase Canadians' interest in moulding bodies into texts of profane representation, but paradoxically our reliance on technology creates feelings of uneasiness among some Canadian tattoo enthusiasts. For these individuals, a preoccupation with virtual worlds and the interface between human and machines is an impending threat to our very humanity. A tattoo artist named Phil (24) stated:

> In twenty or thirty years people will be machines. We'll all have mechanical limbs, other computer-assisted body parts, synthetic skin, and Christ knows what else. Combine that with our interest in generating forms of hyper-space reality and you've got a serious problem with accepting who we naturally are. I'm surrounded by machines, and any way to join body with soul is a positive thing.

Getting back in touch with the physical self through such a primal practice dramatically illustrates enthusiasts' sense of alienation from their own bodies. Recent scientific breakthroughs including the development of wearable technology, replaceable body parts, and other methods of human–machine interfacing clearly strikes fear in the hearts of some Canadian enthusiasts, and is articulated through their tattoos.

However, the most common form of resistance waged through tattooing described by enthusiasts was the contestation of dominant codes about gender and beauty. Unimpressed by mainstream notions of what is aesthetically pleasing, eighteen (20%) of the tattoo enthusiasts interviewed placed importance on considering traditionally outsider forms of body expression and appearance as beautiful. Attempting to break free from what they perceive to be repressive conceptualizations of beauty (based on Judeo-Christian ideologies about the body), scores of the women tattoo enthusiasts I met stressed the importance of taking personal control over the body in a culture that promotes a degree of individual body play, yet regulates, restricts, and prohibits the completely free pursuit of bodily jouissance via rigid beauty codes:

> When I was a kid, I used to draw on my jeans. All the kids did it. Remember that, I bet you did it. But my mom would tear a strip off me when I came home after school and she found pen on my pants. She said it made me

look like trash ... and when I got older I started to wear a pound of make-up everyday, and people had problems with that, calling me a whore or a tramp ... All my life I've wanted to colour myself, design my body into art-work, you know? But every time I tried people hassled me saying it wasn't appropriate or it looked tacky. Like people have the right to make me do what they think is beautiful. So after I had my first tattoo finished, I said to myself, 'This is beautiful, this is me, and it isn't coming off no matter how much people complain.' All of my life I've wanted this, to be a piece of art, and now I am. (Erin, 27)

According to Erin and her peers, Canadian tattoo enthusiasts actively wage resistance to a stagnant and historically Puritanical ethos of body representation that they feel discriminates against outsider/different/ alternative forms of body expression.

In this pursuit, particular enthusiasts in Canada are adamant about how their practices of body modification actively challenge gender codes regarding appropriate femininity and masculinity. As the body is a principal text upon which established standards about gender are inscribed, many women enthusiasts may utilize the radical modification of the body to undermine constraining established codes of bodily idiom and socially prevalent ideas about gender. For example, rituals of the flesh are used to challenge long-standing Western notions of the physical capabilities of the female body to endure pain. They accent the active desire to experience and embrace physical pain as a means of per-sonal growth. Female enthusiasts in Canada are key in this social drama as extravagant forms of body modification explicitly subvert Western conceptualizations of the beautiful feminine body:

I'm so encouraged that more and more women are turning to body mod as a way of flexing their feminine muscles. There's a new understanding that Canadians have about what a woman can be, and I hope that we [at the studio] are playing a role in educating women that 'our bodies, our selves' is more than a catchy feminist slogan ... I think women who are painted [tattooed] are beautiful because the tattoo just exudes confidence. So it's beautiful, but not in the traditional way that women were tattooed as biker molls or circus freaks, and certainly not in any bubble-gum, Betty Boop, 'I'm a helpless bitch' way. (Renata, 25)

Seventeen (34%) of the female enthusiasts I interviewed were quick to emphasize that cultural expressions of beauty and the female body

are varied and historically include a range of body-modification practices. These women point out that women have participated equally with
men in most forms of body modification around the world. They are
aware, for example, that in ancient Egypt men were not allowed to be
tattooed; only women engaged in the practice and used the tattoos as
talismans of fertility and sexuality (Atkinson and Young 2001; Rubin
1988). In the Mayan culture, women were widespread users of tattooing,
piercing, and scarification to enhance the body aesthetically (Camphausen 1997). Women in Borneo tattoo designs on their body as indicators of their social lineage, and Nubian women scar themselves to represent their fertility to males (Lautman 1994). Finally, Tiv women endure
painful rituals of the flesh such as scarification to proclaim individual
qualities of strength, courage, and fearlessness (Mifflin 1997). Thus, as
Mifflin (1997) and Pitts (1998) have suggested, the contemporary
renaissance in tattooing practices within Western cultures confronts
notions of docile femininity by appearing at least consciously theatrical,
and possibly vulgar or 'grotesque' (Bhaktin 1984), when compared to
traditional gender expectations.

Similarly, a few of the male tattoo enthusiasts I met stressed that body
modification can be used as a means of exploring a *variety* of masculine
identities. In the sociological literature, 'queer theory' has repositioned
the study of the male body by focusing on how hegemonic masculinity
(Donaldson 1993) typically marginalizes certain types of male bodies
(Connell 1995; Pronger 1990). Through the use of body modification,
some tattoo enthusiasts in Canada demonstrate that the male body is a
cultural site in which codes of acceptable masculinity are as equally contested as codes of femininity are on female bodies. For these male
enthusiasts (mostly gay men), modifying their bodies through tattooing
can represent a deliberate attempt to struggle with cultural power, sexuality, and established forms of masculinity in Canada:

> People already think because I'm gay, I'm less of a man. They think I'm not
> classically 'macho' because I've chosen a lifestyle that runs contra to what we
> consider to be manly. But I appreciate the male body and being masculine
> more than others *because* I truly love the male body in all its forms. That's why
> I admire male bodies that are marked [tattooed] in ways that question what
> we consider to be manly, and point out that gay men possess qualities of
> strength and courage that straight men egotistically claim ownership over ...
> People need to know that gay men are strong [physically, emotionally], but
> don't have to be overbearing and aggressive to prove it. (Cole, 27)

However, while some Canadian men and women clearly assert a defence against social regulation of the body, the point is perhaps made more by women, whose marked bodies are deconstructed more troublingly in Western cultures (Chernin 1981; Davis 1997a; Duden 1993; Katz 1999; Stafford 1991). For many enthusiasts, though, tattooing becomes a conscious attempt to resist established cultural ideology regarding what counts as beautiful, particularly as it is constructed along gender lines.

While not all tattoo enthusiasts in Canada subscribe to the belief that tattooing should be utilized as a form of cultural dissent or be construed as a process of political identity work, core segments of the figuration in Canada evidently draw on tattooing's long-standing association with rebellion and profanity as a means of drawing attention to many social problems that find their roots in social discrimination. In choosing to mark their bodies with tattoos, which continues to connote a wilful act of disregard to prevailing body norms in Canada for some, these individuals consciously subvert Western constructions of the civilized body in order to point out more culturally disintegrative social processes and conditions in Canada.

3. Strained or Broken Interdependencies

Motivations to become tattooed may also be born out of a series of strained interdependencies, as weakened bonds with significant others often precipitate tattooing body projects. In one way, the freedom to participate in outsider body-modification practices like tattooing is partially facilitated by the loosening or elimination of interpersonal bonds. In Hirschi's terms (1969), with the severance of a series of 'commitments' to, 'attachments' to, and 'involvement' with norm-abiding others, individuals may not feel as constricted by established social norms regarding their bodies. In a cumulative way, when individual relationships with norm-abiding or conservative others are terminated, when employment ties are severed, when family relations are weakened, and interaction with peer groups diminishes, it seems that some individuals become more interested in exploring tattooing. Feeling less constricted by established body norms, they may dabble in body art. Some Canadian enthusiasts suggest that, with the removal of a key series of social bonds and their supporting control structures, then, they drifted into tattooing in reflection of their changing figurational embeddedness:

> After I got fired for like the tenth time, I felt pretty defeated. But I got
> myself together and realized that it could be an opportunity to do all kinds

of stuff that I couldn't have when I was employed. I let my hair grow long, I dressed in track pants everyday, and I got a tiger tattooed all the way down my arm. With no one to care about how I looked, or anyone I had to report to everyday, I could be me and not worry about someone breathing down my neck. (Jerry, 25)

Therefore, some enthusiasts may find tattooing a more viable and attractive social practice, as they do not fear stern reprisal from others for their corporeal transgressions:

I was tattooed fifteen minutes after I moved out of my parents' house. My dad always warned me that if I ever came home with a tattoo he'd kick my ass and kick me out. I didn't know if he was joking, but I couldn't take the risk. Even if he let me stay, he would have hassled me everyday about it. Either way, I'd have lost, right? (Cliff, 29)

Tattooing their bodies as part of sampling previously forbidden fruit, seven (8%) of the enthusiasts I interviewed were partially motivated to become involved in tattooing following a perceived liberation from culturally pervasive body norms. The removal of one's interdependencies with others (self-initiated or otherwise) may act as a gateway to forms of bodily deviance like tattooing. Such a process is well predicted in the criminological literature on the importance of social bonds (Gottfredson and Hirschi 1990; Hirschi 1969; Matsueda and Heimer 1997; Sampson and Laub 1993). This sentiment was expressed by the enthusiast Dan (34), who stated that one of his tattooing projects was motivated by his wife's announcement that she intended to file for divorce:

After that moment when she smashed our lives by telling me she wanted out of the marriage, my whole life was turned upside down ... It was kind of funny because she told me what to do and when to do it, in like every single aspect of my life. So I'm like the kid in the candy store now, eh. I'm free to do whatever the hell I want [laughs] ... My ex-wife hated tattoos, man, so I thought to myself, I need to get one of them. So I had a hula girl tattooed on my back, and oh man, she would've hated that.

From the above quotation, and others expressing similar sentiments, it became evident to me that the motivation to participate in tattooing can partly be contingent upon who initiates the severance of a bond. Among individuals discussing how strained or eliminated interdependencies spurned involvement in tattooing, most implied that (in one way or another) they did not wish the relationship to be terminated. In essence, their participation in tattooing partly articulated feelings of rejection from significant others. The elimination of the bonds might have been prevented in some instances (divorce, break-up, or being fired), while others were entirely impossible to avoid (a family member dying):

> When my mum died, I started thinking about a permanent way of com-memorating her. I took this old picture I had of her from when she was like twenty and went to a tattoo artist in Michigan who is the master of portrai-ture tattoos. After three months of waiting to get an appointment, I went and had her picture put on my left shoulder. It's my favourite tattoo, cause it makes me remember how special she was and how she loved me no mat-ter what I did. (Hunter, 21)

The process of utilizing the tattoo to represent one's alienation from others partially reproduces its deviant status. A tattoo is purposefully selected as the marker of the social misfit, the outcast, the unwanted. Wilfully marking the body with culturally recognized symbols of Other-ness, individuals voluntarily inscribe symbols on their bodies that distin-guish them immediately from the cultural mainstream in Canada. In several respects, the specific symbol(s) chosen for the tattooing project are of secondary importance. Altering one's body through the tattooing process (deviant in comparison to the mutilation experienced in nor-mative forms of cosmetic surgery, dieting, or body-building practices!) is enough to signify that one has experienced a rupture from normative behavioural patterns.

These cases tend to give some empirical support to theoretical expla-nations of social deviance from a classic 'control' or 'self-control' per-spective (Gottfredson and Hirschi 1990; Hirschi 1969). With social bonds removed, individuals may be 'freed up' to participate in a full gamut of non-mainstream body behaviours. In figurational terms, their diminished figurational embeddedness (their reduced interdependen-cies with others) allows them to experiment *more freely* with a series of corporeal practices that were formerly discouraged by controlling oth-ers. These conditions become apparent in their tattooing narratives, and partially structure how they experience the tattooing process. For these individuals, who express little worry about how their tattoos may affect future bonds with others, tattooing the body is a mechanism for expressing emotion. Their tattoos come to symbolize their sense of distance from social others (often along with a sense of personal loss), and articulate a degree of disaffiliation from the mainstream.

4. The Quest for Excitement
A central principle in Elias's research (1994, 1996) on long-term civilizing processes is that Western figurations have become relatively unexciting social environments. A collective need to devise and institutionalize cultural activities that strike a balance between personal pleasure and restraint resulted from the general pacification of figurations over time (Elias 1994). As outward displays of emotion are largely pushed behind the scenes of social life, individuals learn to pursue a range of activities that elicit exciting significance in highly controlled contexts of interaction (Maguire 1992).

Fitting sport into the category of activities that elicit a level of socially accepted excitement for individuals, Elias and Dunning (1986) stated that sport provides an interactive context within which a moderate degree of violence is both permissible and encouraged; individuals (either as competitors or spectators) can participate in that which is strictly taboo in other social spheres (Dunning 1999; Maguire 1999). For example, sport is predominantly a social institution extolling the virtues of competition and physicality (i.e., as part of 'character building'), while providing a source of temporary liberation from diffuse social codes that curtail violence and uncontrolled affective outburst. In this way, sport establishes an outlet for experiencing free-flowing but carefully managed emotions. In the words of figurational sociologists, sports contests fashion an interactive scenario that facilitates a 'controlled decontrolling' of emotional controls among participants and spectators (Elias and Dunning 1986).

Elias and Dunning and Dunning and Rojek (1992) have argued that one of sport's primary roles within complex figurations is to 'de-routinize' social life. Constrained by dense chains of interdependency, individuals are socially expected to engage in (and learn to internalize the merits of) predictable and emotionally controlled behaviour. Sport is a social theatre within which spectators are deliberately aroused by the tension balances (Dunning 1999; Elias and Dunning 1986; Maguire 1993, 1999) created through athletic contests. Sport is referred to as mimetic because it deliberately resembles war-like competition; it is socially and emotionally significant to individuals because it elicits a level of excitement while being structured by an understanding that the outcome of the battle is not as perilous to the participants as a 'genuine' war would be:

> Mimetic activities vary considerably across the globe, both in terms of their intensity and style, but they have basic structural characteristics in common. That is, they provide, a 'make-believe' setting which allows emotions to flow more easily, and which elicits excitement of some kind in imitating that produced by 'real life situations,' yet without their dangers or risks. 'Mimetic' activities, locally constructed or globally generated, thus allow, within certain limits, for socially permitted self-centredness. Excitement is elicited by the creation of tensions: this can involve the imaginary or controlled 'real' danger, mimetic fear and/or pleasure, sadness, and/or joy. (Maguire 1999, 71)

Hence, spectators are excited by the often rough and violent competitive exchange between the participants – yet feel neither guilt nor repugnance in watching the battles since the struggles are not 'real' (Goodger and Goodger 1989).

Elias and Dunning's analysis (1986) of sport and leisure pastimes in England (fox hunting, cricket, boxing, horse racing, rugby, and football) underscored the sociological importance of conceptualizing sport as mimetic activity. Detailing the sociogenesis of sport, they accounted for its role as a mediator between social order and the exploration of emotions. In this way Elias and Dunning cleverly incorporated elements of 'macro' and 'micro' social analysis into their discussion, so as to correspond with and complement their figurational approach. Moreover, research on football hooliganism as a world problem (Dunning 1999; Dunning and Sheard 1979; Dunning et al. 1988) suggests that even socially dangerous forms of sport-related deviance may be mimetic – as hooliganism and other more violent variations of crowd disorder are surrogates for open class conflict (Young 2000). As the ritual 'aggro' that constitutes hooliganism adds excitement to the working-class participants' lives, it quells more serious forms of social outburst.

More recently, Sheard (1999) used a figurational approach to examine the sport of bird-watching as mimesis. Positing the practice ('twitching') to be a further extension of the civilizing processes, he draws attention to the exciting significance created by the activity. According to Sheard, by using a mock-hunt, mock-battle formula of action, bird-watching supplants hunting or killing animals as a collectively exciting social activity. Apart from figurational sociologists, however, few have pursued empirical examinations of mimesis in society.

Participation in the outsider social practice of tattooing may be utilized as a vehicle for experiencing exhilaration in unexciting figurations. Involvement in deviant body-modification practices like tattooing can be mimetic if constructed to replace more serious social transgressions that would jeopardize a person's physical safety, social status, or interpersonal roles. One may wish to get tattooed because it is thrilling, different, and produces pleasure for the individual. The act of tattooing, then, might be a carefully designed form of thrilling risk-taking behaviour. Yet involvement in an outsider practice like tattooing is a relatively safe or controlled form of deviance in this respect – entered into with the knowledge that others will not be physically injured in the process, and that one's status as a deviant can be discursively managed or physically hidden at times. Once more, tattooing allows enthusiasts to walk the tightrope of deviance, appearing physically different but not exceedingly deviant:

> The first few days after I was tattooed were really stressful. I kept looking and staring at my tattoo in the mirror and wished I could go back in time and erase what I had done. It made me look like a freak, and it's strange because that's partly what I wanted to have happen. You know, as soon as my friends started speaking out about my tattoo and every time I saw chins drop though I was all loving it. That's really the reaction I wanted from the get go. You get this rush from looking different, and knowing people are looking at you and wondering what you are like as a person. (Amber, 27)

Narratives offered by five (6%) enthusiasts (all females within the 20 to 23 age range) indicated that much of the excitement gleaned from tattooing derives from the perceived level of pain and trauma involved in the process. While much of the literature on tattooing offers an explanation of the kudos acquired from enduring the painful ritual in relation to the confirmation of masculinity, stories I gathered while studying tattooing among Canadians suggest another way of interpreting the experience of pain. The ability to endure long sessions of tattooing may be considered as a marker of one's extraordinary pain threshold – regardless of one's gender. Moreover, one's ability to withstand the painful ordeal is a flagrant breach of established cultural ideologies that emphasize how pain should be avoided or feared in everyday life. Being able to describe the pain experienced in the acquisition of a large tattoo as 'nothing much,' as 'no big deal,' or as something that is relished can be amazing to others:

> It really is the first question on people's minds, and when you can say, it's [the pain] nothing o.k. ... Some people think you're lying and others have this blank look on their faces. Stunning people, especially when you can show how tough you are, is pretty cool, I think anyway ... When so many people flinch and turn away from you it makes you feel, I dunno, like you are physically and emotionally stronger than people without tattoos. (Jill, 34)

Enthusiasts who are motivated to become involved in tattooing in order to flaunt their unnatural physical ability to encounter self-inflicted physical trauma without trepidation deliberately seek the label of deviant or outsider.

Much as the carnival and sideshow traditions of displaying tattooed freaks did, the tattooed body is designed to shock audiences aesthetically. By tapping into the outsider status of tattooing in Canada, some individuals use tattoos to call attention to themselves through radical body practices. In like manner to the use of the tattoo as a form of social protest, tattooing images across the body may prove exciting as it elicits social curiosity:

> I speak with people everyday who want a tattoo so they can stand out in the crowd. I get to know people a bit when they sit in my chair and let me tattoo their bodies, and one thing that comes up all the time is that being different is important to people. I don't know how they got to that place or why they need to be different or anything, but if you cut through all the crap they might tell you about some deep personal reason why they want a tattoo, they're just telling me they want to look different from every other person and be noticed because of it. (Jones, 27)

Given the continued marginality of the practice, and most individuals' lack of knowledge about tattooing, a tattoo may be a conversation piece or a device fostering social exchange. This is especially evident among individuals who were tattooed as a means of shattering others' perceptions of them as a 'goody-two shoes' or 'square':

> No one ever thought I'd show up some day with a tattoo. I mean, really, I'm an honour student, I still go to church every weekend and my parents are

my best friends. The wildest thing I ever did was have a few too many drinks on my eighteenth birthday ... So, I sort of got off on changing that image people have of me. At least it makes people think twice about me, and not fit me into some neat stereotype. (Allison, 20)

The sociological literature on deviance has focused on how contra-normative forms of behaviour may be instrumental in providing thrills or spontaneous pleasure for participants. Criminologist Jack Katz (1988) suggested that some individuals engage in these types of socially deviant behaviours since they provide an immediate source of pleasure derived from the risk-taking (i.e., physical and social) involved. In this way, forms of deviant behaviour 'seduce' individuals through their emotionally exhilarating character. In their seminal work on the importance of self-control as an aetiological factor in deviance, Gottfredson and Hirschi (1990) also noted that one's lack of self-restraint may lead to involvement in a spectrum of risk-taking behaviours. Asserting that involvement in deviance gratifies an individual's unrestrained quest for excitement, however, they summarily discounted the possibility that forms of deviant behaviour may actually be highly *controlled* excursions into hedonism. Instead, Gottfredson and Hirschi account for what they perceive to be unskilled, haphazard, or unplanned risk-taking behaviour as a symptom of an individual's inability to manage the need to uncover immediate sources of gratification (Wade and Brannigan 1998).

The acceptance and reproduction of tattooing as an outsider social practice serves Canadian tattoo enthusiasts in several different ways. Despite the assumption that the increased prevalence of tattooing in Western cultures is a general indicator of its acceptability among middle-class established groups (DeMello 2000), Canadians' tattoo narratives indicate that such an assumption is not entirely valid. Even though cultural attitudes about tattooing are clearly shifting, it would be fallacious to assume that enthusiasts themselves seek a widespread cultural acceptance of tattoos. Tattoo enthusiasts may wilfully align their identities with social deviance in order to declare outsider affiliations, engage in cultural resistance, mark changing interdependencies, or find excitement in unexciting societies.

Embracing Difference: Marks of Conformity

The preceding discussion of tattooing centred on the ways in which contemporary enthusiasts embrace the deviant status of the tattoo as a means of consolidating their own sense of social isolation or outsider identity. Yet given the flexibility of tattooing as a meaningful cultural practice, we should be careful not to reduce the sociological significance of this body project to the ways in which it bestows socially deviant identities on Canadians. Narratives provided by tattoo enthusiasts in this study indicated that motivations for tattooing may be far less culturally antagonistic.

Tattooing projects may be articulated by enthusiasts as an integral part of their individual repertoires of normative self-representational practices. The body work engaged in through tattooing is not intended to align one's identity with outright deviance, but is rather included in the pursuit of meaningful forms of body expression. This does not, in any way, suggest that the expression of deviance through tattooing is devoid of cultural meaning or interpersonal relevance. Conceptual differences are, however, evident between the meanings given to socially rebellious forms of tattooing and more normative forms deemed to be corporeal voyages of personal discovery – or in Atkinson and Young's terms (2001), their 'flesh journeys.'

The centrality of tattooing and social deviance does not fade into the background when deep personal meaning is expressed through tattooing body projects. Cultural constructions of the tattoo as an indicator of social deviance remain central in providing analytical frameworks for tattooing projects. In these cases, the status of deviance surrounding tattooing is partially disavowed by enthusiasts; that is, their self-professed motivations for tattooing are structured in part by and against established perceptions of tattooing as a disreputable (sub)cultural practice. In wrestling with dominant constructions of tattoos, an enthusiast staunchly proclaims, 'My tattoos are not like *that* [a sign of deviance], they are meaningful.' Motivations are carefully configured by enthusiasts to distance themselves slightly from the so-called outsider traditions of tattooing in Canada (white, male, working-class), and thus become interpretive resources for deciphering the significance underlying tattoo projects. What we are witnessing here is the clash between different 'generations' (Mannheim 1971) of tattoo enthusiasts, and the differing uses and meaning structures they attribute to tattoos. While some embrace and reproduce the more 'traditional' legacy of tattooing in North America, others (and indeed the newest generation) poach the outsider status of the tattoo and rework it into a symbol of 'cultural difference.'

The discursive reconfiguration of tattooing as a sign of personally 'meaningful difference' rather than unbridled social rebellion mostly occurs among middle-class clients. This speaks to the enduring social stereotypes about tattooing held by many in Canada. In some ways, the ongoing discussion and referencing of the deviant stereotype by some middle-class enthusiasts is a way of highlighting their body projects as resistant but respectful, serious but playful, and alternative but socially acceptable (and jibing well with current sensibilities about the body and its modification). Of course, the tattoos of the more marginal social outsiders are certainly meaningful to them, and this is acknowledged by middle-class enthusiasts. But it is the way in which these bourgeois enthusiasts construct their tattoos as somewhat *more* creative, expressive, personally relevant, and artistically pleasing that establishes the difference. In this process, it is not a matter of referring to one another's tattoos as disingenuous, but simply of putting a middle-class spin on tattooing practices. In the current boom in popularity of tattooing in Canada, then, clear 'generational units' (Mannheim 1971) are developing with their own unique tastes and preferences for tattoos.

Therefore, the motivations for tattooing expressed by some enthusiasts are formulated as well-rehearsed justifications (Scott and Lyman 1968). Examining the discursive constructions of tattooing body projects offered by some Canadian enthusiasts, we can see that common justifications are circulated among them as established 'techniques of neutralization' (Sykes and Matza 1957). Denying their involvement in outsider body practices, enthusiasts frequently protest that their tattoos – because of some deep-seeded personal meaning structure – are not signifiers of a lack of conformity. Common sensibilities about modifying the body are tapped into, as are sentiments that the body is an entity meant to be wilfully shaped throughout the life course.

By attending to Mills's understanding (1940) of how 'vocabularies of motive' are constructed in the process of deflecting negative reaction following rule-breaking behaviours, we may understand how justifications of deviance are formed in specific contexts. Equally, however, we must be aware that justifications for deviance are sensitive to both cultural time and space. Among tattoo enthusiasts in the current era, for instance, justifications for tattoos hinge on a desire to be different from the mainstream yet norm-abiding – justifications rarely made, or even considered, among the majority of enthusiasts in previous eras. Through a set of linguistic signifiers, tattoo enthusiasts are able to tell cleverly scripted stories about their tattoos, and manage potentially negative reactions from others. Elaborate stories about one's motivations to become tattooed serve as a type of discursive shield used against being lumped into the undesirable category of the social outsider. Questions about the authenticity of motivations naturally arise, and individuals will occasionally go to extreme lengths to justify their tattooing practices (and their motivations) as genuine.

Through the justification process, however, a clever attempt is often made to co-opt tattooing into established forms of body play. As the majority of enthusiasts offering clear justifications about their tattoos have middle- to upper-class social backgrounds (78%), are relatively well educated, and are tied to conventional roles and responsibilities (family, occupational, religious), we may be witnessing an invasion of the middle-class 'establishment' into this outsider territory. These enthusiasts do not wish to become full-fledged members of an 'extreme' outsider group, yet in walking the deviance tightrope they are not inclined to fully sanitize the body project since the tattoo's deviant status is partly what attracts them to the project (i.e., the tattoo's standing as a symbol of difference allows them to assert a refurbished version of personal difference through their body work). Redesigning the body in this way is a manifestation of a general desire to assert personal/group difference within extended chains of interdependency. Tattooing the skin is a ready-made social practice for this task. Enthusiasts align themselves only superficially to more marginal groups by sharing a common predilection for tattooing, and prefer to rework tattoos into symbols of middle-class difference.

Normative justifications for such involvement in tattooing may be segmented into three major categories. The first category, *role transitions*, includes justifications revolving around the central idea that at key points in the life course individuals encounter transitions involving moments of self-redefinition and doubt. Tattooing the body with symbols denotes one's changing interdependencies with others and corresponding alteration in one's self-conception. The second category, *affect management*, includes types of discourse that detail how tattooing is explored as a method of coping with emotions routinely pushed behind the scenes of social life. The third category, *individual difference*, represents the justifications enthusiasts offer for their tattooing practices that revolve around the desire to be an individual.

1. Role Transitions
The desire to mark changing interdependencies through the skin is not a motivation owned solely by those interested in aligning their identities

with social deviance. At key points in the life course, individuals may be motivated to pursue a tattooing body project as a method of permanently marking significant interpersonal transitions (Sampson and Laub 1993, 2001) or changing identities within groups of others. Utilized in this way, the body is a travelling scrapbook upon which memories are permanently imprinted. The permanence of the tattoo is attractive to the enthusiast, as the recollection of the period in one's life may fade, yet the tattoo endures. Images chosen for these projects vary considerably, ranging from cartoon characters to Greek letters, animals, club mottos, family crests, or portraits.

Paralleling the use of tattooing among deviant subcultural members to confirm loyalties, tattoo enthusiasts may carve symbols into the skin in order to declare a series of bonds with others. The classically deviant social practice is sought out as a method of affirming existing or emerging (normative) interdependencies in an everlasting way. For instance, three (4%) enthusiasts interviewed in the research stated that their tattoos were designed to commemorate their wedding ceremonies or mark eternal bonds with their life partners. The tattoo is a signifier of a new life trajectory, a fresh beginning for the person:

> When Kate and I were married in Hawaii, it was the most perfect experience in my whole life. We were married just before sunset on this little beach with seven of our closest friends. We stood in the water and made our commitment under heaven ... As soon as we got back [home], we were down at the tattoo shop getting our tattoos. We planned it out months in advance, made our appoints with Steve [tattoo artist] and had picked out our designs. They're like another set of wedding rings. We joked about doing it at first, but after some time, and a bit of laughter, we thought it would be a beautiful expression. I have a wave with the sun setting behind it on my shoulder, and Kate chose a palm tree with the date we were married written underneath it. (Stu, 27)

For other enthusiasts, marking the body within specific iconography (e.g., a cross, the face of Jesus, or the Star of David) was instrumental in expressing the strength of their religious convictions:

> The cross on my back really symbolizes my experience of being born again. I was very religious as a child, since my family was, I didn't have much choice. I moved out at eighteen, and took it as an opportunity to really go wild, and let my beliefs sort of slide. Two years later, I found myself going

back to church. The difference was that I was doing it on my own terms. After a lot of thinking, I realized I needed to recommit to Catholicism, and was born again. Even though tattooing is something which is taboo if you read the Bible carefully, there's no better way to show other Catholics how strongly I am committed. (Ethan, 26)

Thirteen (14%) of the enthusiasts interviewed indicated that their tattooing projects were designed to forge a permanent bond between friends, especially in the case where interpersonal affiliations were strained by spatial distance:

Toward the end of university a bunch of the girls from my floor [in residence] who had been together since first year decided to get tattoos of the university logo. I thought they were crazy at first, and that I would never ever do that. But right before the [school] year ended we were all out at a bar and I thought to myself that it might be one of the last times we were all together and having fun. I've been through some of the toughest times of my life with these girls, and they're like my second family ... Two days later I was tattooed with the university logo. Andrea and Kim came down with me and held my hand the whole time ... I cried thinking about how I was going to miss them, and when I look at the tattoo sometimes I still cry. (Renee, 25)

Several of the older (40 to 45 year age range) enthusiasts interviewed noted that their tattooing projects coincided with major role transitions encountered in later stages of the life course – such as their children leaving home, acquiring a new job or career, or returning to university to complete a degree:

The day I walked into Shelley's [daughter] room and knew she wouldn't be coming home that night was one of the emptiest feelings of my life. She was married, she had her own life, and I had to let go. You have a child and watch her grow, only to see her leave and this immense feeling of loneliness slowly sinks in from the head down ... My tattoo, I just wanted a reminder of her, something I could carry with me forever. She came from my body and I wanted to return a piece of her into me ... if that doesn't sound too crazy ... I had this old finger-painting she had done in grade one framed on the wall, and I decided to have that tattooed in my left shoulder. She brought it home to me one day after school and stood there with her little blue dress on. She was so beautiful and so proud. It reminds me of when she was innocent, and when she was mine. (Helen, 45)

While these motivations are linguistically constructed as deeply meaningful – and therefore, supposedly different than the use of tattooing among outsiders – Canadian enthusiasts are not ignorant of the nagging cultural associations between tattooing and social deviance. Techniques of deflecting such negative associations are correspondingly formed so that the enthusiasts' identities are not negatively impacted by their tattooed bodies. Justifications are formulated to account for one's involvement in a traditionally outsider social practice. The underlying motivation behind the tattoo is not subjected to scrutiny in this process; still, the choice of avenues for expressing the bond may be routinely questioned by others. Enthusiasts often deem (or find) it necessary to justify their choice of corporeal practices narratively:

One of the biggest changes in tattooing in the past like ten years or so is that just about everybody coming in feels this need to make up some hodgepodge story about their tattoos. It's weird cause people will sit in my chair and think like they have to cook up a really elaborate story about why they are getting tattooed. I don't know if they are trying to convince themselves or if they're trying to act cool in front of me or whatever. It could be they are just practising a story and looking for a reaction from me, but I feel like tellin' them, 'Look, I've heard it all before and I don't care.' (Butch, 35)

Through the course of my investigation into tattooing in Canada, several recurrent justifications became evident. These were not only conceptually similar, they were linguistically identical in some cases – with the same phraseology being utilized by different enthusiasts to articulate motivations. Take, for example, the excepts from two separate narratives, where the term 'souvenir' is central:

I think tattooing really is probably one of the best ways to define yourself in ways that you can control. Things happen to you in your life and a lot of them are beyond your ability to change, and you just have to accept what you have been dealt with and go from there ... My tattoos are like stickers you put on a suitcase when you travel around the world, they are *souvenirs* of everything happening to me in my life. (Rachel, 35)

> My body is under my control, at least that's what I like to think anyway. You can't control everything that happens to you, but you can take charge of your body and design it however you want. That's what tattooing is for me, a way of taking charge of who I am and who I look like to other people ... I've gone through life-altering events in the last few years, right. I almost died in a car accident, and my girlfriend had a baby. These were sort of the low and high of my whole life, and they happened in a real short span of time ... They were probably the two biggest changes in my life ever, and the memories stick out in my mind. So I have a tattoo of my car on my arm, and a portrait of my boy on my calf ... Both of them changed who I am and I have the tattoos as *souvenirs* to remind myself how far I have come in life. (Kevin, 25)

Although such similarities could be the product of coincidence, a closer inspection of the narratives indicates that justifications are partially learned and distributed among like-minded enthusiasts. Justifications about involvement in deviance are, therefore, products of interpersonal interaction and (as the narratives suggest) circulated among intimate groups of interdependent actors (Sutherland 1937).

Justification for one's involvement in tattooing is learned from two primary subsets of enthusiasts. First, some enthusiasts learn how to justify their involvement in tattooing as part of a normative bonding process with close friends who are tattooed; groups of like-minded others, whom Simmel (1964) referred to as 'organic social groups.' Ready-made scripts of justification are offered by fellow enthusiasts as a way of promoting collective understandings of the practice. Placing only a slight variation on the justifications, enthusiasts eventually formulate their own unique narratives. Compare the following quotes provided by two second-year field hockey players who were tattooed in the process of solidifying their relationships with fellow players:

> I mean, I never thought twice about it, really. The girls all have tattoos on their ankles and that's just part of being on the team. You can't get one until you have finished your first full season with the team, okay, but as soon as you do, you feel like you're really a member of the inner squad cause you get to do it and other players don't ... We feel so close to each other, and yeah it feels just natural to want to go out and get a tattoo to express that ... We're teammates and that means a lot, if you don't play sports and don't know about how important it is to be close to the players on the team, you just can't understand. (Erica, 21)

It's part of being on this team. Well, it's not like that's what we do [tattoo-ing] as a team, but it is something that you get to do after you play your first full season ... I don't have any other tattoos, and probably wouldn't get any more because they just wouldn't be as special. You can't understand unless you play with other athletes and have to go over the whole obstacle course of feelings that come with wins and losses, success and failure. These guys on the team know me better than anyone else in some ways, and I feel close to them – even after playing on the team for only a year. They've seen me at my worst and encouraged me to push myself beyond limits I thought I could never cross ... My tattoo is about my feelings. It's me saying thank you for being considered as a member of this team and being privileged enough to get to compete with them. (Brooke, 22)

Second, enthusiasts will also learn how to justify their involvement in tattooing through interaction with tattoo artists. Spending anywhere from thirty minutes to five hours per session being tattooed, clients reg-ularly inquire about others' tattooing experiences. Due to their unique position in the figuration, artists can provide a treasure trove of infor-mation in this respect – including their perspectives on why other cli-ents are tattooed. I spent hours upon hours in tattoo studios sitting with artists and their clients noting the exchange of information between them. On many occasions the conversation involved a discussion of why people are tattooed – a topic typically broached by clients. One day, for example, I watched a young man named Aaron (23) receive a tattoo of the sun on his back. He had stated that he believed the symbol to be cool, and thought it would render his body more physically attractive/ intimidating. He stood out in my mind because during the hour and a half it took to complete the piece, he posed dozens of questions about why people acquire tattoos. He seemed particularly fascinated by the idea that individuals are tattooed in the process of affirming relation-ships with others. Several months later, I interviewed Aaron in a one-on-one session, and he described his motivation to become tattooed in the following way:

All that stuff I was asking Cliff [tattoo artist] about was made up. I didn't want to tell you or him the real reason why I was being tattooed, you know. It's just like we were talking about, right, like getting a tattoo because you want to be close to someone else. That's how I feel about my girl[friend] Gwen, she's the light of my life and that's why I wanted a sun to show that. She's the only person in the universe for me but sometimes I feel like she's sitting up there in the skies out of my reach. She's up there looking down on me, lighting up the path I am taking.

Through a process of introspection, Aaron learned to justify his tattooing practices using a specific discourse – as a justification that relates significantly more meaning than the aesthetics of tattoo art.

Enthusiasts may also learn how to justify their tattoos by reading articles in tattoo periodicals or on World Wide Web sites. As DeMello (2000) commented, mass-distribution tattoo magazines include testimonials about tattoo projects, and are influential resources in the process of learning how to discursively frame normative meanings for one's tattoos. Justifications are co-opted by enthusiasts and developed into patterned ways of assigning social significance to the body markings. Therefore, while there may be a growing number of types of enthusiasts in the current era (in terms of their biographies or artistic preferences), there are clearly diminishing contrasts between the justifications for their tattooing practices.

Evidently, enthusiasts who promulgate interpretations of their tattoos as normative partially learn how to justify their involvement in a classically outsider practice. The doors to normative social construction of tattooing are opened for individuals if they can begin to conceptualize the process as a deeply meaningful way to mark life transitions on the skin. The justifications and resulting narratives supporting them are, in some cases, far more important than the actual images tattooed. In managing the cultural status of tattoos, enthusiasts offer interpretations of the practice as a form of tolerable deviance. Such interpretations hinge on the idea that the symbols inscribed bear highly personal meanings designed to promote growth and mark the passage of time for wearers.

In retrospect, these Canadian tattoo enthusiasts engage in what might be theorized as an 'appeal to higher loyalties' (Sykes and Matza 1957). In denying their involvement in an outsider form of body modification, enthusiasts employ this technique to minimize the potentially negative reaction to their body projects. Proclaiming that their tattoos are indelible marks of loyalty, love, friendship, empowerment, or shared connections, such enthusiasts outwardly deny any involvement in cultural rebellion. The permanence of the mark is simply offered an indicator of the strength of a bond or the significance of role transitions – and not, in any way, to be read by others as a symbolic act of protest.

This use of tattooing stands in contrast to the practice of those who might tattoo their bodies following a weakening of social interdependencies. Individuals possessing strong interdependencies often tattoo their bodies to signify the importance of social bonds, or their status among others. The permanence of the tattoos and the ability to customize the designs are especially appealing to those wishing to confirm the importance of specific social interdependencies through the skin. What seems to mark the difference between tattoo enthusiasts in this case is the *meaning* assigned to the tattoos by the enthusiasts, and how they are experienced and/or managed in everyday life. Quite simply, the form and content of tattooing body projects seem largely to be underpinned by the type, quality, and character of one's interdependencies with others. Different levels of interdependency bear directly on how, when, and why someone chooses to become involved in tattooing. This demonstrates how social interdependencies *are the common denominator* in the analysis of tattooing practices, and further illustrates how a figurational understanding of corporeal behaviour furnishes a more holistic understanding of tattooing as a highly social act.

2. Affect Management

For some, marking the body with tattoos may also diverge significantly from deviant traditions in that the practice may be utilized as a rather 'civilized' way of managing affect. In Elias's terms (1983, 1994), engaging in this form of body modification may illustrate one's ability to express what we might call 'negative' or painful affect in highly controlled, quasi-normative ways. In figurations where a high degree of internal restraint is expected among individuals (and internalized as personally/socially beneficial), finding acceptable methods for managing emotion is required. The body, as a communicative text, may readily be modified in order to manage emotions that might be otherwise pushed behind the scenes of social life or expressed through destructive avenues.

In the sociological literature, research on emotions and their management (Maguire 1992, 1999; Scheff 1983, 1990; Wouters 1989) has focused on the methods by which individuals curtail the display of affect in everyday life, or on the ways people renounce their own emotions through techniques of impression management (Goffman 1959, 1963). Arlie Hochschild's investigation (1983) of flight attendants typifies the (mainly symbolic interactionist) approach to the study of emotions. She focused on how one's feelings are routinely forced behind the scenes of public life – such that individuals are required to present false personas through social interchange. Affective containment is required when flight attendants are 'on stage' so that airline clients experience flight in the 'friendliest' of skies. Research on the experience of corporeal breakdown similarly suggests that individuals feel social pressure to ritually hide or 'pass' (Goffman 1959, 1963) feelings of fear, frustration, and anger. Conforming with cultural inclinations to shun the open discussion or representation of corporeal disease and decay (Stafford 1991), individuals experiencing ruptures in bodily function are mainly expected to manage emotion privately and silently (Crawford 1994; Frank 1991a, 1991b; Freund and McGuire 1999; Katz 1999; Sontag 1991).

Yet tattoo enthusiasts regularly speak of how tattooing can be liberating emotionally, a way of venting emotions publicly through the body. The outsider practice of tattooing is rationalized in this process as a normative healing mechanism. With pervasive figurational ideologies supporting the idea that 'it's my body, and therefore my choice,' enthusiasts construct their practices as a pro-social, or civilized, way of expressing negative affect stirred through interaction with others. In this way, tattooing the body represents a controlled decontrolling of emotional controls for some enthusiasts.

Robert Agnew's general strain theory (1992) added key insight into how individuals pursue lines of deviant behaviour in responding to affect. For Agnew, the experience of negative emotions results when one's life goals are blocked, when positive stimuli are removed from, or negative stimuli introduced into, one's life. Whereas traditional strain theorists (Chilton 1964; Menard 1995) have zeroed in on the first of these three sources of strain, the examination of the other two sources have been considerably neglected. Moreover, Agnew commented that negative emotions (especially anger toward others) are managed by individuals in different ways, depending on the coping strategies internalized over the life course and whom they blame as the source of their frustration. Agnew hypothesized that people will turn to deviance when the cause of frustration is attributed to others, and emotions like anger are stirred to such an extent that one's coping mechanisms are no longer effective. As Broidy (2001) confirmed, the experience of hostility and other powerful emotions resulting from strain (especially among women) may precipitate a full range of deviant behaviours.

However, theorists like Agnew failed to consider that individuals may partake in social deviance as a culturally tolerable strategy for coping with strain; that is, people may participate in alternative or socially questionable activities in lieu of more serious social transgressions. Indeed, a normative way of coping with anger or other emotions may be to dabble in light forms of social deviance. We should not confuse the term 'normative' here with the proposition that outsider ways of life become habitual or commonplace in groups of like-minded actors. Furthermore, Agnew did not explore the methods by which individuals are able to account for their behaviours discursively as products of strain and their inability to cope with negative affect. Instead, Agnew traced the pathways of criminal behaviour through his general strain model, thereby replicating the idea that individuals simply respond to strain in either normative or hyper-deviant ways.

Regardless of the aforementioned deficiencies, Agnew's ideas about strain and deviant response blend well with a figurational understanding of the management of affect in civilized figurations. If one conjoins the study of how positive and negative social stimuli produce strain for individuals with the notion that people actively construct normative techniques of communication to represent affect (often, in carefully controlled 'decontrolled' ways), one can forge a powerful conceptual tool for explaining how tattooing is interpreted as normative social practice.

The analysis of enthusiasts' narratives indicates that motivations to become involved in tattooing may be shaped by an interest in expressing affect on the body. Through processes similar to those as outlined in the previous section, these motivations form justifications that are learned and disseminated among middle-class enthusiasts who deny their participation in tattooing as social deviance. Thirty-two (34%) of the enthusiasts maintained that their involvement in tattooing – rather than lashing out at others, engaging in physically destructive (to the self or others) behaviours, or further repressing the strain (leading to emotional incapacitation) – was propelled by the experience of negative affect.

For instance, some Canadian enthusiasts claim that for people who have endured emotional pain or stress (through biological illness, sexual assault, or physical abuse), body-modification rituals like tattooing help to cope with such experiences and purge the associated trauma – in many ways indirect relation to the pain inherent in process. For some female respondents, for example, this involved coming to terms with an experience of sexual assault:

I can't believe it, even now when I'm sitting here talking to you [about being raped]. I was out of my body for almost two years. I can't really find any other way of explaining this to you than by saying I felt numb. I tried not to think about my body because I felt dirty, ashamed, and like, you know, I wanted to crawl out of myself ... Then I met the people at Tattoo Mania [studio]. I went in one day with a friend of mine who was getting a tattoo to commemorate the passing of her dad, and after speaking with a couple of the receptionists and one of the artists, I started thinking about getting a tattoo ... I thought a tattoo might help me re-claim my body, bring it back to my control, you know. I lost my body, I was a stranger in my own skin ... I cried the whole time I was being tattooed, all of the fear, and hate, and sorrow came to the surface, and every time the needles struck me I re-lived the pain of the rape. I don't think any amount of talk, with whoever, could have forced me to get back in touch with my body like that ... I consider that day my second birthday, the day I really started to move on with my life. (Jenny, 24)

For some gay male respondents, modifying the flesh through tattooing marked their coming out, a part of the declaration of a gay identity heretofore repressed by others:

I finally mustered up the courage to come out to my family and friends about three years ago, after almost fifteen years of hiding who I am. I'd just entered into a serious relationship with a man I met in the U.S., and after several months of enduring a long-distance affair, he moved to Canada and in with me. I love Charles and want to be with him the rest of my life ... My tattoo [of a Gay Pride flag/banner] symbolizes the commitment I have made to Charles and to myself. This is me, this is who I am and I want people to know that I'm not living in shadows anymore. (Buddy, 31)

A vital part of the tattooing process for these enthusiasts is the ritual cleansing of a previously oppressed body, mind, and soul.

When inspecting the ages of enthusiasts citing affect management as a motivator of their tattooing practices, I noticed that the distribution was relatively bimodal. That is, enthusiasts were overrepresented in the 18-to-22 and 35-to-55 age categories. For the younger category of tattoo enthusiasts, tattooing may help manage emotions frequently experienced through (but not exclusive to) specific stages in the life course, including a lack of confidence in the range of one's abilities, uncertainty about one's future, confusion about one's career choices, or fears about one's sexual attractiveness. In the words of enthusiast Gus (28):

There was a period there for about six or seven months when my whole life was in doubt. My job sucked so I quit, and the whole thing looked like it was going down in fucking flames. I was busy doing nothing, spinning my wheels and getting nowhere fast. I don't think you could call it a deep depression or anything, cause that's not serious enough to describe the shit I was feeling. I was suicidal almost every day, and desperately searched for something to keep me going ... I went into this tattoo shop [in Toronto] with a buddy of mine who was being tattooed, and after I started flipping through the pages of the portfolio in the lobby, I started to think about tattooing. The bodies on those pages looked powerful, and everyone in the photos was smiling like they just won the lottery. I wondered what about it was making them feel so happy. I found out exactly what they were feeling when I got tattooed for the first time, as a rush of power came over me and all the ways that I felt limp in life were gone.

For the older age category of enthusiasts – as some suggest, the fastest growing population of enthusiasts in Canada – tattooing the body with symbols can be a resource for socially displaying emotional strain experienced in later stages of the life course. A tattoo enthusiast named Ernie (41) stated:

After my first heart attack, I started to get in touch with my body. I never exercized or dieted, and when 'the big one' almost killed me I had to go through a long process of recovery. Monitoring yourself [body] every day makes you really think about your relationship with your body parts in every detail. My mentality about my body turned right around from defence to pro-action ... Up until the day I was tattooed I felt like a prisoner in my own body, just like I was waiting to hear from the doctor about what was wrong next. I thought I was going to have another heart attack from all the stress. Instead of waiting around for people to tell me how my body was going to get sliced open or taken apart, I found a way to make my body do what I wanted.

Where the younger generation of enthusiasts are (in some ways) unconcerned about the deviant status of the tattoo, older enthusiasts are keenly aware of its traditionally deviant standing in Canada. Given relaxed social codes about the body, the revitalization and professionalization of the practice, and prevailing social discourses espousing the personal healing potential of tattoos, older enthusiasts find ways of justifying their involvement in tattooing.

By citing personal growth or affective management as germane to their tattooing practices, these enthusiasts offer a central denial of the status of social victim. Rather than passively responding to negative stimuli or the removal of positive stimuli in their lives, enthusiasts grasp the opportunity to work through their feelings through tattooing. By flatly denying the existence of any victim in the process, enthusiasts discursively construct their tattooing practices as methods of managing emotional strain. This process of self-healing reflects broader cultural pressures to engage in inner restraint or control. Tattooing replaces other forms affective display that may weaken or sever interdependencies with others – asserting, again, that forms of body modification like tattooing are highly interpersonal acts.

The use of tattooing to work through emotional experiences seriously challenges Gottfredson and Hirschi's emphasis (1990) on 'persistent heterogeneity' or 'cumulative continuity,' while supporting Sampson and Laub's understanding (1993) of how individuals' involvement in (or attitudes toward) deviance changes over the life course. As body habits transform over time in response to life-course transition, shifting interdependencies, and the experience of affect, sensibilities about tattooing are reconstituted. Involvement in this 'deviant' practice may occur at any age, regardless of one's previous history with deviance or past perspectives about tattooing. The past is not prologue, and individuals do not neatly conform with age-curves or models predicting involvement in the deviant practice. As involvement in tattooing can be justified on the basis of confirming bonds or managing negative affect, Elias's understanding (1994) of interdependencies and their role in influencing understandings of behaviour is a better-suited conceptual model (i.e., in comparison to the discussion of social bonds in deviance literature) for analysing tattooing practices.

In a manner that reaffirms other central tenets of figurational sociology, narratives that highlight how tattooing is used for affective display illustrate how bodies are increasingly rationalized through civilizing processes. The skin is utilized as a communicative text upon which personalized messages about the individual are written. As significant as personal motivations to become involved in tattooing are for grasping the sociological significance of the practice in Canada (and how its outsider status is veritably negotiated), of equal importance is a recognition that established cultural habituses in Canada direct specific uses of tattooing; in this case, as a high degree of inner restraint is required and rewarded, individuals utilize tattoos as signifiers of one's *ability to conform* with cultural edicts (i.e., manage your emotions, don't lash out at others, act in a dignified way, and be in control of your mind, heart, and body). Tattooing is, then, appropriately viewed as a form of mimesis – a body technique designed as a controlled decontrolling of emotional controls.

These flesh journeys of Canadian tattoo enthusiasts represent personal status passages and the ritualistic purging of emotional strains. Ultimately, how publicly an individual chooses to display the passage is unique in each case. A status passage can be kept private and hidden, being shared with only a few intimate others, or may be discussed openly as a means of encouraging others to explore the potential for personal growth associated with tattooing. In either situation, tattooing is both an inward and outward symbol that the person has made a conscious life choice that binds him/her to a desire to move beyond a former identity or experience.

3. Individual Difference

Being and looking different is a widely promoted cultural goal in Canada and in other Western figurations (Simmel 1957, 1964). Whether we are discussing achievement in school, success in the workplace, or distinction in sport, being noticed is an overarching desire for many Canadians. The search for distinction through body modification (Camphausen 1997; Davis 1997a; Featherstone 2000; Pitts 1998; Shilling 1993; Woodward 1997) conforms well with a matrix of established cultural codes detailing how corporeality is to be experienced and represented. Even though it supports dominant consumer discourses about doing identity-work through the body – which tend to homogenize corporeal styles and body shapes (Featherstone 1991; McRobbie 1994; Muggleton 2000; Redhead 1997, 1998) – tattooing can be justified by enthusiasts as part of a private quest for individuality. The rejection of the tattoo as an outsider practice is asserted once more, as enthusiasts interpret their involvement in tattooing as a normative means of personalizing the self through body alteration.

The discussion of one's motivations around the theme of individuality provides enthusiasts with what Hewitt and Stokes (1975) might describe as a 'sin license.' If this outsider form of body modification can be articulated as part of one's pursuit of a genuine (i.e., personally meaningful) way of expressing the 'inner self,' then the practice may be wholly justified. If wrapped in catch-phrases or clichés about capturing meaning or authenticity in life, then the tattooing process is cleverly packaged as a form of cultural conformity. Temporary breaches of class-based body codes are permissible, since the body project is construed as a bourgeois form of self-improvement.

For example, some enthusiasts stated that tattooing represents a desire to expand the cultural boundaries of personal expression and creativity. Feeling that they are prisoners of popular culture, enthusiasts claim that people are limited in the potential range of personal (bodily) expressions available given established Canadian mores. Ironically, while they believe that Canadians are more tolerant of varying cultural beliefs and expressions, they perceive individuality to be in decline in the modern global village, at a time when spatial areas and cultural differences are merging, blending, and losing their uniqueness. In other ways, these individuals feel encumbered by the social rules and regulations brought upon them by the increasing number of 'rational social relationships' (Simmel 1964) they are subjected to in daily life, relationships they feel forced into on the basis of 'social obligation' (such as work relationships). As the sense of community is in decline in the modern urban metropolis, and as people are being dehumanized through mass-marketed body products, some enthusiasts are searching for a method of re-injecting authenticity and personal identification into corporeal practices: 'See this, all of this, this is about me and nobody else. This is like, like another way to introduce myself, another name I have. No one else will look like this, ever, because the designs I have done are custom, that's what I believe in ... It's like another signature or thumb print, it's all about me' (Brian, 27).

For this reason, the tattoos some enthusiasts request are predominantly custom-made. Tattoos are typically designed for (and sometimes by) the individual, taking into consideration the specific biography of the person, the contours and shape of his/her body, and artist-client negotiated ideas about the aesthetic appearance of the prospective work. In a world in which we are often defined by a very specialized job role or task we perform, as the basis of our social identity (see Elias 1991a, 1994; Simmel 1964), wanting to further customize our selves through tattooing makes clear cultural sense:

> Every person who walks through the door comes in because they're searching for something. My job is to lead them down the path of discovery. I have to get to know them, to become friends so I can get into their heads

and help them become who they want to be. So, I think a body mod artist needs to be a shaman, a healer, and a soothsayer that guides a mystic journey ... The mark that remains in the skin is only the end of the process, man, it remains when the journey is over, or to mark that it [the journey] has only begun. That's why I don't tattoo designs off the wall, and it's why we sit down together and draw out something unique for every soul who walks in here. (Andrew, 29)

Again, this fits well with contemporary middle-class sensibilities about tattooing – in that the client purchases the services of an artist who facilitates the individual's flesh journey. Just as the plastic surgeon is a trained flesh artist, a tattooist is a mediator between what individuals perceive themselves to be and what they wish to be:

If you boil it all down, my job is to help people realize their visions. Somebody comes in and has something in their head. It might be a very specific image, but it could be this general style that they like or even a really vague feeling they want to turn into a tattoo. In my opinion, that's what makes a good tattoo artist, someone who can think up art that will help people along with that process. Anyone can trace a design someone brings in but not everyone can sit down and listen to the *person* wanting the tattoo ... Plus, if you can't do that nowadays, and just tell people what you can do for them and that's it, then you aren't going to last in business long. People are really particular, and if you can't meet their demands then someone else will. (Stan, 27)

The motivation to assert individuality through tattooing is also evident among enthusiasts who possess an interest in permanently etching an especially meaningful one-time event on their bodies. For some tattoo enthusiasts, this may be a commemoration of a distinguishing achievement at work:

I had my 'eyes on the prize,' so they say, for close to six years. I'd been busting my ass to become a junior partner in the firm and after a lot of hard work and luck, my ship came in. I'd promised myself I would take a long trip to Tahiti and get a tattoo of the scales of justice to celebrate. As soon as I got back from the trip, my arm was bare and the ink was going in, baby! (Gordon, 39)

In other cases, the tattoo is an indicator of a status passage through a 'first-time event' that symbolically separates the person from unspectac-ular others:

> After three years of pretty intense training, and a shitload of money, I got my pilot's license and was able to take my first solo flight. If you think about how many people fly everyday, but how few people actually know how to fly a plane, it makes you feel like one in a million – because you really are one in a million. It's not like driving a car, right. Everyone can do that and we take it for granted. How many pilots do you know though? ... I have a car-toon drawing of a plane with a cigar hanging out of the propeller as my gift to me. It's all about that day I finished my task and could say that I accom-plished what I set out to. (Gwen, 27)

In the above instances, enthusiasts attempt to differentiate themselves from others by marking specific images on their bodies. Rather than viewing their corporeal inscriptions as symbols of deviant Otherness or blasé acts of cultural conformity, they interpret the tattoos as marks of positive distinction:

> I've never considered that I've ruined myself or anything like that because I have a few tattoos. Each one I have, as we have been talking about, is not only a part of me now, but it reflects a part of who I am. And I mean, if you are doing it for those reasons, how could anyone gripe with you about it? I think, well, as long as you are getting inked for yourself and not to shock the shit out of your parents or something, you've got your head on straight. (Mary, 25)

But if we are to conceptualize tattooing body projects as the search for authenticity and personal meaning (i.e., individuality), then this quest must be located within broader webs of interdependencies and processes of human interchange. As individuality is *only* achieved in a group context (Elias 1978, 1983, 1991; Simmel 1964), a personal sense of uniqueness is crystallized in reference to others' ideologies, practices, and identities. Notice the above comments made by Gordon, which indicate that his sense of individuality was affirmed by the way his work-related success differentiated him from others; similarly, the way Gwen commented that her ability to fly a plane sets her apart from the crowd – with her distinction from others further shown by her involvement in the tattooing process. What makes the tattoo unique (and therefore rep-resents the uniqueness of the self) is the fact that while anyone could have selected the particular image in the process of self-redefinition, these individuals view their tattoos as unique because *they* chose the tattoo and attributed a highly personal meaning structure to the mark.

Yet these enthusiasts conspicuously refrained from discussing how their tattoos conform with established understandings of the body as a text of identity – particularly, in relation to dominant class- and gender-based body codes. Female enthusiasts might, for example, proclaim a sense of individualism through tattooing practices, but closely conform with established codes about acceptable female body play. Although sociologists have examined the increased participation of women in tattooing, and the variation in the tattooing styles worn by women (DeMello 2000; Mifflin 1997; Sanders 1991), few note that women *still* typically select smaller tattoos in comparison to their male counterparts. Moreover, while more women are choosing to have their full bodies tattooed or large segments of the skin filled with tattoos, contemporary female enthusiasts generally choose images encoded with established Western constructions of femininity. For instance, common images include flowers, dolphins and other docile creatures, abstract art, and cosmic imagery (suns, moons, and stars):

> A ring of flowers around my ankle looks a lot more like 'me' than a skull and dagger or a pair of dice with flames coming up from behind them. I'm a girl and I feel comfortable looking like one. I'm not a butch. I have friends who have permanent make-up and that's the same exact thing. My tattoo is kind of like a piece of jewellery that I got to design myself that won't get stolen. I won't lose it someday, and it won't get broken if I hit it against something. (Roma, 23)

The middle of the lower back is the most common location for tattooing body projects among females (38% of the females in this study had at least one tattoo on their lower backs, 33% on their hips or stomach area, 30% on their ankles, 17% on their upper backs/shoulders, and 7% on their arms), mainly for concealment purposes. Even though female participation in tattooing has ascended to unprecedented levels in the past ten years – and with it speculation about the degree to which established gender-based body codes are decaying – one cannot ignore that female enthusiasts often pursue individualism through tattooing *within the parameters* of established femininity in Canada. Hence, established constructions of femininity are visibly reproduced through the tattooing process.

If we compare women's tattooing practices to those of their male counterparts, we see that men equally conform to pervasive gender codes, as they relate to the body, through the tattooing process. Still, Canadian men's tattooing projects tend not to be underpinned by an impetus of concealment – quite to the contrary. For Canadian men, especially those professing that an ongoing quest for individuality is the ideological structure supporting their body-modification practices, tattooing the arms is standard. Among the tattoo enthusiasts I interviewed, 72 per cent of the men had at least one tattoo on their arms, with other popular locations including the upper back/shoulders (41%), chest (30%), and calves (22%). While the practice is often analysed as the product of blind conformity to the cultural association between masculinity and toughness/bravado, tattooing (often in large designs) across these parts of the body tends to symbolize many Canadian men's sense of freedom to pursue a plethora of body-modification activities. In this sense, men actively tap into the cultural permission (and sometimes expectation) they are given to experiment with the skin, and display their projects quite publicly:

> Here I am, I turn twenty a couple of years ago and every one of my friends is getting some kind of ink. All of their girlfriends are asking them what they are going to get, people ask them all the time to see the tattoos they already got. Just about, well, let's see ... yeah, if I count it, like probably ninety per cent of them have tattoos done on their arms. Usually it's right at the biceps on the outside, or smack in the middle of your outside shoulder. It just looks cool there, you know. When I meet a guy and he says he's tattooed, you can almost put money on it that's it's on his arm ... Men are like that, that's where we get them. It's tradition for guys who get tattooed. If you're a guy, and are going to get tattooed, why feel ashamed about it? Chicks are into it, your buddies all have them there, so what's the big deal? I don't think anyone has ever stopped a guy with heavy tattoos and said, 'Man, why did you ever get that on your arm?' You might get a tattoo on the back or something later, but that's when you've already had a couple on your arms already. (Kevin, 23)

Therefore, the pursuit of what enthusiasts interpret to be a quest for individuality should not be taken as a confirmation of tattooing as a socially isolated body project. Despite the justifications and rationalizations enthusiasts offer about their tattoos as declarative acts of individuality, we must not lose sight of the fact that these understandings are circulated and popularized in accordance with established social norms about bodies and their modification – be they bound with cultural sentiment reflecting gender-, class-, sexual-, or religious-based ways of viewing the world. Justifications whirling around the premise of individuality are learned and intersubjectively promoted by enthusiasts in Canada, especially in relation to established discourses encouraging individuals to be different (while conforming!) through body work. Once more, the deviant status of the tattoo (or, more generally, the tattooing body project) is rejected in favour of a position supported by culturally positive goals of self-improvement, self re-definition, and personal growth.

Almost uniformly, by renouncing the tattooing practices of those who appear to modify their bodies without similar motivations and justifications, enthusiasts draw in-group boundaries between the established and outsiders in the tattoo figuration. Definitions of tattooing as a deviant social practice are not denied outright, but rather are negotiated by demarcating established (i.e., normative, culturally conforming, individually beneficial) from outsider (i.e., destructive, hedonistic, or devoid of meaning) uses of the tattoo. Self-defined meaningful tattooing projects, for instance, are judged against those deemed to be meaningless by established middle-class enthusiasts. Whereas the long-standing deviant uses and meaning structures attributed to tattoos (as a form of cultural disaffiliation or resistance) were the historically established interpretations in the figuration, the current middle-class generational encroachment into the figuration poses a significant contestation to these codes to the extent that they are now 'outsider' perspectives in contemporary practice.

By speaking with tattoo enthusiasts in Canada, I noted that justifications and corresponding sensibilities about tattooing are learned during different stages of the life course. Rather than suggesting that predispositions toward tattooing behaviour are formed early in life – rearing their heads in response to key transitions – we must view motivations toward tattooing body projects as malleable. Given unanticipated twists and turns in their lives, individuals often find themselves involved in tattooing quite to their own amazement. Through ongoing sociogenic and psychogenic processes, habituses and resulting body habits are formed over time in unanticipated ways. Illustrating how and why individuals turn to forms of social deviance at various forks or transitions in life trajectories, an examination of enthusiasts' motivations and justifications brings to the fore how discursive techniques are drawn upon in the process of socially managing one's involvement in tattooing.

CHAPTER EIGHT

Shame, Social Control, and Display

One cannot spend extended periods of time in tattoo studios, or living as a tattoo enthusiast, without coming to the realization that people who inscribe tattoos into their bodies often fear negative reactions from others. As shown in the last chapter, narratives provided by tattoo enthusiasts detail how they may construct discursive strategies to minimize or deflect these negative reactions. By justifying the practice with personally significant motivations, enthusiasts often portray their body projects as deeply meaningful cultural expressions. Although scores of enthusiasts actively seek out condemning reactions from people as a means of drawing attention to ideologies of cultural resistance or contempt, their more conforming fellows may regularly avoid public disclosure of involvement in tattooing in fear of stern reprisal.

For some enthusiasts, exhibiting a tattooed body is a precarious social practice. Unsure of how others will interpret their predilections for tattooing, enthusiasts may refuse to display tattoo body projects in most social contexts. Of central concern for these enthusiasts is how and when non-tattooed others will deconstruct tattooed skin as a breach of established body practice. Worried that a tattoo will be interpreted as a sign of a personal inability to conform with social norms and mores, some enthusiasts participate in a series of interaction rituals geared toward protecting their statuses among norm-abiding people.

In the following discussion, two principal themes are addressed in the process of exploring how social life is experienced by a tattoo enthusiast. The analysis is based on how tattoos are incorporated into an enthusiast's sense of self, and on the contexts within which tattoos are wilfully allowed to be read by others. Attention is then directed to the processes through which body-modification projects become purposefully com-

municative gestures. Importantly, if established cultural readings of tattooing tend to underscore the lack of respect the practice enjoys – and
some enthusiasts are adamant about distancing themselves from pejorative labelling – then specific techniques of concealment should be utilized in managing their physical stigmata. As discussed here, for those
enthusiasts especially sensitive to negative reactions from significant
others, carefully regulating the physical appearance of a tattooed body
becomes part of an everyday regimen. Conversely, for enthusiasts who
do not view their tattoos as especially discrediting (such that they feel little shame or embarrassment about their physical modifications), negative reactions from others can be interpreted as either a fringe benefit
or a trivial annoyance unfortunately associated with the practice.

Tattooing and the Reflexive Self

A substantial amount of investigation into the lives of tattoo enthusiasts
is not required to forge conceptual connections between tattooing and
the self. Even if extant sociological research on tattooing (e.g., DeMello
1993, 2000; Mifflin 1997; Irwin 2000; Sanders 1989; St Clair and Govenar 1981; Steward 1990; Vail 1999) failed to address the impact of
the inscriptions on one's self-conception, one does not have to make
a dramatic theoretical leap in conjoining the study of tattooing with a
person's sense of identity. As Sanders wrote: 'Tattooees consistently conceive of the tattoo as having an impact on their definition of self and
demonstrating to others information about their unique interests and
social connections ... [A]ll interviewees spoke at some length about
their social experiences with others and how the tattoo affected their
identities and interactions (1989, 47).

Yet it is worth mentioning that those sociologists curious about the
nature of self-definition and physical representation through tattooing
are largely indebted to the 'sociologies of everyday life' – to name a few,
hermeneutics, symbolic interactionism, ethnomethodology, dramaturgy, phenomenology, and existential sociology. Indeed, the pioneering research statements on tattooing by Sanders (1989, 1991), Vail
(1999), and DeMello (2000) are either squarely or loosely located
within the theoretical traditions of symbolic interaction (Blumer 1969;
Mead 1934) and dramaturgy (Goffman 1959, 1963). Holding firm to
the idea that the self is substantially moulded through the course of
human interchange, sociologists employing one (or a combination) of
the aforementioned sociologies of everyday life generally assume that

one's identity is formed through reflection on the verbal and physical feedback offered by others in situated contexts of interaction over time.

It seems rather commonplace, but still essential, to assert that individuals acquire understandings of the self through social interchange. In Goffman's expositions (1959, 1963, 1967) on the importance of self-definition through social interaction, he suggested that the physical cues offered to others through scripted body performance are pivotal in shaping interpretations of the self. Like Mead (1934) and Blumer (1969), Goffman balanced his arguments on the assumption that the social self is a malleable product, subject to wilful manipulation through situated techniques of body posturing and display. to that extent, individuals are empowered to be their own agents of self-control. Unlike the majority of contemporary analyses of bodies, which claim that resistance to established body standards is the true method of corporeal liberation and agency (e.g., Bordo 1989; Fiske 1989a, 1989b; Davis 1997a; Pitts 1998; Rail 1998), like-minded sociologists of everyday life consider the normative body to be a text of endless social power and self-determination. Rather than pitting a passive individual against domineering and discriminative established norms about the body – common in critical readings of body modification (Balsamo 1996; Featherstone 2000; Woodward 1997) – sociologists of everyday life draw attention to the self-initiated techniques of bodily display engineered by individuals as intersubjectively accepted forms of social communication.

In these analyses, cultural habituses do not fade into oblivion. There are few social actors who are completely indifferent – in the process of either conformity or resistance – to diffuse cultural codes detailing what is more or less acceptable as established body display. These codes are replete with prescriptions confining the individual's range of body choices in regard to their gender, class, sexuality, and religion. The tendency, in the current era, has been to renounce the existence of dominant social codes or habituses as a method of illustrating the breakdown of established meta-narratives and of white, male, patriarchal systems of knowledge (Behar 1999; Deveaux 1994; Featherstone 2000; Mifflin 1997; St Martin and Gavey 1996; Seidman 1994). Simultaneously, though, claims are made about the existence of undeniably oppressive cultural codes that marginalize the body shapes, sizes, or appearances of particular groups – such as certain types of feminine bodies, ethnic bodies coloured by specific skin tones, or unrefined and profane bodies that reflect membership in the working class.

We must concur that in any cultural system an individual is given a finite number of normative options for corporeal projects – *regardless* of the degree of cultural tolerance or curiosity prevalent in a figuration. Since identity is not completely free from established cultural expectations, the self is clearly dialogical with established constructions of bodies (Elias 1983, 1996). If sociologists believe that the 'crisis of identity' is as pervasive as implied (Dunn 1998), that would preclude the possibility that intersubjective communication through the body is even possible. Even though cultural norms about the body (especially those relating to its modification) are loosening or being redefined, it is theoretical misdirection to contend that established codes about body performance and display have been reduced to social rubble. Instead – to reaffirm Elias's axial proposition (1991a, 1991b) that the self is best conceived of as one's sense of 'I' amidst extended groups of WE and THEY others – established cultural standards provide a matrix of interpretation for understanding one's individuality. Simply put, established cultural norms applying to all help provide a sense of individual identity within larger figurational webs.

By drawing upon a pronoun-based model of interpersonal identification, figurational sociologists (Dunning 1999; Elias and Dunning 1986; Elias 1978, 1991a, 1991b, 1994; Maguire 1992, 1993, 1999) suggest that the individual 'I' is formed in conjunction with understandings of the WE and THEY. The 'I' – not to be confused with a Meadian (1934) depiction of the 'I' – is located among a group of mutually identified WE others. Mutual recognition is accomplished through shared cultural systems, including forms of corporeal modification and display. In other terms, the interdependencies one forms over the life course provide the primary basis of identification and are, as such, central to the ongoing development of a person's tastes and preferences for body modification.

As we take into consideration the figurational embeddedness of the individual, emphasis should be given to the normative standards of body display one is exposed to and those that are eventually internalized. As individuals construct their own mosaics of interpersonal involvement (Prus 1997) with groups of others (families, schoolmates, peers, co-workers, social club affiliates, etc.), they pay witness to competing definitions of and reactions to established body play. It is through this blending of understandings that individuals formulate a key component of their habituses, and come to develop personal relationships with their bodies. Therefore, in studying physical performance as the process and product of everyday life, sociologists must consider the interweaving of the personal (self-definition and use of the body), interpersonal (social exchange of communicative gestures through the body), and socio-cultural (existing codes about the body and its display) in order to grasp fully the sociological significance of the body–self relationship.

Through the time I spent interacting with tattoo enthusiasts, they described how others' reactions to their tattooing projects are pivotal in altering their self-conceptions – and, as a result, how and why, in the course of everyday life, tattooing projects are revealed. Reactions to tattoos were mainly decoded by enthusiasts through a series of 'interpretive resources' (Gubrium and Holstein 1997) relating to one's 'I' and WE identifications with others. The statuses and roles an enthusiast possesses among significant others appear to be chief in providing a set of interpretive resources for gauging interpersonal reaction to tattooing projects. As Simmel (1964) suggested, with increased membership in diverse social groups one's sense of individuality is heightened. It became evident to me that drawing upon one's experiences as a mother, a lawyer, a loyal member of a religious congregation, an athlete, or a woman is integral in actively anticipating and assessing others' responses to a tattooed body.

From the moment that an individual begins to think about a tattooing body project, for example, other people enter into the equation. Stories provided by enthusiasts already discussed in previous chapters indicate that others may involved in the process of getting tattooed, or in directing one's motivation to be tattooed. Of equal importance is the idea that a tattoo enthusiast 'takes the role of the other' (Mead 1934) in predicting and interpreting the social reactions to tattooing projects. That is to say, while membership in social groups carves out a sense of individuality for the person, it also has a constricting effect on one's participation in activities like tattooing, which are still deemed non-normative in most social contexts. Based on previous interaction with others (e.g., sisters, fathers, daughters, schoolmates, or employees), including the exchange of physical cues and body language, individuals develop stocks of knowledge (Berger and Luckmann 1966; Schutz 1967) concerning others' attitudes about tattooing the body. From the onset, social reactions figure prominently in deciding how and when to participate in tattooing – including what image will be tattooed, the location of the tattoo, and the size of the design:

> I knew that if I went overboard and had the tattoo take up most of my arm
> or something, then people would go bonkers. It's quite a jump to make
> from having no tattoos to having this massive one. You have to ease people

into it, right, let them get used to the idea that your body is going to be different. I didn't want everybody to think I was basically saying, I'm not myself anymore ... So I started small and if I liked it, and people didn't get screwed up, I could always go back and get something bigger [on another part of my body]. If you let your friends know that you've haven't really changed that much, you can get into it as much as you like. (Rosalyn 22)

If I had come home and shown my dad a big picture of a naked chick riding a rocket he'd have probably slapped me in the head. But how could he argue with me about getting a maple leaf tattooed on my shoulder? I'm Canadian, he's Canadian, and what's wrong with showing how patriotic you are? We should all wear the maple leaf. There's a real problem with our identity in this country that way. No one I know seems to be proud to be Canadian, except in beer commercials ... When he saw it for the first time, I remember him telling me he didn't like that I had been tattooed, but he liked how well it was done, and he approved of my choice anyway. Now, when all his friends come over to the house and they watch hockey, he calls me into the room to show them my tattoo. He yells out, 'See that, that's my boy right there. He loves his country I'll tell ya.' He embarrasses the hell out of me, but at least he's not calling me a scumbag for having a tattoo. (Brian, 26)

Throughout my discussions with tattoo enthusiasts, they pointed out that several groups of individuals are typically considered when a tattooing body project is contemplated or tattooed flesh is displayed in public. While some individuals' opinions about or reactions to tattoos are obviously deemed more consequential than others, immediate family members, close friends (tattooed and non-tattooed), and co-workers play central roles in influencing the extent to which one becomes involved in tattooing.

Family Members

Across academic disciplines, it is widely accepted that the core of an individual's personality structure and corresponding self-identity is forged principally within the family through primary socialization processes (Elias 1991a, 1994). Irrespective of the theoretical orientation, research on social deviance has long correlated one's propensity to commit contra-normative behaviour with weak or malformed family relationships (Gottfredson and Hirschi 1990; Hirschi 1969; Merton

1938; Sutherland 1937; Thrasher 1927; Tittle 1995). It is evident that the socialization occurring in the home (and not simply that confined to the formative years of early biological maturation) plays a central role in creating rule-abiding attitudes. By the same token, individuals who value familial bonds tend to avoid the shame and embarrassment accompanying contra-normative behaviour (Braithwaite 1990; Elias 1994; Scheff 2001; Simmel 1964). Fearing repudiation from family members and a weakening of family ties, people tend to conform with norms, values, and beliefs promoted in the home – such that norm abidance becomes second nature or habit.

To this extent, some enthusiasts who possess incredibly close interdependencies with family members refrain from participating extensively in tattooing. Unless the practice is viewed as normative within the home, or family members are at least habitually tolerant of outsider body projects, enthusiasts generally restrict their involvement in tattooing. Their fear of negative reactions from family members (and anticipation of strained relationships) is grounded in several interrelated concerns. First, for most Canadian families, tattooing continues to be an exotically outsider social practice – demonstrative of one's affiliation (symbolic or otherwise) with social misfits. The prevalence of tattooing in Canada aside, most families containing one or more tattoo enthusiasts are first-generation tattooing families. Since tattooing is not normative according to established habituses in Canada, it is understandably met with some confusion and stereotyping – particularly among the forty-year-old or over generations, for whom tattooing has traditionally denoted membership in nefarious social circles. One tattoo enthusiast, Rena (23), stated that her inclinations to be tattooed were tempered by the fear that her modified flesh would meet with significant disapproval from her family:

> I wanted to get tattooed so bad. All my friends were getting them, and I had so many cool ideas about what I wanted ... like a band of turtles around my ankle, or a couple of Celtic fish on my lower arm. But dad always said that he thought women with tattoos look like whores. And he said that if people look at you like a whore, they'll treat you like one. My mom agreed with him, and even my brother asked me why I wanted to do it. My friend Marcy has a horny devil girl tattooed on her shoulder. My dad won't even talk to her anymore when she comes by the house, and has basically told me he doesn't want me to hang around with her ... So, when I finally screwed up enough courage to be tattooed with the Chinese symbol of

eternity and took the plunge, I thought my butt would be the best place because even in a bikini, my dad would never see it. I had a tough time hiding it from him for the first few days because every time I sat down I would wince and have to sort of sit on the left side of my butt. He's never seen it to this day, and I don't think I could ever bring myself to even tell him.

In Rena's case, she interpreted her family members' negative sentiments about tattooing as a form of social protection. By condemning the body project as outside the norm, family members attempt to impress upon the budding enthusiast the social importance of following established cultural practices within networks of interdependent people. When taking the role of other family members and viewing the tattooed body through their eyes, enthusiasts realize that tattooing is still perceived culturally as a practice that may close social doors and elicit a significant amount of stigmatization outside the home.

Second, and owing to the closeness of family relationships and their impact on the self, condemnation from specific family members carries more weight than other family members' reactions. In particular, parents' negative responses to or intolerant attitudes about tattooing are usually more troubling than siblings' or extended family members' reactions. Sixty-seven (73%) of the enthusiasts interviewed in this study feared negative reaction from their parents at some point in their lives, and suggested that such fear has strained the relationships. Believing that their parents interpret this breach of established body idioms as a sign of their unwillingness to follow social norms and rules (or as a more general rejection of authority), some enthusiasts go to great lengths to conceal their tattooed skin. For the most part, these enthusiasts keep their parents 'out of the loop' in anticipation that the tattoo will become emblematic of a radical self-transformation:

My mom still doesn't know I have a tattoo ... and I have four! She believes that tattoos are scummy, and warned me if I ever got one that she would wring my neck. I've always been perfect in her eyes, and I've really done whatever she wanted me to do no matter what. You know, I went to the college she suggested so she wouldn't be upset, I wore all the clothes she wanted, but I really wanted to go out and do something for myself. She loves me, I never thought twice about that, but I'm terrified about how she would feel if she knew I have tattoos. I have to show her someday, or she might find out by accident, but I'll wait until she's in an old-age home and she can't climb out of her bed to kill me. (Amy, 28)

In fearing such reactions from family members, enthusiasts may cleverly negotiate their involvement in the practice. For instance, by selecting locations on the body that are regularly covered by clothing, enthusiasts are able to pass as normal and remain discreditable deviants. They can further negotiate their involvement in tattooing by choosing an image that, if exposed to others, is not usually decoded as socially challenging or repugnant in any way. If, at some point, family members become privy to the tattoo, the enthusiast's self will not be overly (or negatively) associated with the mark:

> In real estate, the saying is 'location, location, location.' With my tattoo, the saying was, be 'safe, safe, safe' ... My whole family, we're dog lovers. And, by choosing to get a little Labrador puppy tattooed like our dog Chance, I knew I would be safe. I was right too, everybody in the house loves my tattoo, and even my mom now is talking about getting the same one on her ankle. She hated it at first, but she's really come around. I almost fell off my chair when she asked me how to get one, and what it feels like. Up until now she's hated tattoos ... I can't believe it. (Zara, 25).

As confirmed by Zara, the hope is that even if family members initially react to the tattoo with disapproval, their disdain will eventually dissipate into indifference, tolerance, or even respect. It is further hoped that since the marks are only small blemishes – and if the practice is backed by convincing justifications – previous family understandings of the enthusiast as a norm-abider will not be completely dislodged.

Third, tattooing may be socially hazardous if individuals fear that their involvement may precipitate a complete severance of bonds between themselves and their families – such that they would be asked to leave home, or communication between family members would be discontinued. Six (7%) of the individuals interviewed stated that they feared such stern punishment if they revealed their tattoos to their parents. Claiming that their parents possess rigid anti-tattooing attitudes, some enthusiasts hide their bodies in order to preserve their interdependencies. Furthermore, enthusiasts believe it is not the actual tattoo itself that elicits a harsh response, but rather the gesture of insolence connoted by body marking: 'I waited until I left home to get tattooed. My parents always gave me that line that if I was going to live in their house I had to follow all their rules ... It wouldn't have been a big deal to actually have a tattoo while I was living there, but just the fact that I went out and did it against their will, they'd have been really pissed off ...

I'm sure they would have told me to have it removed or kicked me out (Clarice, 26).

It may be argued, then, that based on established habituses in the home, enthusiasts do not encounter much tolerance toward their tattooing projects from family members. Possessing neither 'habitual' nor 'enlightened tolerance' (Stebbins 1996) about the outsider practice of tattooing, family members (mainly parents) have perspectives about this form of body modification that reflect established cultural habituses. Even though tattooing is not a grave violation of established norms, values, or beliefs, the symbolic gesture made by one's participation in tattooing is considered a foreshadowing of future involvement in more deleterious social transgressions. Tattoos are viewed as graffiti on the social temple that is the body. Defacing one's corporeal home in this way, in a highly visible and permanent gesture, is intolerable if it implies a commitment to other forms of social disregard.

Not all family members meet tattooing projects with negative sentiment. For example, brothers and sisters routinely provide key sources of social support throughout the processes of acquiring and living with a tattoo. To such sympathetic siblings, tattooing is clearly a form of tolerable deviance. Since they may be informed about the motivations underlying the body projects and may occasionally participate in the enthusiast's body-modification process, they possess enlightened perspectives about tattooing. For example, enthusiasts often travel with their siblings to the studios to be tattooed, which adds an element of moral support to the process:

> My brother went down with me to the shop on the day I was scheduled to go in and get it [tattoo] done. We have a very close relationship, he's my best friend. I didn't tell him what I was getting done, and it was hard not to cause he kept asking and asking. Mom begged me not to do it, but Charles [brother] talked her down and convinced her my life wouldn't be ruined by it. That was important because I'm the black sheep and he's the golden child, so if he said it was okay, then she would go along with it ... I still remember his face when he saw I planned to get the Kanji symbol for brother tattooed. He almost broke down right there in front of Stu [the tattoo artist]. I love him, and want people to see how lucky I feel to have him in my life as my brother. (Pete, 23)

Close siblings can also help allay the enthusiast's fears about living with ink, as they may constantly affirm the motivations underlying the project or convey that they are impressed by the tattoo – proving their enlightened tolerance:

> My sister has made me think so positively about my tattoo in the last year. After I first got tattooed, I felt kind of ashamed about what I did. I stared at my body and felt like it made me look used. I didn't show it to anybody, and even thought about getting a consultation about having it removed. She started to ask me about what it's like to have one, almost like out of the blue. She said she thought it took so much courage, and since she knows why I did it [marking the death of their mother], she said it was beautiful. I changed my outlook on my tattoo after that, sort of bit by bit. (Annika, 29)

Parents, themselves, may occasionally support the body project either directly – as in the rare case of providing encouragement to become involved in tattooing – or indirectly by refraining from voicing negative opinions about a proposed tattooing project.

Therefore, negative and positive reactions tend to be counterbalanced within the family. Whereas negative reactions from family members may not be sufficient to completely dissuade the enthusiast from acquiring a tattoo, they unambiguously influence how life as a tattoo enthusiast is experienced. Some enthusiasts live in constant fear that their discrediting marks will be discovered (regardless of the age of the enthusiast), while others' self-conceptions are affected only minimally. In other instances, the tattoos are disclosed years after being acquired, when sufficient emotional or geographic space is created between family members. Nonetheless, how family members tolerate tattooing figures prominently in an individual's self-image before and following completion of the body project. More so than with others' reactions, cues about the self given by family members are imprinted like tattoos on the individual over time.

Peer Groups

One of the cornerstone propositions in deviancy literature is that peers are instrumental in promoting pro-deviance definitions of behaviour (Tanner 2001). Irrespective of where we hypothesize peer relations to figure into a causal chain of deviance, the informal social support supplied by peers in the process of doing illegal, contra-normative, or immoral behaviour is critical in providing a person with situated understandings of their actions. While the family is the chief social unit considered in the tattooing process (in terms of others' reactions), peers are the social group among whom tattooing body projects are most regularly discussed. Believing that intimate peers are the most tolerant of all significant others, enthusiasts utilize their chains of friendship interdependencies as a means of gathering more open-minded (and flattering) opinions about tattooing.

Enthusiasts actively seek out reactions from both tattooed and non-tattooed peers, even though these by no means form a homogeneous set. When considering the social impact of their body play, and the image of the self emitted by tattoo projects, enthusiasts place a high value on the assessments made by either group of close friends. Since enthusiasts share intimate details about their lives with peers, and come to trust their reactions as empathetic, the opinions they offer influence how enthusiasts learn to interpret tattooed bodies socially. Billy (25), a tattoo artist, commented:

> When you get right down to it, my two best friends know me better than anybody else on this earth. They don't tell me how I should act, and when I come to them with a problem or something wacky I might be thinking, they give me their honest feelings. We know each other so well, you get to just trust them and their opinions ... When I even started thinking about getting a tattoo, way before I wanted to be a tattoo artist, I asked them what they thought ... like how I would look and if they thought it would be right for me. My buddy Mort gave me the thumbs up right away. Dan and Chuck, two of my best friends from way back, were mixed. Mostly because I wanted something big across my back and then talked me into getting a smaller design ... When somebody knows you real good and can tell you're not doing it on the spur of the moment, they should support your choice if they're real friends.

Enthusiasts believe that their close friends will provide the most honest and objective feedback regarding their redesigned bodies. This is especially true when enthusiasts discuss their tattoo projects among tattooed peers. For enthusiasts who have experienced a series of negative reactions from family members, tattooed peers are a refreshing change of pace. In sharing pro-tattooing perspectives, tattooed peers are mutual advocates of the practice. Although there may be some dissent about the images tattooed, or locations on the body selected for the projects, since people prefer different tattoo styles or admire tattoos strategically placed on certain body parts more than others, fellow enthusiasts are generally considered to be part of the 'own' (Goffman 1963). Enthusiasts share common physical experiences, know how the self is affected by negative reaction from others, and can appreciate the personal commitment involved in being tattooed:

> You can talk to someone with ink differently than someone who has never taken the needle. They know what it's like when some asshole stares at you on the bus because you have this mark on your arm that they don't care for ... When we talk about the work I want to get done, and they tell me they don't feel I should get this or that done, it's not because they want me to do what they say, or look how they look. Like my last tattoo, right, I wanted to get an orchid tattoo and after talking about it for hours with my friends, they reminded me about our road trip to Montreal ten years ago. After that I got it in my head that I wanted to get a road sign tattooed as a reminder of that trip, don't ask why. And that's the way it goes, right, like we can sit around and talk about our tattoos and exchange ideas without somebody calling us weird. (Jill, 34)

As Jill noted, enthusiasts consider their tattooed peers to be somewhat unenlightened sources of identity evaluation – but clearly seek positive affirmation of their tattooing projects from them nonetheless. Since they intersubjectively share particular body-modification attitudes and preferences, their corporeal practices are not viewed as outsider pursuits deserving of social condemnation. The fact that enthusiasts value the support offered by individuals similarly committed to this type of body modification illustrates, once more, that tattooing has not permanently gone mainstream.

Through processes of interaction within groups of fellow enthusiasts, important lessons about one's identity are learned. In some cases, the negative reactions experienced in other social spheres are offset by the support offered from like-minded tattoo enthusiasts. Concerns about one's altered body and uninvited feelings of cultural dislocation from established others are assuaged by the acceptance granted by fellow enthusiasts:

> Whenever somebody makes me feel dirty for having tattoos, I go down to the tattoo shop. All I have to do is start talking with the people down there, and all is good in the world again. They're so nice, some of the best people I've ever met. And you know, when you see different types of people being tattooed and realize it's something for a lot of people, you don't feel like

an island unto yourself. I'm not a bad person for having tattoos, but a few narrow-minded people try to make me feel that way because of their own insecurities about their bodies. (Claire, 27)

The significance of being involved with others in the tattoo figuration is further evidenced here. The more enthusiasts interact with individuals who share a perspective that the body is a canvas to be coloured, the more they come to envision tattooing body projects as normative. This partially explains the fact that, among the 18-to-25-year-old category of enthusiasts, tattooing is only marginally a outsider practice. This generation of Canadians, for whom tattooing has attained a quasi-normative status, has received more exposure to tattooed skin than any other in our social history. The increased prevalence of tattooing in this age group also illustrates the idea that the body-modification habits among younger generations of Canadians are dramatically shifting.

At the same time, tattoo enthusiasts experience a litany of reactions from non-tattooed peers. Non-tattooed persons' opinions of and reactions to the projects are deliberately sought for a number of reasons – all relating to the enthusiast's self-definition. Some enthusiasts actively elicit negative reactions from their peers as a means of confirming their status as free-thinking individuals (as discussed previously). The negative reactions from peers become a validation of one's sense of uniqueness among conforming others:

When people see my full sleeve [of tattoos], I know they wonder how much it hurts. You really do get used to it [pain] after a few sessions, but it's cool that when people are looking at my arm, their eyes glaze over and their brows furrow because to them the pain is unimaginable ... You feel that after a year or so of wearing your tattoos. Some say it's like a suit of armour. It's a symbol of strength among people who hate to feel physical pain. (Harland, 26)

In a conceptually similar way, tattoos may not be a symbol of personal deviance, but are intended to signify one's unique identity among peers who are deemed to be trend followers or uncritical consumers of mass-marketed body fashions and cultural proscriptions about the body:

You're not going to walk into a mall and buy this [points to tattoo] off the rack. People sit at home and watch TV, or go to school and people walk by, and they see what clothes they have on and then just go by 'em. I can't sit here and tell you that I don't shop at the Gap and Banana Republic, because I do, and I'll admit that ... No one else is ever going to have this tattoo though. I designed it and I tell people that when they ask, 'What is that anyway?' It's an abstract interpretation of a phoenix in flight, and it's all mine. When people see my body and it looks different from theirs, there's an automatic response to see me as more of an individual than a person who looks like they stepped out of the pages of a summer catalogue ... I have my own mind, and I want people to respect me. (Jamie, 25)

Narratives provided by tattoo enthusiasts also suggest that while non-tattooed associates' opinions and reactions are affirmations of the underlying motivations structuring the projects, they are taken with a grain of salt. Many enthusiasts believe that, without first-hand experience in tattooing, one simply cannot comprehend the psychological, emotional, physical, and social impacts of the practice on the self. The cues offered by non-tattooed others are not entirely dismissed, but are interpreted with this disclaimer in mind. Since non-tattooed peers are incapable of accurately taking the role of the tattooed other, reactions from the uninvolved are influential yet not monumental to the self.

On the other hand, reactions supplied by tattooed peers (positive or negative) are valued and closely incorporated into the self. In possessing what is believed to be an enlightened tolerance of tattooing body projects, fellow enthusiasts are utilized as pillars of social support. Reactions from tattooed peers are doubly meaningful in this respect, since intimate peers' evaluations of the self are significant, and fellow enthusiasts' opinions about tattooing are viewed as non-judgmental and experience-based. Positive (supportive) or negative (critical) reaction to tattoo projects from fellow enthusiasts come to be understood as both valuable and valid assessments of the self.

Co-workers and Employers

The reactions to tattooing body projects (experienced or anticipated) offered by co-workers can be more tenuous than those provided by members of other social groups. The primary concern for enthusiasts, especially in neo-conservative business environments, is that negative reactions from co-workers will interfere with their achieved statuses at work. In recognizing the steadily growing interest in the tattooing body project, some organizations have instituted policies prohibiting the display of tattooed skin in the workplace (Lienert 1998). While the constitutional validity of such policies is questionable (Drohan and Toneguzzi 1998; Lindores and McClearn 1998), enthusiasts must consider the implications of such a stigma on their career aspirations. For the most part, enthusiasts come to view their own tattooing habits as a form of intolerable deviance in the work setting – a profane form of representation carrying immediate career-related ramifications.

With only a few exceptions, the employed tattoo enthusiasts I interviewed expressed a degree of concern about how co-workers might react (or have reacted) to their tattoos:

> When I go to work I'm not there completely on my own terms. I feel like the company pays my salary, and therefore they get to tell me how to behave. That's the price you pay to get paid ... I work in an office as a personal assistant and if you come in looking different from all the stuffed shirts who hit on you all day, you can catch hell. You have to maintain a real business persona at work, and apparently you can't have a tattoo and be professional ... I've had nightmares about going to work naked – not because everyone can see my breasts, but because everyone could see the tattoos on my breasts. [The company] gives off this image like they're hip and young and urban, but we'd see how hip they are if I came in with a low-cut top on. I'd be the hippest girl on the unemployment line. (Laura, 24)

As the first line of corporate defence, co-workers operate as informal agents of control in the workplace. The majority of one's immediate office mates have no authority to administer company policy or punish transgressors, but they are the foot soldiers regulating corporate standards and practices. By instilling fear in enthusiasts' minds about their corporeal projects, co-workers act as liaisons between enthusiasts and occupational superiors. Rationalized warnings about the possible implications of one's tattooing projects are given, or constant teasing may suggest that the enthusiast risks being ostracized:

> One guy up the hall from me [in the office] saw me changing in the gym down the street. I never knew we both worked out there or I would have used a lot more discretion in the changing room. It's funny that I can't even feel safe while I'm on my own lunchtime. I felt like the kid who gets caught with his hand in the cookie jar – busted city. No one knew I had a huge back piece [tattoo]. I don't even wear white shirts at work in case they are even the slightest bit see-through. This guy's eyes bugged clean out of his head, he was really thrown off kilter. I didn't know whether to go over

and explain, or play it off like it was nothing. He hurried away so I didn't get a chance to say anything. Two weeks later, he starts making comments about my back in front of our boss. Nothing specific about the tattoo, more like, 'Is that something on your back?' or 'Is there ink on your shirt?' We've never really gotten along, and he's trying to hold this one over on me. I thought I met my last tattletale in the second grade. The truth is I don't know how they [superiors] would take it, but I don't want to risk it ... I basically grovel at this guy's feet and do whatever he wants, even though he's below me. (Gill, 29)

Depending, of course, on the size of the tattoo and the images inscribed on the skin, co-workers' derisions may have little effect on the enthusiast's daily regimen. If the tattoo is cleverly placed on a highly private part of the body, or tiny enough that it cannot be viewed easily, enthusiasts do not fret over reprisal from their superiors:

We have a 'no tattoo' policy at work, but it's never really been an issue. I work at a desk down in the basement of the building and I don't deal with the public everyday. They [company] don't want any of their employees coming in with sick tattoos on their necks or someplace in the open. As long as you don't get foolish, you're probably going to be fine. It's a 'don't ask, don't tell' rule as I see it. (Robin, 30)

If the tattoo is large, or may be exposed through the course of everyday movement or one's regular posture at a workstation, enthusiasts find debriefing co-workers (including one's superiors) about the body project to be an effective strategy. A tattoo enthusiast named Amber (27) approached her immediate supervisor before to being tattooed to test the waters and negotiate her involvement in the body project:

I went to my manager Doug and sat him down. I explained myself to him, and mentioned that I was planning on having a small tattoo put on my ankle. I was kind of scared since we have a no-tattoo rule, but we have a strong working relationship. I've made an impression on him that I'm a solid and dependable employee. He was so-so about it at first, asking me where I wanted to get it done, and what I wanted to have tattooed. I could tell he didn't want to give me his approval at first, and then I offered to wear a skin coloured band-aid underneath my nylons everyday to cover it up. I wanted one on my arm at first. I've seen so much beautiful tattoo art in magazines, and all the best work is on people's arms. Totally out of the question for me [laughs]. There's no way I could keep my job with a tattooed arm. That would never fly where I work ... My boss told me to come in [to work] sometime that week with a bandage on, and if it wasn't so noticeable he'd give me the green light. I wore one everyday and he completely forgot about it ... When it came time to get tattooed, he was so interested he even came down to the studio with me. I've never had a problem with it. I mean, sure, people were inquisitive the first few days after they knew I had one, but they haven't commented on it in, God, forever.

In recognizing that an individual's particular body habits may not be intersubjectively appreciated in the workplace, enthusiasts may restrict or negotiate their involvement in tattooing as a matter of personal necessity; that is, enthusiasts are not oblivious to their economic interdependencies and restrict their body-modification projects accordingly.

The impetus to negotiate one's involvement in this personally meaningful form of self-expression can create internal tensions for enthusiasts who perceive their conformity to body politics as a character deficiency (Sennett 1998). Enthusiasts frequently use the term 'selling out' to describe their sense of inauthenticity in the workplace. By complying with pressures created by established habituses in the workplace, enthusiasts compromise a part of their identities in putting on a front every day for co-workers:

I step into the elevator to go up to the eighth floor and I start to suffocate. I love my tattooed body and am proud of the way I look. I can't show people that at work, I have to be a soulless peon who fills in space at his cubicle, and can only speak when spoken to. I can put on a suit, but I can't put on another skin ... What really sucks is that I'm starting to hate myself. I was tattooed to make my body something more pleasing, and by covering it up, I'm not just denying what I look like, I'm denying who I am. (Marc, 32)

In Berreman's (1962) and Goffman's (1959, 1963) analysis of social interaction, the process of hiding an aspect of one's identity illustrates how the self is physically displayed in the front and back regions of a figuration. In socially presenting a false persona in the front regions of everyday work settings, enthusiasts push their authentic sense of self into the back regions of social life.

In other cases, enthusiasts do not fear being dismissed from their employment positions outright, yet are emotionally troubled by the potential loss of status following discovery of their tattooed bodies. Even where no formal policies or standards prohibit an employee in an office from being tattooed or displaying a tattoo, the body project may still be a significant breach of middle-class workplace convention. As in Weber's classic understanding (1930) of bodily discipline and work, and Sennett's more recent analysis (1977, 1998) of public body display, tattooing is a violation of established body idiom on the job. Through the stigmatization of tattooed bodies in the workplace the cultural status of tattooing as an outsider social practice is undeniably reproduced, since a tattooed body is labelled inappropriate and unprofessional. The association between tattooed skin and social outsiders is further highlighted, as the tattoo is interpreted to be a violation of established business etiquette:

If someone comes into the shop and I find out that they want a tattoo somewhere really visible like the hand, forearm, or high up on the back or neck, I try to find out where they work. If they have a job in a conservative business or have to meet with customers all day, I try to talk them out of it. In this business you need to protect people from themselves sometimes ... A girl came into the shop this week. A real nice-looking kid about eighteen or nineteen, probably in university or just started a real job and still green about life. And she wants, get this, she wants a tattoo on the front of her neck right above the collarbone. I shake my head and ask her if she is planning on becoming a tattoo artist or has just been sentenced [to jail]. That's a whole other league of commitment, my friend. I ask her why, and she stumbles around a bit, and it finally comes out that she saw it on a tattoo artist, and thinks it's cool. Ridiculous, absolutely ridiculous. She may think it's going to be no problem, and her bosses or teachers will be cool with it, but my experience tells me different. What's the matter with getting a small piece done for your first tattoo, and see how you can live with one? About five or six years ago, this guy phones me and starts yelling that he got fired because his boss gave him shit for the tattoo I put on him. He called me a fucking prick, and asked how I could let him do it to himself. It's like handing a loaded gun to some idiots and telling them to go and swing it around it public. You know, somebody is going to make you pay if you're irresponsible ... Now, I say who I will tattoo and where on their bodies, so if I don't think it's in their best interests and they won't budge with the location, I tell them to go see another guy. You can see all the tattooed people you want, Chief, that doesn't mean you can become one. It's pretty depressing I have to educate people about their own lives and remind them they have to live with it as soon as I'm finished doing my thing. (Archie, 30)

As deviance and social interpretations of the modified body are both contextual and audience-specific (and thus tolerated to varying degrees), a series of rationalized concessions or techniques of body management must be undertaken at work in order to hide a physical condition that may be completely unproblematic in other social spheres. While tattooing the body, particularly as a form of resistance, is a permanent transformation of the skin that affects one's life in all social spheres including work, we must remember that individuals often intend to reveal their tattoos only in the spare-time spectrum (except for, of course, tattoo artists). What is especially important, as the above stories suggest, are the constraining effects that work commitments have on the ways individuals may express themselves through tattooing projects. The line between spare time and work is not absolute, then, as individuals always carry the physical trappings of their preferences for tattooing with them on a daily basis.

Narratives provided by Canadian tattoo enthusiasts do suggest, however, that reactions from co-workers or supervisors (as part of rational social relationships) are not as deeply incorporated into the self as are those from family members (as part of organic social relationships). Since enthusiasts do not typically hold co-workers as significant others, they decode their reactions as inflexible middle-class sensibilities about how a body should be displayed at work:

> We strut around in little bourgeois shirt-and-tie uniforms and pretend that we are different from each other. If you said 'no more suits at work' we'd be lost. It's part of the capitalist mentality. You have to look this way to be one of us, and if you can't, get out and drive a cab. If these guys [co-workers] have problems with my tattoos, then what does that tell you? I'm not a stooge that fits the model of the go-getter. Sure it does. Hey, if they don't like who I am, they should have to deal with it. If they came to me and showed me my efficiency ratings were low, or my productivity had declined dramatically, they'd have reason to complain. I would correct my behaviour, because that's what I was hired to do. No one can tell me what to do with my body, and I'll be damned if it's the guy signing my paycheque who dictates how I should look. (Carl, 26)

Furthermore, enthusiasts see corporate policies about the body and its appearance as reflective of broader capitalist tendencies to homogenize corporeal experience and suppress cultural interests in bodily difference:

The rule my company has about tattoos is theirs, not mine. I thought we lived in a culture of choice. I guess that's the lie you're supposed to swallow. We don't appreciate difference in body shapes at all. I've learned that from being tattooed. It's the nature of our economy to find different physical shapes, isolate them, redefine them by our standards of beauty, and then sell it to millions of people. When it comes right down to it, we all look the same. (Ingrid, 24)

Thus, reactions made by parents, peers, and co-workers to one's tattoos are valued and utilized as measures of the self. It's no surprise that reactions from individuals sharing close affective relationships and interdependencies with enthusiasts are held in the highest regard, and are reflected upon with greater deliberation. Other interdependencies are neither ignored nor downplayed by enthusiasts, but are evaluated in reference to alternative criteria.

Reaction to tattooing projects, then, is experienced by Canadian enthusiasts in ratios. Since there seems to be a sliding scale of tolerance in Canada toward this traditionally outsider activity that is tilted in situated contexts of interaction, enthusiasts are presented with conflicting and complementary reactions to their tattoo projects on an everyday basis. In a process mediated by the sources supplying, the veracity behind, and perceived meanings of the reactions, enthusiasts contemplate a full spectrum of social cues provided about their respective selves. Some of these reactions have a lasting effect on one's self-conception. Negative reactions may dissuade one enthusiast from participating in the body project in the future, or may encourage another to accept the labelling, thereby stimulating the process of secondary deviance (Lemert 1967). If they are perceived to be impartial and genuine assessments, however, favourable reactions toward the body project are evaluated by an enthusiast and incorporated into his or her sense of self. By living with tattoos over time and experiencing a mix of reactions to them, enthusiasts can begin to predict when and among whom reactions will be favourable or condemning. Steering their public exposures of tattooed skin on this basis, enthusiasts further mould their body-modification habits.

Elias's idea (1983, 1994, 1996) that bodies are increasingly rationalized over the course of long-term historical processes is supported by understanding how Canadian enthusiasts experience cultural reactions toward their tattoos. Through accepting the idea that one's corporeal performances will elicit a range of responses from others, enthusiasts learn to anticipate how and when their tattooed bodies (and tattooed selves) will be tolerated. Whereas some tattoo enthusiasts feel free to participate in tattooing when bonds or interdependencies are severed (the form and content of the tattooing projects reflecting this), those feeling bound by extensive social relationships reveal markedly sensitive understandings of how reaction to tattooing affects the self. Their tattooing body projects become reflections of their relationships with others, and expressions of how others react to tattoos in specific contexts. The body is viewed thereby as the organic, living, moving self – a text for immediately communicating one's identity within dense cultural webs of human interdependencies. Since the body is modified through tattooing in self-directed ways, the resulting symbols are culturally interpreted as outer reflections of the true self. For both enthusiasts and their audiences, the symbols inscribed upon the skin are representations of identity given to be read by others.

Giving the Body to Be Read

Depending on the social scenario, enthusiasts may be more or less willing to reveal their tattooed bodies. As noted in the preceding discussion, thanks to the range of responses encountered over time, one learns when the exposure of a tattooed body is precarious social practice. Drawing upon a series of interpretive resources (used to evaluate among whom tattooing will be tolerated), enthusiasts select appropriate social contexts for displaying their tattoos. In brief, in perceiving how tattoos are decoded by parents, children, peers, co-workers, or those sharing interdependencies, tattoo wearers attribute significance to their body projects. Enthusiasts learn to interpret how their bodies appear to actors in the course of social interchange – including how others' decodings of tattooed bodies are both context- and audience-specific. Therefore, one's social statuses and roles largely influence the practice of self-representation through corporeal manipulation.

Yet the situated judgment to expose tattooed skin also reflects the motivations structuring the body projects. Enthusiasts deliberately bare their bodies to be 'read' (Barthes 1972, 1975; Fiske 1989a, 1989b) for a series of personal, political, and cultural reasons. For example, if one of the main goals underlying a tattooing body project is cultural protest, Canadian enthusiasts will likely reveal the body project to others and discursively explain the inscription as a form of resistance. This is not true in all contexts of social interaction, for even those committed to social protest through the skin are well aware that there is a time and place for effective dissent. Assessing when and among whom the resistance will be the most effective – and the least disastrous to their social interdependencies – individuals are selective about representing their ideologies of resistance:

> There's a responsibility that comes with having a tattoo that you can't understand unless you have one. Well, I mean, for people who have part of their life philosophies permanently scratched into their skin, you've got to be sensitive to other people's space. I wouldn't want to be at a party and have a person cramming their politics on me, or going on about their religious beliefs. Sometimes you want to go out in public and not have to deal with noise from everyone ... And I know when most people see the swastikas I have tattooed on my arms, they immediately think I'm a Nazi. They don't get it that it's one of the oldest symbols used by men, and I'm trying to steal it back as a meaningful cultural symbol. I hate all that white power bullshit, but I am not stupid enough to believe I don't look like that to people on the street. Most everywhere I go, I wear long-sleeve shirts, you know. (Doug, 26)

Keenly aware that public identity is routinely decoded with respect to one's repertoire of corporeal representations, enthusiasts committed to social resistance rely on past experiences to gauge when their ideologically coloured bodies will spawn interpersonal tolerance or hostility:

> Just because I treat my body like a message board, that doesn't mean this guy does, or that girl does. Why should I try to provoke a fight with somebody for that reason? I pick my fights, and if I can have a conversation with someone, like their mind is open to new ideas, then I'll show them mine. Some people aren't ready to rethink the way they look at the world, and it's not like I respect that or anything. It's about not wanting to hit my head against the wall while I'm trying to get them to change their minds. (Claire, 27)

Although restraint is occasionally interpreted as a form of self-denial or ideological submission, enthusiasts who utilize the outsider status of tattooing to engage in cultural commentary rationalize those instances in which tattooed skin is hidden as an unfortunate necessity. Enthusiasts are neither ashamed nor embarrassed about tattoos or the meanings attributed to them – quite the contrary. Depending on how deeply the tattooed skin figures into the person's self-conception, justifications are made regarding the benefits of hiding the true (socially belligerent) self:

A couple of weeks ago I was sitting in my room after a real depressing night out and broke down and cried. When I'm with my friends at the club, I feel so alive and free to do whatever I want with my body. Or I could be strolling down the aisle at the mall happy with who I am and how I look. All it takes is one person to burst my bubble. I know most women don't have their arms tattooed, and I accept how I'm different from them. I want to be different from them. I can't be sad about being different, I chose this. I was crying because I don't feel like myself when I hide my tattoos, when I need to look more feminine to other people. Why can't I be admired for what I look like? I had a blind date that night, and the guy shows up to my apartment. For one time in my life I decided to wear a tank top on a first date. My friend Josie assured me the guy was cool, so I get it in my head that I can be myself in front of him ... no surprises. He knocks on the door, I take a peek through the hole, and he's real cute. I'm totally revved up, and the door swings open. His eyes meet mine, and it's a click right from the start. He looks down at my arm and his expression changes from excitement to terror. What the fuck, I think to myself. Here we go ... again. We went out to play pool and his eyes are not going off my arm all night. For once, I'd have liked it if a guy stared at my tits ... I won't make the same mistake again. It's part of the job, as they say, it goes with the territory. I can look at my arms in private and get off in knowing I'm not a girly-girly, but it sucks that I have to hide it to get along with men. (Allison, 20)

The intended cultural discord underpinning the project does not come to fruition when tattoos are concealed, but the *potential* for the enthusiast to assert resistance remains. Such restrictions are viewed as only partial limitations, and actually reaffirm the enthusiasts' conceptions of the banality of Canadians' body practices.

For enthusiasts choosing to be tattooed in the process of declaring symbolic affinities with others, how and when they select to display the tattoo is contingent upon similar social factors. Here, the nature of the affiliation principally sways the person's decision to reveal tattooed skin. If, for instance, the affinity is something that draws envy from others, or signifies membership in a social group revered by many in a social figuration, the symbols might be shown with gusto:

I go into the gym for a workout, and for sure I wear a low-cut top to show off my tattoo. It's right up here on my back and you can't see it unless I wear something sort of low ... I play hockey and you can't see my face on the ice. Unless you're really into the sport, you don't get to know the players well. Names maybe, but our masks cover up the face ... I love the game but I'd be kidding myself and lying to you if I didn't admit that showing you're a member of the team doesn't have extra benefits. When we were kids we all used to wear our hockey jackets and pick up girls. Having a tattoo of the team logo is the same kinda thing. So many girls have come up to me in the gym and asked what position I play. I don't need an opening line, my tattoo is all I need. I figure, everybody is looking at everybody else in the gym, so if I advertise who I am, the sort of girls I want to meet will pick up on it. (Kurt, 22)

Of course, the marked body may not elicit favourable response if the symbols are highly abstract or open to myriad interpretations. This basic fact is taken into consideration when a project is designed, as images are chosen that carry preferred cultural meanings:

The worst part of my job is that I'm an artist, and everyday clients come in and ask for the same run-of-the-mill tattoos. I barely ever get a chance to test my boundaries and grow as an artist. They all want the same crap. For a few weeks in a row I might be doing Tasmanian devils or maple leafs. That'll stop for a month and clients all want Bart Simpson or a band of barbed wire. I'm convinced that it's more pleasing for people if they don't have to put mental effort into wearing a tattoo or looking at somebody else's tattoo. You have to really go out of your way to screw up what those tattoos mean, right. What else could a maple leaf stand for other than being Canadian? (Jack, 25)

The tattooed skin may more readily be displayed to others when in-group norms are such that individuals are expected to model their altered bodies publicly. Take, for example, membership in a youth gang or a deviant syndicate in which individuals place a high value on declaring their loyalties publicly. If the act is interpreted as a tool for fostering in-group cohesion and distance from the established cultural mainstream, displaying the tattooed body is compulsory social practice. Like donning braces, Doc Marten boots, or closely cropped hairdos in Punk and Skinhead figurations (Baron 1989, 1997; Hebdige 1979; Polhemus 1994; Young and Craig 1997), wearing the standard uniform of the tattooed body is a relished (and demanded) signifying practice:

> We're talking about a group of guys who were with each other all day, every
> day. The guys I used to run with, they did everything together. They stole
> together, got drunk together, beat people up together, had sex with the
> same girls, and lived in the same house. Having the same tattoo was no big
> deal. And, we all put it on our left arm, just about the bicep, no exceptions.
> We wore 'wife beaters' [T-shirts] all the time to show them off, and when
> we'd go to a bar to hang out, people backed the fuck off. (Quentin, 23)

Therefore, if intended as a universal and unabashed declaration of
social identity, the tattoo will be exhibited in most contexts. Where the
tattoo might draw condemnation from others – as a breach of established body idiom or sign of membership in outsider circles – this is offset by the personal satisfaction of being a loyal member of the group.

Yet not all affiliations consolidated through the tattooing process are
intentionally given to be read by audiences. Even though the projects represent interdependencies nurtured between people, they may be semi-
private relationships divulged to only a handful of privileged others. As
one example, the tattoo may symbolize a relationship that is meant to
remain secretive since it revolves around non-normative activities. Rather
than being considered an abomination of the body, the tattoo represents
participation in a social activity that is stigmatizing in and of itself:

> I'm not afraid of showing people my tattoos at all. I'm sitting here right
> now and you can see the butterfly I have tattooed on my ankle, or the stars
> on my arm. Being tattooed hasn't changed my life in that way. They don't
> make me embarrassed. In fact, I get stopped on the street all the time to
> get asked who did the work and how long I've had them ... The tattoo on
> my inner right hip is another story. It's a small tattoo of a ball gag and a
> pair of handcuffs. You see, I got into the leather culture in town a while
> back, and you don't make mistakes about showing your interest in leather
> culture recklessly. Some of the domme [dominatrix] women I know have
> tattoos, and keep them covered too. Part of it's that we don't share this
> side of ourselves with others, and it's nobody's business anyway. There's a
> mystique to keeping the practice hidden, like an underground flavour
> making it even more arousing ... I didn't get off a banana boat, though.
> Telling, or I guess showing, your friends you like to be restrained or
> choked in sex play can be a problem. It can cut you off from the rest of
> the world. (Erin, 27)

With public display of a tattoo, and bringing to light one's involvement
in deviance, the individual passes from the discreditable established

actor to the discredited outsider. Tattoos are best hidden, cherished as body ornamentation among groups of like-minded others and appreciated as esoteric symbols of difference.

Similarly, a tattoo can attain heightened personal meaning if kept hidden from a majority of others. Enjoying one's tattoo in semi-seclusion indicates how special the symbol is for the enthusiast. This is particularly true of tattooing projects intended to symbolize physically an intimate bond between family members or sexual partners:

> The tattoo I had driven into my skin isn't for anyone else except my wife and me. I wouldn't have sat in a chair going through that grief if I didn't know in my soul that we have been in love across time. I had this dream once that we knew each other in the Middle Ages. We were lovers from two families from different countries and ran away together to be married. That probably never happened, I know, but I feel an eternal bond with her and decided to put it on my skin ... No, I don't tell everyone about my tattoo, and barely anybody else has seen it up close. My wife and I sometimes stare at the tattoo, and she kisses her fingers and rubs them across it. How could I explain that to people and expect them to understand? (Stu, 27)

For these enthusiasts, disclosing the tattoo to others would violate the sanctity of the relationship symbolized through the markings. Opening up the possibility for outward criticism or condemnation of the tattoo as the symbol of the outsider could further reduce its integrity. In those rare cases wherein the tattoo is discovered by another, the emotional significance of the mark is rarely described:

> If someone asks me about my tattoos I don't feel obliged to give them a full story. I don't lie about the tattoo or anything, but if someone asks that doesn't mean they have the right to pry into my personal life ... If my shirt moves a bit or one of my pant legs rides up an inch or two you can see my tattoos as plain as day. That isn't an invitation to invade my privacy or an agreement to let somebody grill me about my innermost feelings. I do my best to cover them up most days, but I can't avoid it sometimes. They'll never get it [the meanings behind the tattoos] anyway. Unless they know me and some facts about my life, they're wasting their time trying to get in my head ... I would never even dream of walking up to a total stranger and asking them about what their necklace symbolizes or why they gelled their hair in the way they were wearing it. Bizarre, you know, some people are bizarre to me. (Lucy, 23)

For Canadian enthusiasts utilizing a tattoo to mark the passage from one self to another, the extent to which the tattoo becomes public domain is highly variable. Where one enthusiast seizes the opportunity to boldly boast he or she has successfully passed through a rite of passage, another recoils from social commentary. What distinguishes certain enthusiasts' preferences for public display, as in the cases above, is a willingness to have both the mark and the social connotations of the mark associated with the self. For Cole (27), a tattoo enthusiast who partially utilized a tattoo to symbolize his coming out, his tattoo is eagerly given for social consumption. However, as a narrative provided by Rachel (35) suggested, tattooing projects may be cautiously exhibited to a choice few:

> My tattoo is personally empowering for me. The visceral experience of being tattooed kick starts your mind, and you wake up about how much your body means to people. I always intended to walk around showing it off, but changed my mind about that only a few days after it healed. I got tattooed, and in some ways that was good enough. Nobody needed to validate the fact that I felt changed and when I looked in the mirror, I saw a new person standing in front of me. I was transforming from the outside in ... I was tattooed in the process of reclaiming my femininity, as we discussed, and I took charge of how my body was going to look. Changing your body shape, or the way it is coloured, sinks into who you are in your heart. I don't have a flair for the dramatic, so a tattoo is a good place to start ... Having other people see a strong woman with a tattoo is important to me sometimes. I won't pretend that being tattooed doesn't mean something to me as a woman, as someone who you don't expect to see with a painfully scarred body. When I'm in a group of men and they're acting all macho, I might roll up my sleeves and let them see I'm tougher than them. It may sound like a pissing contest, but men need to learn women can challenge them physically – it's healthy.

Social context and audience are equally important in these cases. If individuals involved in a situated context of interaction are deemed capable of empathically grasping the motivation behind the tattoo, the body is exuberantly given to be read. However, if the enthusiast does not share similar backgrounds, experiences, or body habits with those others, it is typically assumed that intersubjective understandings about the mark cannot be reached – and the body project remains concealed behind clothing or another physical prop:

I never let most people see the 'XXX' [Straightedge] tattoo ... Why? Who among us can really stand in my shoes and tell what it's like to give up all our socially popular poisons. Giving up the social devices like booze and drugs that give people euphoria isn't the easiest program to go through ... I choose to leave my tattoo under a shirt to save myself from being singled out by hypocrites and the self-proclaimed beautiful people. I might be called a skid mark because I have tattoo, but my life is a lot more pure than the guy shoving coke up his nose on the way to his office job in a big high rise. Go through the trials and tribulations of my life, and then we'll talk about my tattoo, my friend. (Carl, 26)

Depending, once more, on how centrally the status passage and its physical representation fits into one's 'master status' – or simply the main person they see themselves to be (Becker 1963) – these enthusiasts purposefully choose the terms under which full disclosure of the tattoo is given.

It is evident once again, then, that reactions to tattooing body projects experienced by individuals are stored in their respective memories, and are instrumental in orienting their everyday body practices. In plain terms, feedback from others is consequential for grasping how representational techniques impact the sense of self. In furthering the conceptual understanding of body projects as highly interdependent acts, we continue to uncloak the socio-cultural relevance of tattooing in Canada. If one attends to the way tattoos are experienced in everyday life, the *social* nature of the tattooing process comes plainly into view. By treating the body as a three-dimensional text of identity formation and dialogue, enthusiasts draw our attention to the uniquely human methods of, and reactions to, self-transformation. Through the process of interacting with tattoo enthusiasts, and developing my own preferences for tattooing in this process, I realized just how deeply perspectives about tattooing are affected over the life course. A significant part of developing an orientation to tattooing comes from experiencing life as an enthusiast – a fact germane to any social activity or form of physical transformation. Indeed, arguments presented at the beginning of this book outline how tattooing is theoretically comparable to other forms of corporeal modification – such that we may develop conceptual schematics to link together seemingly dissonant journeys of the flesh.

In extending the lessons I have learned about tattooed bodies, and the body habits of Canadian tattoo enthusiasts, I can propose a theoretical model of habitus (trans)formation. If we remember that habituses are both culturally and historically contextual – and as such transform in unintended ways over time within any given figuration – a working model for researchers critically interested in the social construction and deconstruction of body-modification projects may be constructed. Having the structure of the model upon a figurational foundation, our overriding goal is to lobby for concatenated research efforts on body modification alongside the ongoing development of integrated theories of the body.

CHAPTER NINE

The Body-modification Habits of Canadians

The purpose of my personal and sociological foray into the world of tattoo enthusiasts has been manifold. First and foremost, for close to ten years I have felt that a preliminary description and analysis of tattoo enthusiasm in Canada has been long overdue. Feeling that few have taken the subject matter seriously, I wanted to attend to the lived experiences of tattoo enthusiasts and to how they construct meanings about their body project. Second, through the exploration of enthusiasts' narratives about tattooing, and their self-described relationships with their bodies, I have sought to contextualize sensibilities about modifying bodies within broader sociogenic trends in Canada. Third, in conjoining the previous two tasks within the theoretical direction provided by figurational sociology, this investigation of tattooing in Canada emphasizes the interconnection between sociogenic and psychogenic change. Fourth, the case study of tattooing illustrates the more general benefit of examining body-modification practices through integrated theoretical ideas rather than narrowly focussed opinions or streams of theory.

Based on what I have learned as a sociologist/tattoo enthusiast, I firmly believe that figurational sociology provides a set of core principles for accomplishing the above tasks. Although by no means the only theoretical lens through which tattooing may be viewed, figurational sociology offers several central ideas for re-examining our body modification practices, such as tattooing. One of the cornerstone ideas in Elias's research (1983, 1994, 1996) on long-term civilizing processes is that through the sociogenesis of specific state formations, individuals in Western figurations have internalized a need to regulate carefully their public behaviour. As central states developed monopolies of violence and taxation in figurations, the major mechanism of social control shifted from external to internal restraint – largely displayed through corporeal performance. Affective outburst and repugnant forms of interpersonal display are pushed behind the scenes of social life, as demanded by established discourses and prevailing cultural habits. In these pacified social spaces, chains of interdependency are extended and diversified, economies flourish, people develop mutual recognitions (I, WE, THEY) with one another, and foresight becomes critical in formulating lines of personal and collective action. In studying the extent of a figuration's civilization, we look to the collective ability of its members to engage in highly controlled interaction.

Cultural habituses, then, partly change over generations to reflect our pursuit of a triad of social controls: control over nature; control over others' actions; and self-control (Elias 1978, 156). Whereas humanity struggled through the Middle Ages to master a working control over nature, later to be complemented by the pacification of violent social spaces (Elias 1994), the project of the last two hundred years has been that of cultivating self-control as the hallmark of 'civilized' personality structures (Dunning 1999; Maguire 1992). Self-restraint provides predictability in social life, a standard for behaviour in complex figurations that preserves and promotes the growth of human interdependencies. While Elias (1996) argued that individuals in Western societies have not reached the pinnacle of self-restraint or affective control, people do exhibit a high degree of civilized control in everyday social practice.

These axial principles of figurational sociology lay the conceptual groundwork for grasping how personality structures, or habituses, develop over an individual's life span. Furthermore, they furnish sociologists with considerable guidance for examining how established standards of behaviour develop into cultural habits over time. These processes, as examined throughout this study, are inexorably intertwined. Since we are born into figurations that precede our births, socialization processes tend to imprint established cultural tastes, preferences, and habits on us. While this does not preclude the possibility of individuals developing unique personality structures that reflect their individual biographies, it illustrates how social interdependencies are pivotal in shaping what becomes a person's second nature. In this study, emphasis has been placed on how body-modification habits form over the life course, and how people come to develop preferences or tastes for body projects like tattooing.

A working model of habitus formation can be constructed by analysing data collected on tattooing practices. The purpose of the model is not to reduce the complex processes constitutive of habitus formation to a series of causal factors. Instead, the goal is to provide an integrated model of habitus development that facilitates more extended exchange between those committed to the inspection of corporeality. Through his argument that individual personality structures are both similar and distinct in a given figuration, Elias directed our attention to how a habitus steers one's daily actions:

> This make-up, the social habitus of individuals, forms as it were, the soil from which grow the personal characteristics through which an individual differs from other members of his society. In this way something grows out of the common language which the individual shares with others and which is certainly a component of his social habitus – a more or less individual style, what might be called an unmistakable individual handwriting that grows out of the social script. (1991a, 63)

In order to examine critically the research on diverse corporeal projects and performances – that is, to press for substantive and theoretical integration across research efforts on cultural body play – a useful point of departure may be found in the specification of how and why body-modification habits are formed.

Conceptualizing Body-modification Habits

If one places a figurational perspective on habitus formation at the centre of the analysis, several theoretical perspectives may be synthesized to provide a more encompassing perspective on corporeal modification. Here, the model of habitus formation is structured around an individual's biological characteristics, figurational embeddedness, exposure to figurational discourses, and lifestyle interdependencies. The aim is not to reinvent the proverbial wheel (concerning theories about bodies and habitus formation), since much may be gleaned from existing thought on issues pertaining to corporeality. Instead, the proposed model is best envisioned as an attempt to summarize how our bodies, and cultural body habits, are socially constructed and experienced.

Biological Characteristics

In the contemporary rush to scrutinize the social significance of bodies, we must not forsake the body as it emerges biologically. While sociologists should be commended for 'rediscovering' corporeality over the past twenty years, we must be cautioned against limiting the analysis of bodies to their representations and textual deconstructions. Similarly, while research in the areas of gender, illness, and sport have taken the physical body seriously by exploring the body–self interrelationship, there has been a tendency to ignore the fact that human beings are born with bodies possessing natural characteristics – such as drives, impulses, and emotions. If we are to configure a well-rounded and empirically sensitive model of habitus formation, the characteristics and components of our biological bodies should be addressed in sociological theory.

The claim that we as a species are born with natural characteristics can be a slippery slope if it is used to reinforce exploitive social relationships or ideologies predicated on interpersonal discrimination. Claims about natural differences between groups can thinly veil the most insidious of pseudo-scientific 'truths.' For instance, the 'race logic' in sport is founded upon the principle that individuals of darker skin possess a deficiency in mental abilities and an abundance of muscular power (Coakley 2000). Manifesting in a system of structured inequality in sport – including the stacking of racial minorities in so-called non-thinking positions – the race logic is a product of social stereotype and bigotry. In a related way, so-called essentialist constructions of gender are underpinned by an assumption that men are born with natural characteristics and biological tendencies that make them more suited for leadership, social roles demanding strength and courage, and economic responsibilities (Bartky 1988; Bordo and Jaggar 1989). In this way established/institutional patriarchal systems of control are justified as natural forms of figurational order (Bordo 1993; MacKinnon 1987; Sanford 1992).

A theoretical balance must be reached between the body as a biological entity and the socially constructed body. In theorizing about corporeality, sociologists need to accept the idea that inborn drives and impulses are as important as social constructions of the body. For figurational sociologists, this recognition stands at the centre of an integrated approach to the habitus-formation process. More specifically, a fruitful point of departure for deciphering how body-modification habits develop over the life course is found in the idea that human biology figures into the assembling of personality structures.

The road to body-modification habitus formation is perhaps first paved by one's biological make-up (or physical characteristics), which we may refer to as a complex system of drives, impulses, emotions, and organic compositions. Humans are born with skin, bones, and organs that give us physical shapes and structures. However we are able to function as beings (i.e., to move, think, and feel) is directly related to our biological structures. Humans are also equipped with affects and impulses that steer conduct and provide a biological basis for understanding the social world (again, our ability to think, learn, and reflect). They influence how people perceive social interaction (including individuals' perceptions of their place in a figuration) and are key in facilitating ongoing learning and personality formation throughout the life course (Elias 1978, 1994, 1991a). Rather than suggesting that the individual is born, and then stuck with, a set of hereditary biological characteristics, we can best view humans' physical characteristics as malleable; thus, so too are habituses.

Yet an individual is certainly not born with an extensive desire to modify the body through tattooing, or alter its natural structure in many other ways – that is, to modify the body as part of performing culturally. However, people possess bodies that demand ongoing modification and maintenance in order to survive – including the intake of food or the securing of shelter (clothing and domiciles). We learn from an early age to protect and alter the natural structures of our bodies through primary socialization processes, not as culturally expected tasks, but as requisite functions (Elias 1994). When cultural techniques and preferences for preserving the corporeal are conjoined with a strong internal drive to modify the body so that it might prosper and grow healthier, the basic building blocks of the habitus are set in place.

As evidenced through the data collected on tattooing practices, biological characteristics play orienting roles in the (ongoing) formation of body-modification habits. First, body modification is actively employed by some enthusiasts in the process of managing potentially destructive drives and emotions. If one of the defining features of Western civilizations is that inner restraint is the major mechanism of social control, then those impulses or emotions humans naturally possess that run contrary to socially demanded self-control must be kept in check (Elias 1983, 1994, 1996). On a wide social scale, individuals learn to internalize the social benefits of curtailing affective outbursts or self-gratifying actions, as they may serve to injure a person's physical or social well-being. As discussed here, drive economies are transformed such that self-control is both a conscious and unconscious part of the habitus.

But as Canadian tattoo enthusiasts point out, inner restraint does not alleviate emotional crises or completely mute human impulses; it does not entirely remove feelings of anger, sorrow, or frustration from a person's life, nor will it prevent an individual from experiencing aggression or libidinal impulses. There are occasions over the life course when the desire to express impulses through body performance simply cannot be contained. For some Canadian tattoo enthusiasts, modifying the flesh is a controlled method of emotional decontrolling. Whereas cultural ideologies and practices maintain that the ability to regulate physical behaviour in public is a signifier of a person's social respectability, tattoo enthusiasts rationally employ the body as a text for publicly revealing a high degree of inner control. Physiologically experiencing emotions like rage, frustration, depression, or elation, some enthusiasts may tattoo their bodies as a means of managing feelings or drives in socially acceptable (or at least tolerable) ways. Tattooing, then, is a highly controlled healing mechanism for enthusiasts who wish to vent emotions that are typically pushed behind the scenes of social life. Contrary to the classic psychological construction of tattooing as a sign of a person's lack of self-control, the body project is a carefully orchestrated form of emotional dialogue.

Narratives provided by Canadian tattoo enthusiasts also suggest that tattooing may be sought out by people who experience overwhelming affect at key transitional phases of the life course. Wishing to express or overcome sentiments of anxiety, doubt, fear, dislocation, isolation, pride, or exuberance, a tattoo enthusiast may choose to modify the body through this redesigning body project as a tactic of emotion management during specific social-role transitions or status adjustments. Importantly, this process illustrates that not only are impulses naturally (i.e., physiologically) felt by individuals, but that the desire to express emotion is equally experienced throughout the stages of social life. Whether tattooing articulates trauma suffered following a sexual assault, death in the family, or divorce, modifying the flesh through this social practice is interpreted by some Canadian enthusiasts as a normative form of self-management.

Sociologists should not discount, then, the extent to which impulses and emotions figure into the personality structures of individuals. A core part of the individual habitus, biological characteristics cannot be dismissed as a psychological Pandora's box. Not only should sociologists devote attention to how biological characteristics influence body-modification habits, we must also understand how this relationship transforms over time in response to sociogenic change. The life histories of Canadian tattoo enthusiasts reveal how drives and affect are moulded through social interchange and dynamic changes in human interdependencies across periods of time. In truth, Elias's research (1994, 1996) on the long-term civilizing process is anchored by the proposition that, in this respect, human beings today are qualitatively different than (although not entirely dissimilar to) our ancestors.

Even more basically, we must recognize how cultural body-modification habits are affected by the actual ability to alter our physical selves. If we could not modify our bodies virtually at will, a discussion of body projects would be moot. But our flesh is permeable and subject to boundless structural change. Perhaps coinciding with our distrust in material absolutisms, the body has become a site of manipulation, creativity, and experimentation. Our bones and muscles may be broken down and rebuilt in more aesthetically pleasing shapes and sizes, and a significant portion of the habitus is formed upon this principle. One's body-modification habits are irrefutably linked to the ability to transform the corporeal with the aid of technological devices and commercial products. For example, individuals with darker skin have lagged behind in the contemporary renaissance in tattooing because the inks used in the process do not appear as clearly or with as much depth as in people with lighter skin. Other tattoo enthusiasts often refer to their bodies as canvasses waiting to be coloured in with tattoos. In people's search for individuality among groups of fellow human beings who possess similar body shapes, colours, and sizes, tattooing is a method of stamping uniqueness onto the skin. Or, in the case of individuals who cover scarred or disfigured bodies with tattoos to improve their aesthetic appearance (Atkinson and Young 2001), body-modification habits reflect the experience of bodily breach, invasion, or ageing over the life course.

In brief, as the biological body emerges in a number of ways, body habits concomitantly shift. In this respect, the habitus is accurately understood as a *process* rather than a static structure – illustrating that a person's second nature is both malleable and naturally fluctuates through unanticipated life trajectories that affect biological performance. Research on health and illness (Frank 1991b; Juengst and Koenig 1994) and the pain and injury process in sport (Young 1993; Young et al. 1994) teaches us that individuals learn to adjust their daily bodily practices following the onset of a physical pathology or some form of bodily implosion. By all indications, modifying the body to protect its integrity, repair any deficiencies in its performance, or enhance its natural appearance are common activities in human cultures. These activities stand at the base of one's habitus, and play a role in orienting individuals' perspectives about corporeal performances such as tattooing.

Figurational Embeddedness

Socialization processes are obviously one of the most significant contributors to the ongoing development of one's second nature. The lessons learned about corporeality and how to manage the emerging biological body partly organize an individual's understanding of physicality. In Bourdieu's terms (1984), socialization provides a system of instruction whereby individuals are exposed to techniques of 'bodily hexis.' Just as the mind is stimulated and disciplined through socialization processes, the body is brought under control by social agents (Foucault 1977, 1979).

It stands to reason that a person's body-modification habits are processually affected by changing interdependencies over the life course (Elias 1994). As an individual becomes more or less figurationally embedded, social influences on the habitus vary. For those individuals who are extensively tied to others through bonds, intimate relationships, or other meaningful forms of sustained interaction, a certain stability of influences on body-modification habits is to be expected (Elias 1994, 1996). While all individuals in complex figurations are relatively interdependent with one another (Braithwaite 1990; Durkheim 1951; Elias 1994, 1996; Simmel 1964), the stability of socializing influences provides a constant and generally consistent set of cues concerning appropriate techniques of body performance and display.

We should look, though, to how variation in figurational embeddedness alters the habitus over time. Research on social deviance is critical in educating sociologists about the impact on a person's behaviour of fluctuating bonds and relationships with others. A long-standing correlate with criminal or delinquent activity (Matsueda and Heimer 1997; Sampson and Laub 1993, 2001), a paucity of interpersonal bonds is often taken as a predictor of involvement in deviant behaviour. According to the seminal works of Hirschi (1969) and Gottfredson and Hirschi (1990), the social bond is the primary mechanism for instilling self-control in individuals. The more normative bonds an individual shares with others (particularly in the home), the more a person learns the benefits of restrained behaviour. Since the individual comes to depend on others, learns to share their beliefs, participates in normative social activities with them, and is emotionally tied to them, a high degree of self-control (i.e., the renunciation of activities that may be personally gratifying, yet jeopardize one's social bonds) results. If this personality 'switch' is not turned on early in the life course, one can expect that the individual will engage in an steady flow of contra-normative behaviours throughout adolescence and into early adulthood (Gottfredson and Hirschi 1990).

Figurational sociologists would take issue, however, with some social-control theorists' perspectives about the nature of self-control and affective restraint. By locating the early development of inner restraint in the family and other socializing agents, social-control theorists stress that bonds are immediately consequential in constructing a person's habitus. Elias (1991a, 1994) suggested that the family is the primary social group wherein inner control, foresight, and mutual recognition are taught. With instruction in the home, a person learns how to use the body in everyday life. Parents and siblings are the chief role models for the young person, who constantly learns how to move limbs, protect the body, and understand the social benefit of exhibiting inner restraint through corporeal performance. Body-modification habits morph as family members live and interact with one another, intersubjectively exchanging cultural body techniques and preferences for physical display.

According to my personal and sociological exploration of tattooing in Canada, the lived experiences of tattoo enthusiasts indicate that parents and siblings' perspectives on this form of body modification provide an orienting set of influences on the enthusiast's body-modification habits. Negative attitudes about tattooing may not be sufficient to dissuade a person from participating in the practice (although in many cases they are), but they clearly affect how an enthusiast interpretively constructs opinions of tattooed bodies. Even though enthusiasts may not entirely share family members' sentiments about the body project, their opinions are imprinted on the enthusiast's habitus. For example, tattoo enthusiasts may relish the practice because it stands in opposition to family members' tastes for body display. In fact, breaching established body codes promoted in the home may be a surrogate for more serious forms of intra-family dissent. In other cases, enthusiasts desperately conceal their tattoos from family members and other social actors in reflection of the lessons learned about this profane form of body marking in the home.

If family members are the reconnaissance agents of social control – acting as the first platoon of troops responsible for stimulating self-control in individuals – the family is the nexus of the societal super-ego as it disseminates codes about established social behaviour. As one might expect, if a person receives adequate instruction in regard to the importance of foresight and affective control, a strong sense of mutual interdependence and belonging among others can be fostered. For social-control theorists, then, a person's sense of figurational embeddedness starts in the home, and habituses are thus squarely located in the primary cultural lessons learned there. Figurational sociologists would find little fault with this theoretical position. However, for social-control theorists, primacy is given to the formative years of biological maturation. The overriding assumption is that, by a relatively young age, all aspects of the personality structure are cemented. Following early adolescence, there is little room for significant alteration of the habitus, irrespective of any sliding interdependencies or redefined social statuses/roles (Gottfredson and Hirschi 1990; Hirschi 1969).

Figurational sociologists would argue that habituses are far more malleable. When a person experiences natural variation in figurational embeddedness, the habitus (while anchored in early life-course interaction) is altered as social interdependencies change. Preferences and attitudes for activities such as body modification transform as life-course transitions influence individuals to reconsider their body habits. What may have been unproblematic body practice at one stage in the life course becomes tenuous if it threatens a person's memberships in extended relationship chains. Take, as an example, the tradition of binge drinking on North American university and college campuses. The practice, while no way socially normative, is a tolerated form of bodily deviance among students. Upon exiting university, however, students are aware that such behaviour cannot continue if one wishes to develop and retain certain emergent bonds and social responsibilities. Marriage, peer, and economic relationships, which all carry cultural statuses and expected role performances, may be strained by excessive drinking, and hence intoxication is not a body project bringing many social benefits to the actor.

Narratives provided by employed tattoo enthusiasts indicate that involvement in work environments characterized by rigid codes of acceptable body display clearly influence one's body habits. Not only will chains of employment interdependencies restrict the range of body projects in which an individual may participate, they may similarly dictate how a person displays a modified body in daily life. The very nature of work transforms one's everyday regimen, as individuals discipline their bodies to engage in daily work activities (itself a rationalized form of body modification). The nature of a person's employment and the established social codes about the body proffered at work largely dictate how modified bodies are displayed in the occupational sphere. Tattoo enthusiasts note that a person may be required to engage in a significant amount of body covering at work, wearing clothing or other tools for hiding a modified body. The habitus is impacted in such a way that perspectives about when and how to display certain non-normative forms of corporeal play are created. Body habits are also influenced by the very fact that individuals may perceive that their ability to freely express themselves through diverse forms of body display is confined by work interdependencies.

Stories collected from tattoo enthusiasts further suggest that perspectives about body modification are affected by transition in the dominant forms of work in Canada. With the increased reliance on information and communication technologies characteristic of post-industrial economies, some Canadian tattoo enthusiasts experience a perceived need to communicate with others through body modification. Work settings replete with technological equipment and advanced forms of communication may instil a desire to explore the parameters of the body through its modification. With increased exposure to how the body may be enhanced through technology (alongside the importance of communicating and representing the self to others through technological apparatuses), possibilities for body modification are opened. Life transitions into social statuses and roles demanding extended levels of conformity and self-discipline thus expose people to alternative ways of thinking about their bodies. With the ongoing sociogenesis of work structures, combined with an individual's increased embeddedness in work relationships, body modification habits are transformed.

Changing interdependencies (either tightened or loosened) within friendship networks also influence the ongoing evolution of our body-modification habits. Discounting the blanket assertion of social/self-control theorists (e.g., Gottfdredson and Hirschi 1990) that peers' attitudes or behaviours do not greatly sway the personality structure (i.e., create a propensity for non-normative behaviour), information gathered on tattoo enthusiasm in Canada indicates precisely the opposite. Rather than affirming that habituses are wholly configured before interaction within friendship networks, one finds a more empirically representative observation to be that relationships with an array of peers play an ongoing role in the creation of personal preferences for body practices.

First, friends may be the agents responsible for initiating a person's career in a specific form of body modification. By supplying information on, advice about, techniques for, and justifications concerning a particular body project, friends can be sponsors of a corporeal activity like tattooing. Many of the enthusiasts I encountered in Canada point out that tattoo neophytes may first learn about the practice through friendship networks, and are often escorted to tattoo studios by friends. Likewise, a person's first exposure to tattooed skin may come from interaction with tattooed peers. Whereas tattooing the body, or participating in any form of outsider behaviour, was not contemplated in the past (i.e., the habitus did not include preferences for these types of body projects), interaction with tattooed friends may alter a person's inclinations for the practice.

Second, if peers supply social support for a body practice, and promote it as a normative form of self-expression, body habits can be transformed in a lasting way. People do not simply seek out friends who share similar body-modification habits, neither do they blindly accept particular perspectives offered about the body by their peers. Still, friends' techniques of and interpretations about body-modification projects provide a set of interpretive resources for individuals. In particular, friends' opinions about and involvement in body projects like tattooing can have a normalizing effect on personal interpretations of them. When one is faced with negative social reactions about a specific genre of body-modification activities from other social groups (e.g., family members and co-workers), definitions of body-modification projects as normative supplied within friendship networks may counteract other socializing influences. As a person develops a mosaic of friendship networks and acquires a surfeit of definitions about body-modification, preferences about varying body modification activities are incorporated into the habitus.

Canadian tattoo enthusiasts often find that both tattooed and non-tattooed peers are the most sympathetic receptors of their body projects. Meeting tattoos with curiosity, tolerance, or ambivalence, peers make evaluations of the body project that are ingrained in the enthusiast's habitus. Therefore, the extent of a person's association (especially in the spare-time spectrum) with peers can be pivotal in creating and altering body-modification habits. Constantly referencing their own body-modification preferences against those of their peers, enthusiasts are aware of how others in their social circles interpret body-modification projects like tattooing.

Embeddedness in the tattoo figuration, occurring through the development of friendship chains therein, also figures into the ongoing formulation of perspectives about tattooing. If a person becomes more centrally involved in the figuration as a client, travels to tattoo studios in spare time, ventures to tattoo conventions, or devotes portions of weekly activities to reading tattoo magazines or visiting tattoo Web sites, friendship chains in the figuration are lengthened and strengthened. When one becomes more involved as a 'career' (Becker 1963) enthusiast, a person's everyday activities and overall body perspectives may come to be realigned around the corporeal project. Linking identity more closely to practice (and one's tattooed body), and interacting with friends who intersubjectively share pro-tattooing attitudes, a person changes body-modification habits. Even if a person chooses to remain on the periphery of the figuration, interaction with other tattoo enthusiasts exposes a person to diverse opinions about how corporeality can be reshaped in the process of self-representation.

In brief, as friendship networks both inside and outside of the tattoo figuration change throughout life, a person's body-modification habits become a tapestry of previous and current interaction within social networks. Tattoo enthusiasts indicate that while parents' and other family members' definitions of body-modification activities must be managed or conformed with to a degree, friends' preferences for body modification are equally influential on the habitus. Importantly, if an individual cultivates extensive and diverse friendships chains with others (and thus increases their figurational embeddedness), any castigation of tattooing body projects common in one social sphere may be negated by favourable evaluations made by friends or acquaintances in another sphere. Whereas family members' or co-workers' body-modification practices have a lasting influence on an individual's techniques of bodily expression and display, definitions of body modification learned from friends are equally used by tattoo enthusiasts.

Simultaneously, the interdependencies an individual shares with others (family, friends, co-workers, etc.) should be located within broader established-outsider relationships within a figuration. As regularly expressed in the sociological vernacular in terms of social stratification or structured inequality, membership in socially identified established or outsider groups plays a role in configuring the habitus. In some cases, a person is born into an established or outsider group, while membership in other groups is founded upon achieved statuses or characteristics. Regardless, individuals learn and internalize perspectives about body modification relative to their membership in both established or outsider groups. Quite simply, our body-modification habits are reflective of class, gender, religions, ethnicity, and many other group-based ideas concerning body modification. Taken as methods of communicating social status and identity to others, body-modification practices reflect a person's social positions and roles in a figuration. Like the Maori moko tattoo, which symbolizes a warrior's achieved status within the group, body projects symbolize and reproduce established and outsider relationships between people.

For example, body-modification projects like dieting, breast augmentation, liposuction, and wearing make-up are culturally meaningful because they produce and highlight characteristics typically associated with established constructions of femininity. These characteristics, defined through an established male gaze, serve to produce passive and hyper-sexualized images of women – thus, creating images of women as the cultural Other (Bordo 1993; Grosz 1994; MacSween 1993). In this case, the established patriarchal order in a figuration creates a standard for body-modification practices that supports existing social relationships of power between men and women. Over time, these standards become integral components of women's body-modification habits. To conform with established social codes regulating femininity brings social favour, to resist or challenge these codes elicits marginalization as an outsider.

Similarly, current cultural dictums about exercising are underpinned with middle-class moral sentiment about the body. Given the current access to physical-training equipment and cutting-edge dietary regimes, a moral tag is attached to exercising as a middle-class pastime (White et al. 1995). The individual choosing not to participate in exercise or cultivate a healthy (firm, toned, tanned, or muscular) body risks being labelled a member of a morally inferior class. Since many members of the working class possess neither copious amounts of time nor the money to devote to aerobics classes or Nautilus clubs, this cultural ideology becomes a self-fulfilling prophecy – furthering the established positions of the middle and upper classes. In a conceptually parallel way, since standards defining the 'body beautiful' (Maguire and Mansfield 1998) are mainly set by the racial majority in Western cultures, individuals of non-white descent often engage in full list of body projects to shape the body according to white standards. Cloaking the natural shapes of the outsider body can be an advantageous social practice in figurations where individuals are discriminated against on the basis of their membership in an racially outsider social group. Non-white individuals who straighten their hair, colour or tint their skin, remove skin from their eyelids, or have rhinoplasty and other forms of cosmetic surgery illustrate the fact that racial outsiders in Western figurations develop relationships with their bodies that reflect their membership within culturally marginalized groups.

Thus, membership within collectivities of mutually identified WE actors provides various interpretive resources for understanding cultural preferences about body-modification. By situating individuals within groups of interdependent actors we are able to examine common threads creating and binding together body-modification habits. Postmodernist claims about the disintegration of these social categorizations aside (Best 1995; Denzin 1991, 1992; Hall 1997; Jameson 1991; Lash 1990), membership in established or outsider social groupings appears to partially shape body-modification habits. Since individuals understand the body through a series of interpretive resources furnished by mutual identification with others, preferences about body modification reflect a person's ascribed and achieved social statuses, roles, and identities.

Narratives indicate that personal preferences for tattooing indeed reflect membership in an array of social groups. In keeping with the traditions of tattooing in Canada, there remains a strong (but now minority) working-class contingent in the tattoo figuration. As noted by Steward (1990) and McCabe (1997), some tattoo enthusiasts from working-class backgrounds, by embracing the tradition as an outsider body practice, have incorporated a preference for such projects into their habituses. However, by carefully wrapping the tattooing body project in New Age justifications and rationalizations, many in the middle-class group of tattoo enthusiasts have co-opted the practice as a bourgeois form of identity expression. By juxtaposing their tastes for tattooing against the profane traditions of the working class so as to accentuate the significance of the new guard of tattoo enthusiasts, middle-class clients are supplanting traditional discourses surrounding tattooing with contemporary sensibilities and ideologies about the body.

Historically, participation in tattooing has also been constricted by established gender codes. Joining the ranks of tattoo enthusiasts as a circus sideshow attraction, sexual curiosity, or political protester, women have found their involvement in the body project confined by dominant cultural constructions of femininity both inside and outside of the tattoo figuration (DeMello 2000; Mifflin 1997; Wroblewski 1992). Extensively covering the body with tattoos – a masculine rite of identity confirmation – has been strictly taboo for the majority of women in Canada. However, sociogenic changes inside and outside of the tattoo figuration over the past three decades have brought scores of new female enthusiasts to the practice. Some would be quick to cite women's increased participation in the body project as a marker of a changing cultural landscape, that is, as a symbol of the breakdown of social barriers separating the body play acceptable for men and women. Narratives provided by female Canadian tattoo enthusiasts indicate that while women account for a sizable portion of the new tattoo clients in the current era, women's tattooing practices remain tightly bound by established constructions of femininity. Even though habituses continue to change in Western figurations – as individuals are socially encouraged to practise a host of body-modification activities – established constructions of gender continue to bear cultural weight on body-modification practices.

Established constructions of corporeal modification clearly influence how individuals interpret the body and its display. As such, established standards are measuring sticks by which bodily practices are gauged, and partly form the backbone of body-modification habits. Established codes about the body are both enabling and constraining. On the one hand, as people share basic orientations and perspectives toward body modification, dominant social norms, values, and beliefs are reproduced. Individuals use communication through the body as a method of confirming social interdependencies with others – drawing on common WE and THEY images connoted through forms of body modification. When we identify with other social actors through physical manipulation, bonds are solidified over time. On the other hand, by internalizing and conforming with established social codes about the body, an individual finds his or her freedom to pursue *any* form of body modification deemed personally satisfying to be substantially restricted. What provides the basis for cultural inclusion and a sense of belonging among interdependent others in a social figuration is something of a personal trade-off.

Figurational Discourses

The impact of figurational embeddedness on the habitus is compounded by the extent to which it exposes a person to established and outsider figurational discourses. Although I do not wish to reduce the experience of corporeality, and the formation of body habits, to culturally disseminated systems of language, prevailing social discourses do provide 'maps of meaning' (Williams 1965, 1977) for understanding body practices.

Feminist and pro-feminist research on body modification draws to our attention the power of social discourses on cultural body-modification habits. Discourses constructing gendered bodies are cultural tools utilized in everyday life that provide meaning for specific body shapes. In demarcating what is appropriate body play for men and women, these discourses also legitimate figurational relations of power and social control. Research on the cultural significance of discourse and linguistic ways of knowing the world (Miller 2000) has pointed out that superstructural relationships of power are supported by ideologies promoted by key societal institutions including the family, school, economy, and media. Taking the lead provided by conflict and other neo-Marxist theoretical orientations (including postmodernist and post-structuralist ideas), discourse analyses of body modification practices first locate everyday experience within broader relations of power distribution and structured inequality. Relying heavily on Foucauldian thought (1977, 1979, 1980, 1987), the analyses of gendered forms of body-modification commence by assuming that all forms of corporeal modification are expressions of bio-politics.

Without question, the theoretical stir created in the past twenty years by discourse analysts has stimulated fresh insight into the cultural significance of body modification. Focusing on the ways in which cultural relationships and systems of social power are embodied in representational practices, textual deconstructions of corporeality home in on the political messages about society inscribed through the skin (Woodward 1997). By addressing the ways in which culture is intextuated into everyday body practice and habit, discourse analysts reveal how seemingly banal body movements, gestures, and expressions are in fact teeming with ideologies and systems of knowledge. Through the process of reading textual bodies – which articulate one's social status, position, cultural inclusion, and political ideologies – discourse analysts stress how linguistically framed ways of viewing the world form the basis of the habitus (Miller 2000; Potter 1996; Van Dijk 1993).

However, in limiting the analysis of body experience to a system of signs and signifiers, there is a very real risk of losing sight of the *lived* body amidst a waterfall of textual images and decodings. Sociologists must not become preoccupied with erudite theoretical depictions of the body as a sign while dismissing the need to inspect how physical bodies are experienced in the here and now of everyday life. Empirically responsible analyses must interconnect bodies as they are managed and expressed in life with bodies as they are linguistically constructed and represented (Elias 1983, 1994, 1996). The uncovering of power relations in figurations that produce ways of discursively framing corporeality becomes sociologically relevant only if conjoined with the study of the lived body. Discourses affecting corporeal experience are fundamental for conceptualizing how habituses are formed, as long as they are studied conjointly with experiences lived with the flesh.

A figurational perspective on habitus development would therefore include an examination of how variation in a person's figurational embeddedness affects exposure to social discourses (and vice versa). If habituses are influenced by both established and outsider discourses about the body and its representation, we must ask how the figurational positions and identities individuals hold throughout life expose them to competing definitions of body performance. Along with the study of how 'interpretive resources' (Gubrium and Holstein 1997) influence a person's conception of the body in situated contexts of interaction, figurational sociologists would examine how established and outsider ideologies about the body are discursively formed and circulated through chains of social relationships (Maguire and Mansfield 1998).

As noted in the previous section, transformation in a person's figurational embeddedness ultimately affects the habitus. In one way, it does this because individuals with a greater degree of involvement in a figuration (i.e., many roles and responsibilities, various social statuses, and a high degree of affective attachment to others) will most likely be inundated with differing constructions of appropriate body modification. Whereas established cultural discourses about the body will be depicted (white, male, Christian, middle-class) as the norm, involvement with myriad others undoubtedly exposes people to culturally outsider ways of knowing the body. Canadian tattoo enthusiasts' sensibilities about their bodies, for instance, indicate that sociogenic transformation in the ethnic milieu in Canada have led some to be more experimental with body display and inquisitive of traditionally outsider body styles.

More generally, it seems that with increased figurational embeddedness in normative institutions (family, school, work, religion, sport, or leisure) and the cultivation of extended chains of interdependency with norm-abiding others, a person's body-modification activities become habitual reproductions of established social constructions of the body.

Potentially risking achieved and ascribed roles or statuses by violating established body practice (being labelled a member of an outsider social group), individuals steer their body-modification behaviours on the basis of established cultural expectations. Body-modification habits are not simply affected by discourses detailing what established body modification involves, they create and embody discourses. The corporeal activities of one person do not supersede the importance of any other's, since it is the interweaving of body-modification practices among and between groups of individuals that (re)produces established cultural discourses and body-modification habits.

Many of the tattoo enthusiasts I encountered staunchly argue that proponents of the established Christian, middle-class body idiom in Canada flatly discount tattooing as a beneficial cultural practice. They believe that dominant ideas about and descriptions of tattooing cling to the circus, prison, gang, or primitive (anti-civilization) traditions of tattooing. Here, tattoo enthusiasts are represented in social discourse as deviants, those incapable of following social rules. Perceiving this declaration to be based on outdated and stereotypically white, middle-class, conservative preferences for body presentation, some Canadian tattoo enthusiasts pose what they frequently articulate as resistance to such an ideology. While they do not always conform with established cultural ideals about the body, their body habits are evidently dialogical with them – as body projects are sought out that violate, resist, negotiate, or overturn established ideologies. It seems that enthusiasts who feel particularly oppressed within a figuration (i.e., as they are deeply embedded, follow established norms about body display, and perceive their possibilities for free body expression to be confined) are most receptive to tattooing body projects – since it is a symbolic resistance to cultural ideologies and discourses.

Nonetheless, the extensive body concealing that some tattoo enthusiasts perform in everyday life speaks of their understanding of established discourses about tattooing (or the normative body for that matter). As they have internalized the awareness that such body marking may be repugnant to others, and an unmistakable transgression of body idiom in certain social circles, enthusiasts may avoid the shame and embarrassment associated with baring tattoos for public inspection. Though body-modification habits may include preferences for outsider body practices, they simultaneously reflect the need for enthusiasts to at least appear as norm-abiding in the presence of conforming others – an established idea learned through socialization processes and buried within the habitus. The more figurationally embedded a person is, the more reactions from established others figure into everyday body performance, since mutual recognition and cultural identification are valuable components in social interchange.

The habitus, then, reflects discourses about the body promoted as normative in a variety of figurational contexts. Narratives provided by many employed tattoo enthusiasts, for example, underline how constructions of tattooing as an outsider practice permeate work-related settings. A tattooed body offers a stark contrast to discourses promulgated in the occupational sphere, and is typically hidden away from the prying eyes of potential critics. Discussions with other Canadian tattoo enthusiasts highlighted how tattooing is considered deviant or at least intolerable in most family settings. However, within esoteric subcultural scenes (e.g., a sports team or a Rave figuration) tattooing can be undertaken as a normative signifying practice. Tattoos that are hidden at work, at school, or in the home can be displayed in these contexts with pride. Therefore, the mosaic of interdependencies a person develops, and the corresponding degree of figurational embeddedness, partly configure one's body-modification habits. The tastes for modifying and displaying the body of individuals with extensive, recognized, and valued interdependency chains show a keen sensitivity to the established discourses found in an abundance of social settings.

In social environments where established discourses bear little validity, alternative forms of body play pose minimal threats to relationships with others. Tattoo enthusiasts with working-class backgrounds, and who were unemployed at the time of interviewing, expressed a sense of disregard for established body discourses. Alienated from others (i.e., as an expression of their lack of figurational embeddedness), these tattoo enthusiasts are not dissuaded by the established body idiom, since they do not feel constrained by established social discourses. Ultimately, the form and content of their tattooing practices reflect this freedom from social control. The alternative body practices of individuals carrying only a handful of conventional relationships with others (e.g., criminal gang members, prisoners, or others) become discursively constructed as outsider forms of corporeal performance – hence, the long-existing construction of tattooing as a form of deviance is reinforced by conservative critics.

Nonetheless, the idea that tattooing is (still) not entirely normative *precisely* explains why some Canadian enthusiasts are attracted to the body project. In a figuration where images of outsiders and tattoos go hand-in-hand, the body project continues to be a method of asserting one's difference among culturally homogeneous others (i.e., perceived followers of the established body idiom). By accepting and reproducing the outsider status of tattooing, these enthusiasts reaffirm established cultural discourses about normative body modification. Quite simply, many Canadian tattoo enthusiasts have seemingly internalized dominant cultural habituses, and utilize this outsider form of body marking to plant a social flag of individuality among established others. Ironically heeding established cultural discourses that encourage individuals to perform identity work through body modification, outsider forms of body manipulation provide enthusiasts with ready-made forms of what they describe as authentic identity construction and display. Because uniqueness and individuality are culturally revered in Western figurations, it stands to reason that a tolerable amount of bodily deviance will be incorporated into the habitus.

Contrary to conclusions often made in the deviancy literature, then, a high level of figurational embeddedness does not act as a firewall preventing one from participating in 'contra-normative' activities. Instead, variation in figurational embeddedness shifts and rearranges a person's exposure to and internalization of established and outsider discourses delineating acceptable body behaviour. Even though a person may be surrounded by established ideologies about corporeal practice, and come to orient daily activities around such belief systems, interaction with a diverse cast of social actors over the life course introduces competing understandings of how one may modify the body. Alternative discourses may provide individuals with new maps of meanings for interpreting the body through the cultivation of friendship networks and the establishment of roles among peers. Changes in body habits occur as interdependencies morph and take on new significance for people.

With the tattooing body project as the example, figurational embeddedness appears to open individuals to discourses through which the normative nature of the body project may be judged. The tattooing stories and life experiences I became privy to illustrate how embeddedness in class groups, gender groups, and other mutually identified social conglomerates expose people to specific discourses about the body and its modification. With membership in various social groupings, individuals encounter both established and outsider definitions of body practices such as tattooing. In this way, personal motivations toward, preferences for, and constructions of tattooing come to reflect one's membership in these groups. The habitus is, then, influenced by a rich mosaic of the discourses circulated within groups of people over time. Rather than implying that the habitus is formed only in relationship to a person's identification with a specific social or status group (class, gender, religion, etc.), we must look to the collection of social groups influencing one's body-modification habits, and to how competing discourses about the body across social groups are evidenced in a person's body-modification preferences.

Lifestyle Interdependencies

The fourth major set of influences on the habitus are rooted in personal lifestyles. By drawing on Stebbins's definition (1997), 'lifestyle' sociologists may give attention to the self-directed activities in which an individual participates with others sharing similar life perspectives or orientations. Often associated with the spare-time spectrum or consumptive activities (Stebbins 1997), lifestyle is a conceptual moniker attached to a complex pastiche of activities and interrelationships with mutually recognized WE others. Although by no means capturing the sum total of the concept, the idea of lifestyle brings to the fore the idea that certain patterned behaviours are intentionally sought out and incorporated into a person's life. By pursuing involvement in specific social circles (clubs, teams, scenes, etc.), participating in group activities because they provide members with socially recognized identities and statuses (i.e., as an enthusiast of some social activity), and promoting world views through joint social action, personal lifestyles coalesce around shared behaviours and ideologies.

Lifestyles become culturally meaningful for people within specific generations because they establish outlets for exploring personal interests and fostering social relationships. Joining a hockey team, becoming an avid pottery maker, enlisting as a fund-raiser for a charity organization, affiliating with members of the Rave scene, or participating in a religious community are lifestyle pursuits in that they may partly (or wholly) restructure a person's daily activities or outlook on life. If we cast the concept in figurational terms, a lifestyle is a framework of interdependencies entered into by people that revolve around intersubjectively shared WE activities and belief systems. Whereas lifestyles based on social class, ethnic identification, or racial background are rightfully examined by sociologists as the basis of one's social orientation, equally significant are those lifestyles chosen by individuals as particularly exciting, intriguing, provocative, or relaxing – such as hobbies, spare-time fascinations, and other leisure activities (Stebbins 1997).

The importance of lifestyle for one's body habits is grounded in a rationale similar to that of figurational embeddedness. Lifestyles (although there are notable exceptions) are generally interdependent social activities. They involve other people as fellow participants, spectators, judges, hosts, critics, and confirmers of status. Just as relationships with family members or co-workers imprint preferences for specific forms of corporeal activity on the habitus, relationships with peers situated in similar lifestyle engagements can influence a person's definition of normative body performance. For instance, the lifestyle associated with nudism advocates (at its core) an unabashedly open perspective about the body and its display (Ilfeld and Lauer 1964). Enthusiasts of spare-time lifestyles based on participation in outdoor activities (e.g., hiking, swimming, skiing, rock-climbing, camping, snowboarding, or fishing) often emphasize the benefits of physical exertion in the process of communing with nature. Even social actors who construct lifestyles around the consumption of illicit drugs often construct drug-taking as an activity geared toward extending the parameters of the senses (Hathaway 1997a, 1997b).

The very term 'tattoo enthusiast' conjures images of tattooing as something of a lifestyle pursuit. In describing the tattoo figuration as a community of actors, DeMello (1995, 2000) partially described enthusiasm for tattooing as a lifestyle. To DeMello's analytical credit, it is true that tattoo artists mainly experience the practice as a distinctive lifestyle. In wearing many tattoos, cultivating friendships with tattoo artists and clients, reading literature about tattooing, and travelling the globe to meet fellow enthusiasts, many artists are committed to the tattooing lifestyle. However, not all enthusiasts orient their activities and identities around the body project, or view their tattoo-collecting (Vail 1999) activities as a lifestyle.

Using the case study of tattooing, we may conclude that a person's lifestyle choices alter preferences for body projects. If we hold firm to the notion that tattooing itself is not a lifestyle for the vast majority of enthusiasts, preferences for tattooing as a body project must be located in other lifestyle orientations. Figurational embeddedness in normative institutional activities provides one grouping of influences on the habitus, and helps to arrange a person's perspectives about tattooing. Yet, involvement in social lifestyles deemed interesting or in some way advantageous to the individual are *equally* influential in the ongoing development of body habits like tattooing.

Tattoo enthusiasts' experiences presented in various chapters of this book reveal that the self-initiated affiliations formed with generational

WE groups over the life course furnish maps of meaning for interpreting the body. Using the body as a text of self- (and group) representation, mutually oriented WE affiliates solidify social bonds through the skin. Attracted as they are by the permanence of tattooing, and its status as an outsider social practice, the body project serves as a beacon of in-group solidarity and individuality. Since corporeality is inexorably linked to identity, groups of interdependent people utilize body alteration to galvanize collective identity around an intersubjectively meaningful lifestyle practice. When individuals participate in such body ritual, and learn to appreciate the communicative potential of body modification, their body habits are transformed. The tattoos act as symbols of involvement in an overall lifestyle or generational condition, a consciously chosen pattern of behaviour and supporting ideologies adopted by an individual. Orientations about representation through physical transformation are changed as people are expected to represent their self-directed lifestyle choices through body practice.

Understandably, tattooing fits into lifestyles viewed culturally as contra-normative in some way. Here, the long-standing association between tattooing and social malcontents is reproduced as tattoos are utilized to denote disaffiliation with established peers and their lifestyles. Outsider lifestyles around practices that pose some type of social resistance to existing figurational power relationships or ideologies and tattooed bodies become signatures of cultural protest. Common symbols are worn by lifestyle affiliates or generational sub-units (Mannheim 1971), as is common in the Hip-Hop, Skinhead, Punk, Rave, or Skater scenes. Tattooing is doubly meaningful for fellow lifestyle proponents, since it facilitates a mutual WE recognition among participants, and challenges conforming THEY others who view such body practices as repugnant. Once again, body modification is understood as a vehicle for circulating social commentary and exploring alternative forms of identity work. Correspondingly, the biological body is further viewed as an entity to be shaped, restructured, marked, and accentuated in the process of interacting with and communicating among both established and outsider groups.

The dialectic relationship between the biological body and lifestyle orientations is also evidenced here. As the biological body is continually transformed into a text of representation, individuals learn to orient their body-modification preferences around the practice of self-representation. This is not a ground-breaking sociological conclusion (Goffman 1959, 1963), but the principle is worth reiterating. Yet even though sociologists actively explore the relationship between discourse, social stratification, and body-modification preferences and practices (Lash and Urry 1994; McRobbie 1994; Muggleton 2000), rarely are lifestyle orientations included in the examination of corporeal modification. Conspicuously absent from pioneering and subsequent research on youth lifestyle activities and deviant subcultural affiliations (Cohen 1973; Hall and Jefferson 1976; O'Bireck 1996) is the idea that choosing to modify the body as part of a group (life)style is central to the way attitudes about and constructions of corporeality are created over time.

The lifestyles adopted by individuals (and how they affect body-modification habits) are equally reflective of their embeddedness in established social roles, statuses, and identities (and vice versa). Without question, lifestyle activities may be complementary to those interdependencies shared among family members, peers, co-workers, or a variety of established others. Lifestyle orientations can further ensconce people in established social roles and identities if they reinforce dominant social relationships and established cultural ideologies. For example, physical exercise and healthiness as lifestyle orientations can strengthen relationships between norm-abiding peers (i.e., as a social ritual), signify a moral message about individuals (i.e., the desire to improve and protect the physical body), and illustrate conformity in a figuration where muscular bodies are hyper-sexualized (White and Young 1997). Hence, lifestyle orientations (particularly those accounting for a sizable amount of a person's spare-time activities) may reinforce established body preferences and discourses. Research on youth deviance (Gottfredson and Hirschi 1990; Wade and Brannigan 1998) has consistently correlated unsupervized or undirected leisure time with involvement in contranormative behaviour and the belief in subaltern social values – including those relating to the body and its modification (e.g., drug use, alcohol consumption, violence, and other types of risk-taking behaviours).

Lifestyles may therefore function as a conduit of established bodily order in a figuration. If people are exposed to similar lessons about the body in self-chosen lifestyle activities, as they are in more forced social spheres, the habitus forms as a unified whole. That is, when consistent norms, values, and beliefs about body modification are imprinted in varying social settings (family, work, leisure, etc.), body-modification preferences will be homological. Although one may dabble in risqué body practice, as in a tattooing body project, outsider forms of body modification are either hidden from plain view or justified by elaborate narratives that construct a positive cultural meaning for the practice. The extent of

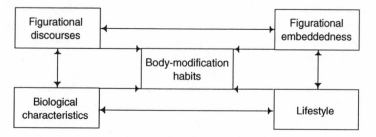

Figure 9.1   Habitus formation

a person's 'established' way of viewing the body is underscored, since techniques of neutralization or 'passing' are practised to preserve the individual's status as a discreditable outsider – and this process further illustrates how a person feels or anticipates feeling shame or embarrassment about the body project in the company of established others.

The conceptual model of habitus formation developed through the case study of tattooing is summarized in figure 9.1. The four major nexuses of habitus formation are created through a series of interconnections and reciprocal effects. While the focus of attention in the current analysis is the body and its modification, we could easily replace preferences for body modification with tastes for other forms of social behaviour including, for example, criminal activities. The model proposed is not a definitive causal model of the habitus-formation process, but is intended to be utilized as a working tool for sociologists interested in how personality structures or second natures for social behaviours are created.

Concatenating Research Efforts on the Body

A concatenation (Stebbins 1992) of efforts around the proposed model above would be worthwhile for expanding on the ideas developed through this investigation of tattooing, and for stimulating fresh theoretical insight into body-modification practices. Rather than treating case studies of body modification as islands unto themselves, sociologists must build more conceptually relevant links between studies of corporeality. Indeed, research on the tattooed body is already connected by central themes such as gender, class, technology, or illness. Furthermore, empirical examinations of corporeality are often housed within the postmodernist, interactionist, feminist, or phenomenological theoretical camps – which establishes some semblance of cohesion in the literature. But a closer inspection of the existing literature indicates that comparative and cross-fertilizing research efforts (i.e., over empirical studies spanning extended time periods) are long overdue. In order to 'flesh out' methods for integrating substantive and theoretical issues related to the body (so that our conceptual understanding of bodies and their modification may be both theoretically powerful and empirically responsible), alternative approaches to research are needed.

A beneficial methodological first course of action would be, of course, to triangulate data-collection strategies within given research efforts on the body. This would require sociologists to grip much less tightly their favourite or preferred methods of data collection. Instead of structuring an entire research agenda around interviewing, content analysis, surveys, participant observation, or archival methods alone, body theorists would develop more elaborate understandings of corporeality through a combination of many methods. Blumer (1969, 44) wrote that to inspect a social phenomenon critically, we must set it on an analytical table and observe it from all angles. Methodologically speaking, this means drawing on divergent ways of measuring, observing, or interpreting a phenomenon of interest. In the case example of tattooing, semiotic readings of tattooed bodies, interviews with individuals about their tattooed bodies, historical analyses of tattoo art and its representation, and the unobtrusive observation of the moving tattooed body in public spaces are all fruitful methods to be incorporated into individual research programs with tattooing as the subject.

The concatenation of research on the modified body should include the linking together of diverse substantive interests in corporeality. For example, an interconnected stream of studies on body modification might critically examine various camouflaging, extending, adapting, and redesigning body projects. A series of investigations might focus on several variations of extending body projects, while another might conceptually compare camouflaging and adapting body projects by searching for similarities and differences between them. A coherent and goal-oriented research agenda designed to amend and expand a model of habitus formation (such as the one offered in this book) can be established. Instead of producing accounts of body modification that will be used to further political standpoints or reaffirm avant-garde theories, concatenated studies of corporeality should press for extended theoretical integration and innovative insight.

A concatenated program of research on body modification would also involve a scheduled revisitation of specific research topics over time. Given the frequency with which social phenomena change (in their form, content, and social meaning), sociologists often find that exploratory research is periodically required to gather updated empirical understandings of the world. For instance, even though Sanders's study (1989) of tattooing is an incredibly descriptive and theoretically intriguing piece of sociology, his data (and segments of his analysis) simply do not reflect contemporary tattoo practices and their cultural constructions. Repeated forays into the tattoo figuration across an extended time period would allow sociologists to study the cultural development of the body project. To that extent, changing preferences for tattooing could be contextualized within sociogenic change, and processual shifts in cultural body-modification habits could be noted.

The tenets of figurational sociology establish a theoretical grid for accomplishing these research tasks. By using principles that include figurational sociology as a supporting theoretical pillar for concatenated research on bodies, the study of habituses and their physical representations could reinvigorate our sociological conceptualization of corporeality. Without reifying figurational sociology or disregarding the need to develop grounded theory through empirical research, a long-term program of research on the body could use figurational sociology as the theoretical centrepiece.

The integration of theories about the body within the general rubric of a figurational sociology would accomplish what Tittle (1995) refers to as 'synthetic integration' – or the interweaving of disparate theories into a unified conceptual whole. If one treats figurational sociology as a theoretical meta-narrative in the integration process, alternative theories of the body can be sutured onto a cohesive assemblage of ideas – culminating in the working models of habitus formation proposed here. While much theoretical integration in sociology merely amounts to adding variables to causal models, a truly integrated theory (of body modification, for example) would restructure existing theories into an unambiguous and parsimonious whole.

At present, we are parked at a crossroads in both our cultural interpretation of body modification and sociological contemplations about bodies. Exciting technological and scientific discoveries have smashed the parameters of what our bodies may become if trained, protected, disciplined, and repaired through basic techniques of reconstruction. Around the corner are human cloning projects, the creation of fully cybernetic virtual people, and the ability to move bodies across vast periods of time and space. What we interpret natural bodies to be, or how we should use our bodies, has never been more subject to contestation. Our cultural curiosity to camouflage, redesign, extend, and adapt our bodies is only limited by our collective imagination. Ironically, our own quest to achieve body perfection has exacerbated our confusion about corporeal matters. In a time when myriad social, biological, and environmental risks confront the long-term existence of bodies on this planet, it is perhaps our own desire to expand bodies that poses the gravest threat to their natural integrity.

Body-modification habits have never been more pliable. Family members, gym teachers, peers, spouses, doctors, television commercials, magazine articles, news stories, and movies all encourage us to participate in journeys of the flesh. Preferences for body projects like tattooing (and the diverse explanations or justifications offered in their social construction) that indicate our hunger to modify our natural bodies know no satiety. Outsider forms of body modification like tattooing are creeping out of the social shadows and into the cultural limelight. Established forms of body modification like exercising, dieting, or wearing fashion have become commodified, ritualized, and etched into our cultural habituses. Even with the multitude of sociological explanations of body projects, it is impossible to predict what forms of body modification will ascend in popularity in the next ten, twenty, or fifty years. Perhaps genetic manipulation and dramatic forms of chromosomal alteration may be the next body plateau to be explored, or the separation of the mind and body through virtual reality. History teaches us that as long as we live in bodies, we will find creative, expressive, and culturally meaningful methods for transforming their shapes, sizes, and appearances.

References

Adorno, T. 1991. *The Culture Industry*. London: Routledge.

Aggerholm, B. 2000. 'Body Art Goes Mainstream.' *Kitchener-Waterloo Record*, 10 February: B2.

Aggleton, P., G. Hart, and P. Davies. 1989. *AIDS: Social Representations, Social Practices*. London: Falmer Press.

Agnew, R. 1992. 'Foundation for a General Strain Theory of Crime and Delinquency.' *Criminology* 30: 47–87.

Althusser, L. 1971. *Lenin and Philosophy and Other Essays*. London: New Left Books.

Andes, L. 1998. 'Growing Up Punk: Meaning and Commitment Careers in a Contemporary Youth Subculture.' In J. Epstein, ed., *Youth Culture: Identity in a Postmodern World*. Oxford: Blackwell.

Andrews, D. 1993. 'Desperately Seeking Michel: Foucault's Geneaology, the Body, and Critical Sport Sociology.' *Sociology of Sport Journal* 10: 148–67.

Appadurai, A. 1990. 'Disjuncture and Difference in the Global Cultural Economy.' *Theory, Culture & Society* 7: 295–310.

Armstrong, M. 1991. 'Career-oriented Women with Tattoos.' *Journal of Nursing Scholarship* 23: 215–20.

– 1994a. 'Adolescents and Tattoos: Marks of Identity or Deviancy?' *Dermatology Nursing* 6: 119–24.

– 1994b. 'Tattoos: A Risk-Taking Art.' *Texas Nursing* 68: 8–9.

– 1995. 'Adolescent Tattoos: Educating and Pontificating.' *Pediatric Nursing* 21: 561–4.

Armstrong, M., and C. McConnell. 1994. 'Tattooing in Adolescence, More Common than You Think: The Phenomenon and Risks.' *Journal of School Nursing* 10: 22–9.

Arnold, D. 1970. *Subcultures*. Berkeley, CA: Glendessary Press.

Arnold, M. 1932. *Culture and Anarchy*. Cambridge: Cambridge University Press.

Atkinson, M. 1997. 'Rounders or Robin Hoods? Questioning the Role of the Ticket Scalper in Urban Marketplace Activity.' Unpublished master's thesis, McMaster University, Hamilton, Ontario.

– 2000. 'Brother Can You Spare a Seat?: Developing Recipes of Knowledge in the Ticket Scalping Subculture.' *Sociology of Sport Journal* 17: 151–70.

Atkinson, M., and B. Wilson. 2001. 'Subcultures, Bodies, and Sport at the Millennium.' In J. Maguire and K. Young, eds, *Theory, Sport and Society*, 375–95. London: JAI Press.

Atkinson, M., and K. Young. 2001. 'Flesh Journeys: Neo Primitives and the Rediscovery of Radical Body Modification.' *Deviant Behavior* 22: 117–46.

Baker, C. 1998. 'Membership Categorization and Interview Accounts.' In M. Silverman, ed., *Qualitative Research: Theory, Method, and Practice*, 99–112. London: Sage.

Baker, W. 1982. *Sports in the Western World*. Totowa, NJ: Rowman and Littlefield.

Balsamo, A. 1996. *Technologies of the Gendered Body: Reading Cyborg Women*. Durham, NC: Duke University Press.

Baron, S. 1989. 'The Canadian West Coast Punk Subculture: A Field Study.' *Canadian Journal of Sociology* 14: 289–316.

– 1997. 'Canadian Male Street Skinheads: Street Gangs or Street Terrorists?' *Canadian Review of Sociology and Anthropology* 34: 125–54.

Barthes, R. 1972. *Mythologies*. London: Jonathan Cape.

– 1975. *The Pleasure of the Text*. New York: Hill and Wang.

Bartky, S. 1988. 'Foucault, Femininity and the Modernization of Patriarchal Power.' In I. Diamond and L. Quinby, eds, *Feminism and Foucault: Reflections on Resistance*, 61–86. Boston: Northeastern University Press.

Baudrillard, J. 1983. *Simulations*. New York: Semiotext(e).

– 1988. *America*. London: Verso.

Beal, B. 1995. 'Disqualifying the Official: An Exploration of Social Resistance through the Subculture of Skateboarding.' *Sociology of Sport Journal* 12: 252–67.

Beck, U. 1991. *Risk Society: Towards a New Modernity*. London: Sage.

Becker, H. 1963. *Outsiders: Studies in the Sociology of Deviance*. New York: Free Press.

– 1970. *Sociological Work: Method and Substance*. Chicago: Aldine.

Beezer, A. 1992. 'Dick Hebdige, *Subculture: The Meaning of Style*.' In M. Barker and A. Beezer, eds, *Reading Into Cultural Studies*. London: Routledge.

Behar, R. 1996. *The Vulnerable Observer: Anthropology That Breaks Your Heart*. Boston: Beacon.

– 1999. 'Ethnography: Cherishing Our Second-Fiddle Genre.' *Journal of Contemporary Ethnography* 28: 472–84.

Belk, R. 1988. 'Possessions and the Extended Self.' *Journal of Consumer Research* 14: 139–68.

Bennis, W., and I. Mitroff. 1989. *The Unreality Industry*. Oxford: Oxford University Press.

Berger, P., and T. Luckmann. 1966. *The Social Construction of Reality*. New York: Anchor.

Berreman, G. 1962. *Behind Many Masks*. Ithaca, NY: Society for Applied Anthropology.

Best, J. 1995. 'Lost in the Ozone Again: The Postmodernist Fad and Interactionist Foibles.' *Studies in Symbolic Interaction* 17: 125–30.

Bhaktin, M. 1984. *Rabelais and His World*. Bloomington: Indiana University Press.

Blake, A. 1997. *The Body Language: The Meaning of Modern Sport*. London: Lawrence and Wishart.

Blishen, B. 1967. 'A Socioeconomic Index for Occupations in Canada.' *Canadian Review of Sociology and Anthropology* 4: 41–53.

Blomert, R. 2001. 'The Second Pillar of State Power: Figurational Explorations of the State and Money.' In T. Salumets, ed., *Norbert Elias and Human Interdependencies*, 213–25. Montreal and Kingston: McGill-Queen's University Press.

Blumer, H. 1969. *Symbolic Interactionism: Perspective and Method*. Englewood Cliffs, NJ: Prentice-Hall.

Bordo, S. 1989. 'The Body and the Reproduction of Femininity: A Feminist Appropriation of Foucault.' In S. Bordo and A. Jaggar, eds, *Gender/Body/Knowledge: Feminist Reconstructions of Being and Knowing*, 13–33. New Brunswick, NJ: Rutgers University Press.

– 'Feminism, Postmodernism, and Gender Scepticism.' In L. Nicholson, ed., *Feminism/Postmodernism*, 133–56. New York: Routledge.

– 1993. *Unbearable Weight: Feminism, Western Culture and the Body*. Berkeley: University of California Press.

Bordo, S., and A. Jaggar. 1989. *Gender/Body/Knowledge: Feminist Reconstructions of Being and Knowing*. New Brunswick, NJ: Rutgers University Press.

Borgman, A. 1992. *Crossing the Postmodern Divide*. Chicago: University of Chicago Press.

Bourdieu, P. 1984. *Distinction: A Social Critique of the Judgement of Taste*. Cambridge, MA: Harvard University Press.

– 1990. *In Other Words: Essays Toward a Reflexive Sociology*. Cambridge, UK: Polity.

Bourette, S. 1998. 'Tattoo Studios Make a Mark on the Mainstream.' *Globe and Mail*, 27 April: B13.

Boyd, N. 1991. *High Society: Legal and Illegal Drugs in Canada*. Toronto: Key Porter.

Brain, R. 1979. *The Decorated Body*. New York: Harper and Row.

Braithwaite, J. 1990. *Crime, Shame, and Reintegration.* Cambridge: Cambridge University Press.

Brake, M. 1985. *Comparative Youth Culture: The Sociology of Youth Culture and Youth Subcultures in America, Britain, and Canada.* London: Routledge and Kegan Paul.

Brohm, J. 1978. *Sport, A Prison of Measured Time.* London: Inter-Link Books.

Broidy, L. 2001. 'A Test of General Strain Theory.' *Criminology* 39(1): 9–36.

Burchett, G., and P. Leighton. 1958. *Memoirs of a Tattooist.* London: Oldbourne Book Co.

Burstyn, V. 1999. *The Rites of Men: Manhood, Politics, and the Culture of Sport.* Toronto: University of Toronto Press.

Butler, J. 1990. *Gender Trouble: Feminism and the Subversion of Identity.* London: Routledge.

– 1993. *Bodies That Matter.* London: Routledge.

Camphausen, R. 1997. *Return of the Tribal: A Celebration of Body Adornment.* Rochester, VT: Park Street Press.

Caplan, J. 2000. *Written on the Body: The Tattoo in European and American History.* Princeton, NJ: Princeton University Press.

Carter, K. 2000. 'Cool Characters.' *Calgary Herald,* 28 August: C6.

de Certeau, M. 1984. *The Practice of Everyday Life.* Berkeley: University of California Press.

Chambers, I. 1990. *Border Dialogues: Journeys into Postmodernity.* London: Routledge.

Chapman, G. 1997. 'Making Weight: Lightweight Rowing, Technologies of Power, and Technologies of the Self.' *Sociology of Sport Journal* 14: 205–23.

Chernin, K. 1981. *Womansize: The Tyranny of Slenderness.* London: Women's Press.

Chilton, R. 1964. 'Continuity in Delinquency Area Research: A Comparison of Studies in Baltimore, Detroit, and Indianapolis.' *American Sociological Review* 29: 71–83.

Clarke, J. 1976. 'Style.' In S. Hall and T. Jefferson, eds, *Resistance through Rituals: Youth Subcultures in Post-War Britain,* 175–92. London: Hutchinson.

Clifford, J. 1992. 'Travelling Cultures.' In L. Grossberg, C. Nelson, and P. Treichler, eds, *Cultural Studies,* 96–116. New York: Routledge.

– 1999. 'On Collecting Art and Culture.' In S. During, ed., *The Cultural Studies Reader,* 57–76. London: Routledge.

Clifford, J., and J. Marcus. 1986. *Writing Culture: The Poetics and Politics of Ethnography.* Berkeley: University of California Press.

Cloward, R. 1980. 'Illegitimate Means, Anomie and Deviant Behaviour.' In K. Stoddart, ed., *The Sociology of Deviance Book 1,* 295–306. Richmond, BC: Open Learning Institute.

Cloward R., and L. Ohlin. 1986. *Delinquency and Opportunity*. New York: Free Press.

Coakley, J. 2000. *Sport in Society: Issues and Controversies*. New York: McGraw-Hill.

Cohen, A. 1955. *Delinquent Boys: The Culture of the Gang*. New York: Free Press.

Cohen, L., and M. Felson. 1979. 'Social Change and Crime Rate Trends: A Routine Activity Approach.' *American Sociological Review* 44: 588–608.

Cohen, P. 1972. 'Subcultural Conflict and Working Class Communities.' *Working Papers in Cultural Studies 2*. Birmingham, UK: Centre for Contemporary Cultural Studies.

Cohen, S. 1973. *Folk Devils and Moral Panics*. London: MacGibbon and Kee.

Cohen, S., and J. Young. 1973. *The Manufacture of News*. Beverly Hills, CA: Sage.

Cohen, T. 2000. *The Tattoo*. London: Greenwich Editions.

Cole, C. 1993. 'Resisting the Canon: Feminist Cultural Studies, Sport Sociology and Technologies of the Body.' *Journal of Sport and Social Issues* 17: 77–97.

– 1998. 'Addiction, Exercise, and Cyborgs: Technologies of Deviant Bodies.' In G. Rail, ed., *Sport and Postmodern Times*, 261–75. Albany: State University of New York Press.

Connell, R. 1995. *Masculinities*. Cambridge, UK: Polity Press.

Connery, L. 2001. 'Too-da-loo Tattoo.' *Calgary Herald*, 28 January: C1.

Coupland, D. 1991. *Generation X: Tales for an Accelerated Culture*. New York: St Martin's Press.

Coward, R. 1985. *Female Desires*. London: Paladin Books.

Crawford, R. 1994. 'The Boundaries of the Self and the Unhealthy Other: Reflections on Health, Culture, and AIDS.' *Social Science and Medicine* 38: 1347–65.

Critical Art Ensemble. 1998. *Flesh Machine: Cyborgs, Designer Babies, and New Eugenic Consciousness*. Brooklyn, NY: Autonomedia.

Crosset, T., and B. Beal. 1995. 'The Use of "Subculture" and "Subworld" in Ethnographic Works on Sport: A Discussion of Definitional Distinction.' *Sociology of Sport Journal* 14: 73–85.

Dalrymple, T. 2000. 'Tattoos and Modern Britain.' *London Times*, 21 June: 8.

Davis, K. 1994. *Reshaping the Female Body: The Dilemmas of Cosmetic Surgery*. London: Routledge.

– 1997a. 'My Body Is My Art: Cosmetic Surgery as Feminist Utopia?' *European Journal of Women's Studies* 4: 23–37.

– 1997b. *Embodied Practices: Feminist Perspectives on the Body*. Newbury Park, CA: Sage.

DeMello, M. 1993. 'The Convict Body: Tattooing among Male American Prisoners.' *Anthropology Today* 9: 10–13.

- 1995. '"Not Just for Bikers Anymore": Popular Representations of American Tattooing.' *Journal of Popular Culture* 29: 37–52.
- 2000. *Bodies of Inscription: A Cultural History of the Modern Tattoo Community.* Durham, NC: Duke University Press.

Denzin, N. 1991. *Images of Postmodern Society.* London: Sage.
- 1992. *Symbolic Interactionism and Cultural Studies.* Oxford: Blackwell.
- 1997. *Interpretive Ethnography.* Thousand Oaks, CA: Sage.

Derrida, J. 1976. *Of Grammatology.* Baltimore: Johns Hopkins University Press.

Deveaux, M. 1994. 'Feminism and Empowerment: A Critical Reading of Foucault.' *Feminist Studies* 20: 223–47.

Dewalt, K., and B. Dewalt. 1998. 'Participant Observation.' In R. Bernard, ed., *Handbook of Methods in Cultural Anthropology,* 259–99. Walnut Creek, CA: Altamira.

Donaldson, M. 1993. 'What Is Hegemonic Masculinity?' *Theory and Society* 22: 643–5.

Donnelly, P. 1996. 'The Local and the Global: Globalization in the Sociology of Sport.' *Journal of Sport and Social Issues* 20: 239–57.
- 2000. 'Interpretive Approaches to the Sociology of Sport.' In J. Coakley and E. Dunning, eds, *Handbook of Sport and Society.* London: Sage.

Driedger, L. 1996. *Multi-ethnic Canada: Identities and Inequalities.* Toronto: Oxford University Press.

Drohan, P., and M. Toneguzzi. 1998. 'Co-op Issues Ban on Facial Jewellery.' *Calgary Herald,* 21 August: B4.

Duden, B. 1993. *Disembodying Women: Perspectives on Pregnancy and the Unborn.* Cambridge, MA: Harvard University Press.

Dull, D., and C. West. 1991. 'Accounting for Cosmetic Surgery: The Accomplishment of Gender.' *Social Problems* 38: 54–70.

Duncan, M. 1994. 'The Politics of Women's Body Images and Practices: Foucault, the Panopticon, and Shape Magazine.' *Journal of Sport and Social Issues* 18: 48–65.

Dunn, R. 1998. *Identity Crises: A Social Critique of Postmodernity.* Minneapolis: University of Minnesota Press.

Dunning, E. 1999. *Sport Matters: Sociological Studies of Sport, Violence, and Civilization.* London: Routledge.

Dunning, E., P. Murphy and J. Williams. 1988. *The Roots of Football Hooliganism.* London: Routledge.

Dunning, E., and C. Rojek. 1992. *Sport and Leisure in the Civilising Process.* London: Macmillan.

Dunning, E., and K. Sheard. 1979. *Barbarians, Gentlemen, and Players: A Sociological Study of the Development of Rugby Football.* Oxford: Martin Robertson.

During, S. 1999. *The Cultural Studies Reader.* London: Routledge.

Durkheim, E. 1951. *Suicide.* Chicago: Glencoe Free Press.

Dutton, K. 1995. *The Perfectible Body: The Western Idea of Physical Development.* London, UK: Cassell.

Dworkin, S., and F. Wachs. 1998. 'Disciplining in the Body: HIV-Positive Male Athletes, Media Surveillance, and the Policing of Sexuality.' *Sociology of Sport Journal* 15: 1–20.

Ebin, V. 1979. *The Body Decorated.* London: Thames and Hudson.

Eco, U. 1972. 'Social Life as a Sign System.' In D. Robey, ed., *Structuralism: The Wolfson College Lectures 1972.* London: Cape.

Edward, T. 1997. *Men in the Mirror.* London: Cassell.

Eichberg, H. 1998. *Body Cultures: Essays on Sport, Space, and Identity.* New York: Routledge.

Eldridge, C. 1989. 'Navy Traditions.' *Tattoo Archive,* Winter: 51–3.

– 1990. 'The Marlboro Man.' *Tattoo Archive,* Spring: 7–9.

– 1992. 'Tattoo History from A to Z.' *Tattoo Archive,* Fall: 1–4.

– 1993. 'American Circus 1793–1993.' *Tattoo Archive,* Winter: 17–19.

Elias, N. 1978. *What Is Sociology?* London: Hutchinson.

– 1983. *The Court Society.* Oxford, UK: Basil Blackwell.

– 1987. *Involvement and Detachment.* Oxford: Basil Blackwell.

– 1991a. *The Society of Individuals.* Oxford: Basil Blackwell.

– 1991b. *The Symbol Theory.* London: Sage.

– 1994. *The Civilizing Process.* Oxford: Basil Blackwell.

– 1996. *The Germans: Studies of Power Struggles and the Development of Habitus in the Nineteenth and Twentieth Centuries.* Oxford: Polity Press.

Elias, N., and E. Dunning. 1986. *Quest for Excitement: Sport and Leisure in the Civilizing Process.* Oxford: Basil Blackwell.

Elias, N., and J. Scotson. 1965. *The Established and the Outsiders.* London: Sage.

Emanuel, S. 1992. 'Culture in Space: The European Cultural Channel.' *Media, Culture & Society* 14: 281–99.

Eskes, T., C. Duncan, and E. Miller. 1998. 'The Discourse of Empowerment: Foucault, Marcuse, and Women's Fitness Texts.' *Journal of Sport and Social Issues* 22: 317–44.

Evans, C. 1997. 'Dreams That Only Money Can Buy ... Or, the Shy Tribe in Flight from Discourse.' *Fashion Theory: The Journal of Dress, Body, and Culture* 1: 169–88.

Falk, P. 1994. *The Consuming Body.* London: Sage.

Faulkner, R. 1975. 'Coming of Age in Organizations: A Comparative Study of the Career Contingencies of Musicians and Hockey Players.' In D. Ball and J. Loy, eds, *Sport and Social Order,* 521–58. Reading, MA: Addison-Wesley.

Featherstone, M. 1991. 'The Body in Consumer Culture.' In M. Featherstone, M. Hepworth, and B. Turner, eds, *The Body: Social Process and Cultural Theory,* 157–95. London: Sage.

– 2000. *Body Modification.* London: Sage.

Ferguson-Rayport, S., R. Griffith, and E. Straus. 1955. 'The Psychiatric Significance of Tattoos.' *Psychiatry Quarterly* 29: 112–31.

Fine, G. 1987. *With the Boys: Little League Baseball and Preadolescent Culture.* Chicago: University of Chicago Press.

– 1996. *Kitchens: The Culture of Restaurant Work.* Berkeley: University of California Press.

– 1999. 'Field Labour and Ethnographic Reality.' *Journal of Contemporary Ethnography* 28: 532–9.

Fine, G., and S. Kleinman. 1979. 'Rethinking Subculture: An Interactionist Perspective.' *American Journal of Sociology* 85: 1–20.

Fiske, J. 1989a. *Understanding Popular Culture.* Boston: Unwin Hyman.

– 1989b. *Reading the Popular.* Boston: Unwin Hyman.

– 1992. 'Cultural Studies and the Culture of Everyday Life.' In L. Grossberg, C. Nelson, and P. Treichler, eds, *Cultural Studies,* 154–65. New York: Routledge.

Ford, C. 1942. 'Culture and Human Behaviour.' *Scientific Majority* 44: 546–57.

Foucault, M. 1977. *Discipline and Punish: The Birth of the Prison.* London: Penguin Books.

– 1979. *The History of Sexuality, Volume 1: An Introduction.* London: Allen Lane / Penguin.

– 1980. *Power/Knowledge: Selected Interviews and Other Writings 1972–1977.* Brighton, UK: Harvester Press.

– 1987. *The Use of Pleasure: The History of Sexuality, Volume 2.* Harmondsworth, UK: Penguin.

Frank, A. 1990. 'Bringing Bodies Back In: A Decade Review.' *Theory, Culture, and Society* 7: 131–62.

– 1991a. *At the Will of the Body: Reflections on Illness.* Boston: Houghton.

– 1991b. 'For a Sociology of the Body: An Analytical Review.' In M. Featherstone, M. Hepworth, and B. Turner, eds, *The Body,* 36–102. London: Sage.

Frank, G. 1967. *Capitalism and Under-development in Latin America.* New York: Monthly Review Press.

Freund, P., and M. McGuire. 1999. *Health, Illness, and the Social Body: A Critical Sociology.* Upper Saddle River, NJ: Prentice-Hall.

Friday P., and J. Hague. 1976. 'Youth Crime and Post-industrial Societies: An Integrated Perspective.' *Criminology* 14: 331–46.

Friedman, A. 1996. 'From Subcultural Sign to Fashion Statement: The Changing Meaning of Tattoos.' Paper presented at the annual meetings of the Popular Culture Association, 10–13 April, Las Vegas, Nevada.

Gallick, R. 1996. 'The Tattoo: An American Pop Art Form.' *Mid-Atlantic Almanac* 5: 1–13.

Gans, H. 1999. 'Participant Observation in the Era of Ethnography.' *Journal of Contemporary Ethnography* 28: 540–8.

Garber, M. 1992. *Vested Interests: Cross-dressing and Cultural Anxiety.* London: Routledge.

– 1997. 'Sign, Co-Sign, Tangent: Cross-dressing and Cultural Anxiety.' In K. Gelder and S. Thornton, eds, *The Subcultures Reader,* 454–9. London: Routledge.

Garfinkel, H. 1956. 'Conditions of Successful Degradation Ceremonies.' *American Journal of Sociology* 61: 20–424.

– 1967. *Studies in Ethnomethodology.* Englewood Cliffs, NJ: Prentice-Hall.

Gartner, R., and B. McCarthy. 1991. 'The Social Distribution of Femicide in Urban Canada, 1921–1988.' *Law and Society Review* 25: 821–40.

Gathercole, P. 1988. 'Contexts of Maori Moko.' In A. Rubin, ed., *Marks of Civilization,* 171–8. Los Angeles: Museum of Cultural History, University of California.

Geertz, C. 1973. *The Interpretation of Cultures.* New York: Basic Books.

Gell, A. 1993. *Wrapping In Images: Tattooing in Polynesia.* Oxford: Oxford University Press.

Giddens, A. 1991. *Modernity and Self Identity.* Cambridge, UK: Polity Press.

Gilbert, S. 2000. *Tattoo History: A Sourcebook.* San Francisco: Juno Publishing.

Gillespie, R. 1996. 'Women, the Body and Brand Extension in Medicine: Cosmetic Surgery and the Paradox of Choice.' *Women and Health* 24: 69–85.

Gittleson, N., and G. Wallfn. 1973. 'The Tattooed Male Patient.' *British Journal of Psychiatry* 122: 295–300.

Gittleson, N., G. Wallfn, and K. Dawson-Butterworth. 1969. 'The Tattooed Psychiatric Patient.' *British Journal of Psychiatry* 115: 1249–53.

Glaser, B. 1992. *The Basics of Grounded Theory Analysis.* Mill Valley, CA: Sociology Press.

– 1995. *Grounded Theory 1984–1994.* Mill Valley, CA: Sociology Press.

Glaser, B., and A. Strauss. 1967. *The Discovery of Grounded Theory: Strategies for Qualitative Research.* Chicago: Aldine.

Goffman, E. 1959. *Presentation of Self in Everyday Life.* Garden City, NY: Doubleday.

– 1963. *Stigma.* Englewood Cliffs, NJ: Spectrum.

– 1967. *Interaction Ritual: Essays on Face-to-Face Behaviour.* London: Allen Lane.

Goldstein, N. 1979. 'Laws and Regulation Relating to Tattoos.' *Journal of Dermatologic Surgery and Oncology* 5(11): 913–15.

Gomme, I. 1998. *The Shadow Line: Crime and Deviance in Canada.* Toronto: Harcourt Brace.

Goode, E. 2001. *Deviant Behavior.* 6th edition. Upper Saddle River, NJ: Prentice-Hall.

Goodger, J., and B. Goodger. 1989. 'Excitement and Representation: Toward a Sociological Explanation of the Significance of Sport in Modern Society.' *Quest* 41: 257–72.

Gordon, M. 1947. 'The Concept of Sub-culture and Its Application.' *Social Forces* 20: 40–2.

Gottfredson, M., and T. Hirschi. 1990. *A General Theory of Crime.* Stanford, CA: Stanford University Press.

Govenar, A. 1988. 'The Variable Context of Chicano Tattooing.' In A. Rubin, ed. *Marks of Civilization,* 209–17. Los Angeles: Museum of Cultural History, University of California.

Gramsci, A. 1971. *Selections from Prison Notebooks.* London: Lawrence and Wishart.

Gray, J. 1994. *I Love Mom: An Irreverent History of the Tattoo.* Toronto: Key Porter.

Grills, S. 1994. 'Recruitment Practices of the Christian Heritage Party.' In M. Dietz, R. Prus, and W. Shaffir, eds, *Doing Everyday Life: Ethnography as Human Lived Experience,* 96–108. Toronto: Copp Clark Longman.

Grognard, C., and C. Lazi. 1994. *The Tattoo: Graffiti for the Soul.* London: Sunburst Books.

Grosz, E. 1994. *Volatile Bodies: Toward a Corporeal Feminism.* Bloomington: Indiana University Press.

Grumet, G. 1983. 'Psychodynamic Implications of Tattoos.' *American Journal of Orthopsychiatry* 53: 482–92.

Gubrium, J., and J. Holstein. 1997. *The New Language of Qualitative Method.* New York, NY: Oxford University Press.

– 1999. 'At the Border of Narrative and Ethnography.' *Journal of Contemporary Ethnography* 28: 561–73.

Gumpert, L. 1983. *Jamie Summers: Metamorphic Rite.* New York: New Museum of Contemporary Art.

Gurke, B., and M. Armstrong. 1997. 'D-Tag: Erasing the Tag of Gang Membership.' *Journal of School Nursing* 13: 13–17.

Haas, J. 1972. 'Binging: Educational Control among High Steel Workers.' *American Behavioural Scientist* 16: 27–34.

Haas, J., and W. Shaffir. 1987. *Becoming Doctors: The Adoption of a Cloak of Competence.* Greenwich, CT: JAI Press.

Hall, A. 1996. *Feminism and Sporting Bodies: Essays on Theory and Practice*. Champaign, IL: Human Kinetics.

Hall, S. 1980. 'Encoding/Decoding.' In S. Hall, ed., *Culture, Media, and Language*, 128–39. London: Hutchinson.

– 1997. *Representations: Cultural Representations and Signifying Practices*. London: Sage.

Hall, S., and T. Jefferson. 1976. *Resistance through Rituals: Youth Subcultures in Post War Britain*. London: Routledge.

Hannerz, U. 1990. 'Cosmopolitans and Locals in World Culture.' *Theory, Culture & Society* 7: 237–51.

Haraway, D. 1991. *Simians, Cyborgs, and Women: The Reinvention of Nature*. London: Free Association Books. Press.

Hargreaves, J. 1986. *Sport, Power and Culture*. Cambridge: Polity Press.

Harvey, D. 1989. *The Condition of Postmodernity*. Oxford: Blackwell.

Hathaway, A. 1997a. 'Marijuana and Tolerance: Revisiting Becker's Sources of Control.' *Deviant Behavior* 18: 103–24.

– 1997b. 'Marijuana and Lifestyle: Exploring Tolerable Deviance.' *Deviant Behavior* 18: 213–32.

Hathaway, A., and M. Atkinson. 2001. 'Tolerable Differences Revisited: Crossroads in Theory on the Social Construction of Deviance.' *Deviant Behavior* 23.

Haug, F. 1987. *Critique of Commodity Aesthetics: Appearance, Sexuality, and Advertising in Capitalist Society*. Minneapolis: University of Minnesota Press.

Hearn, J., and D. Morgan. 1990. *Men, Masculinities and Social Theory*. London: Unwin Hyman.

Hebdige, D. 1979. *Subculture: The Meaning of Style*. New York: Methuen and Co.

Hewitt, J., and R. Stokes. 1975. 'Disclaimers.' *American Sociological Review* 40: 1–11.

Hill, R. 1992. 'One Part Per Million: White Appropriation and Native Voices.' *FUSE* 15: 12–22.

Hirschi, T. 1969. *Perspectives on Delinquency*. Berkeley: University of California Press.

Hladki, J. 1994. 'Problematising the Issue of Cultural Appropriation.' *Alternate Routes* 11: 95–119.

Hoberman, J. 1992. *Mortal Engines: The Science of Performance and the Dehumanisation of Sport*. New York: Free Press.

Hochschild, A. 1983. *The Managed Heart: Commercialisation of Human Feeling*. Los Angeles: University of California Press.

Hoggart, R. 1958. *The Uses of Literacy*. Harmondsworth, UK: Penguin.

Homans, G. 1961. *Social Behaviour: Its Elementary Forms*. New York: Harcourt Brace.

Horkheimer, M., and T. Adorno. 1972. *The Dialectic of Enlightenment.* London: Allen and Lane.

Houghton, S., K. Durkin, E. Parry, Y. Turbett, and P. Odgers. 1996. 'Amateur Tattooing Practices and Beliefs among High School Adolescents.' *Journal of Adolescent Health* 19: 420–5.

Howell, R., R. Payne, and A. Roe, 1971. 'Differences among Behavioural Variables, Personal Characteristics, and Personality Scores of Tattooed and Non-tattooed Prison Inmates.' *Journal of Research in Crime and Delinquency* 8: 32–7.

Humphreys, D. 1997. 'Shredheads Go Mainstream?: Snowboarding and Alternative Youth.' *International Review for the Sociology of Sport* 32: 147–60.

Ilfeld, F., and R. Lauer. 1964. *Social Nudism in America.* New Haven, CT: College and University Press.

Ingham, A. 1975. 'Occupational Subcultures in the Work World of Sport.' In D. Ball and J. Loy, eds, *Sport and Social Order,* 333–89. Reading, MA: Addison-Wesley.

Irwin, J. 1977. *Scenes.* Newbury Park, CA: Sage.

Irwin, K. 2000. 'Negotiating the Tattoo.' In P. Adler and P. Adler, eds, *Constructions of Deviance,* 469–70. Belmont, CA: Wadsworth.

Isajiw, W. 1999. *Understanding Diversity: Ethnicity and Race in the Canadian Context.* Toronto: Thompson Education.

Jameson, F. 1991. *Postmodernism, or the Cultural Logic of Late Capitalism.* London: Verso.

Johnson, R. 1983. 'What Is Cultural Studies Anyway?' *Theories and Methods Series* 74. Stencilled occasional paper.

Johnson, S., and U. Meinhof. 1997. *Language and Masculinity.* Oxford: Blackwell.

Juengst, E., and B. Koenig. 1994. *The Meaning of AIDS.* New York: Praeger.

Kaeppler, A. 1988. 'Hawaiian Tattoo: A Conjunction of Genealogy and Aesthetics.' In A. Rubin, ed., *Marks of Civilization,* 157–70. Los Angeles: Museum of Cultural History, University of California.

Kalbach, M., and W. Kalbach. 2000. *Perspectives on Ethnicity in Canada.* Toronto: Harcourt.

Kalbach, W. 2000. 'Ethnic Diversity: Canada's Changing Cultural Mosaic.' In Kalbach and Kalbach, *Perspectives on Ethnicity in Canada,* 59–72.

Kaplan, D., and A. Dubro. 1986. *Yakuza: The Explosive Account of Japan's Criminal Underworld.* Reading, MA: Kaplan & Dubro.

Kasarda, J., and M. Janowitz. 1974. 'Community Attachment in Mass Society.' *American Sociological Review* 39: 328–39.

Katz, J. 1988. *Seductions of Crime.* New York: Basic Books.

Katz, P. 1999. *The Scalpel's Edge: The Culture of Surgeons.* Toronto: Allyn and Bacon.

Kellner, D. 1992. 'Popular Culture and the Construction of Postmodern Identities.' In S. Lash and J. Friedman, eds, *Modernity and Identity.* Oxford: Blackwell.

Kemple, T. 2001. 'The Trials of Homo Clausus: Elias, Weber, and Goethe on the Sociogenesis of the Modern Self.' In T. Salumets, ed., *Norbert Elias and Human Interdependencies,* 137–48. Montreal, PQ, and Kingston, ON: McGill-Queen's University Press.

Kent, D. 1997. 'Decorative Bodies: The Significance of Convicts' Tattoos.' *Journal of Australian Studies* 53: 78–88.

Kimbrell, A. 1995. *The Masculine Mystique: The Politics of Masculinity.* New York: Ballantine Books.

Kimmel, M., and M. Messner, 1992. *Men's Lives.* New York: Macmillan.

King, M. 1972. *Moko: Maori Tattooing in the 20th Century.* Wellington, VA: M. King.

Kitamura, T., and K. Kitamura. 2001. *Bushido: Legacies of the Japanese Tattoo.* Atglen, PA: Schiffer Publishing.

Kleese, C. 1999. 'Modern Primitivism: Non-Mainstream Body Modification and Radicalized Representation.' *Body & Society* 5: 15–38.

Klein, A. 1993. *Little Big Men: Bodybuilding Subculture and Gender Construction.* Albany: State University of New York Press.

Kleinman, S. 1979. 'The Significance of Human Movement: A Phenomenological Approach.' In E. Gerber and W. Morgan, eds, *Sport and the Body,* 177–80. Philadelphia: Lea & Ferbiger.

Kom, K. 1996. 'Body Adornment and Tattooing: Clinical Issues and State Regulations.' *Physician Assistant* 20: 85–100.

Kotarba, J. 1991. 'Postmodernism, Ethnography, and Culture.' In N. Denzin, ed., *Studies in Symbolic Interactionism* 12: 45–52. London: JAI Press.

Kratz, C., and B. Reimer. 1998. 'Fashion in the Face of Postmodernity.' In A. Berger, ed., *The Postmodern Presence: Readings on Postmodernism in American Culture and Society.* London: Altamira.

Krohn, M. 1986. 'The Web of Conformity: A Network Approach to the Study of Delinquent Behavior.' *Social Problems* 33: 581–93.

Kroker, A., and M. Kroker. 1987. *Body Invaders: Panic Sex in America.* New York: St Martin's Press.

Labarre, W. 1947. 'The Language of Emotions and Gestures.' *Journal of Personality* 16: 49–68.

Lacan, J. 1977. *Écrits.* London: Tavistock.

Lander, J., and H. Kohn. 1943. 'A Note on Tattooing among Selectees.' *American Journal of Psychiatry* 100: 326–7.

Larrain, J. 1989. *Theories of Development.* Cambridge, UK: Polity Press.

Lash, S. 1990. *The Sociology of Postmodernism.* London: Routledge.

Lash, S., and J. Urry. 1994. *Economies of Signs and Space.* London: Sage.

280   References

Laumann, E. 1976. *Networks of Collective Action: A Perspective of Community Influence.* New York: Academic Press.

Laumann, E., J. Gagnon, R. Michael, and S. Michaels. 1994. *The Social Organization of Sexuality: Sexual Practices in the United States.* Chicago: University of Chicago Press.

Lautman, V. 1994. *The New Tattoo.* New York: Abbeville Publishing.

Lemert, E. 1951. *Social Pathology.* New York: McGraw-Hill.

– 1967. *Human Deviance, Social Problems and Social Control.* Englewood Cliffs, NJ: Prentice-Hall.

Lenskyj, H. 1986. *Out of Bounds: Women, Sport and Sexuality.* Toronto: Women's Press.

– 1994. 'Sexuality and Femininity in Sport Contexts: Issues and Alternatives.' *Journal of Sport and Social Issues* 18: 356–76.

Lesieur, H. 1977. *The Chase.* New York: Anchor.

Lévi-Strauss, C. 1966. *The Savage Mind.* London: Weidenfeld and Nicoloson.

– 1969. *The Raw and the Cooked.* Chicago: University of Chicago Press.

Li, P. 1999. *Race and Ethnic Relations in Canada.* 2nd edition. Toronto: Oxford University Press.

Lian, J., and D. Matthews. 1998. 'Does the Vertical Mosaic Still Exist? Ethnicity and Income in Canada, 1991.' *Canadian Review of Sociology and Anthropology* 35: 461–82.

Lienert, A. 1998. 'Pierced and Tattooed Employees Showing Up.' *Great Falls Tribune,* 26 July: B1.

Light, D.W. 1972. *Tattooing Practices of the Cree Indians.* Calgary: Glenbow Alberta Institute.

Lindores, S., and M. McClearn. 1998. 'Facial Jewellery Gains Ground.' *Calgary Herald,* 18 July: K1.

Liska, A., and B. Warner. 1991. 'Functions of Crime: A Paradoxical Process.' *American Journal of Sociology* 96: 1441–63.

Lofland, J. 1966. *The Doomsday Cult.* Englewood Cliffs, NJ: Prentice-Hall.

Lofland, J., and L. Lofland. 1995. *Analysing Social Settings.* Belmont, CA: Wadsworth.

Loland, N. 2000. 'The Art of Concealment in a Culture of Display: Aerobicizing Women's and Men's Experiences and Use of Their Own Bodies.' *Sociology of Sport Journal* 17: 111–29.

Lombroso-Ferrero, G. 1972. *Criminal Man: According to the Classification of Cesare Lombroso.* Montclair, NJ: Patterson Smith.

Lorde, A. 1985. *The Cancer Journals.* London: Sage.

Lupton, D. 1996. *Food, the Body, and the Self.* London: Sage.

Lyotard, J. 1986. *The Postmodern Condition: A Report on Knowledge.* Manchester, UK: Manchester University Press.

MacAfee, M. 2000. 'Tattoos and Body Piercing: Side-effects Can Be Ugly.' *Calgary Herald*, 3 July: D2.

MacCannell, D. 1992. *Empty Meeting Grounds: The Tourist Papers.* London: Routledge.

MacDonald, D. 1957. 'A Theory of Mass Culture.' In B. Rosenberg and D. White, eds, *Mass Culture.* Glencoe, NY: Free Press.

MacKinnon, C. 1987. *Feminism Unmodified: Discourses of Life and Law.* Cambridge, MA: Harvard University Press.

MacSween, M. 1993. *Anorexic Bodies: A Feminist Sociological Perspective on Anorexia Nervosa.* New York: Routledge

Maguire, J. 1992. 'Towards a Sociological Theory of Sport and Emotions: A Process-Sociological Perspective.' In E. Dunning and C. Rojek, eds, *Sport and Leisure in the Civilizing Process*, 96–121. London: MacMillan.

– 1993. 'Bodies, Sport Cultures and Societies: A Critical Review of Some Theories in the Sociology of the Body.' *International Review for the Sociology of Sport* 28: 33–50.

– 1999. *Global Sport: Identities, Societies, Civilisations.* Cambridge, UK: Polity Press.

Maguire, J., and L. Mansfield. 1998. '"No-Body's Perfect": Women, Aerobics, and the Body Beautiful.' *Sociology of Sport Journal* 15: 109–37.

Mannheim, K. 1971. *From Karl Mannheim.* Ed. K. Wolff. Oxford: Oxford University Press.

Marcuse, H. 1964. *One Dimensional Man.* Boston: Beacon Press.

Martin, E. 1994. *Flexible Bodies.* Boston, MA: Beacon Press.

Martischnig, M. 1987. *Tattooing the East-Asian Way.* Vienna: Akademie der Wissenschaften.

Marx, K. 1977. *Karl Marx: Selected Writings.* Trans. D. McLellan. Oxford: Oxford University Press.

Mascia-Lees, F., and P. Sharpe. 1992. *Tattoo, Torture, Mutilation, and Adornment: The Denaturalization of the Body in Culture and Text.* Albany: State University of New York Press.

Matsueda, R., and K. Heimer. 1997. 'A Symbolic Interactionist Theory of Role-Transitions, Role-Commitments, and Delinquency. In T. Thornberry, ed., *Developmental Theories of Crime and Delinquency*, 163–213. New Brunswick, NJ: Transaction Publishers.

Matza, D. 1961. 'Subterranean Traditions of Youth.' *Annals of the American Academy of Political and Social Sciences* 338 (October).

– 1964. *Delinquency and Drift.* Berkeley: University of California Press.

Mauss, M. 1973. 'Techniques of the Body.' *Economy and Society* 2: 70–88.

McCabe, M. 1997. *New York City Tattoo: The Oral History of an Urban Art.* Honolulu: Hardy Marks Publications.

McCallum, D. 1988. 'Historical and Cultural Dimensions of the Tattoo in Japan.' In A. Rubin, ed., *Marks of Civilization.* Los Angeles: Museum of Cultural History.

McGill, N. 1998. 'Tattoos, Piercing, No Longer Just a Fad.' *Calgary Herald,* 10 January: J9.

McKerracher, D., and R. Watson. 1969. 'Tattoo Marks and Behaviour Disorder.' *British Journal of Criminology* 9: 167–72.

McLaughlin, J. 1973. 'Hawaiian Tattoo Motifs.' Manuscript in Bishop Museum Library, Honolulu.

McLung Lee, A. 1945. 'Levels of Culture as Levels of Socialization.' *American Sociological Review,* August: 485–95.

McQuail, D. 1994. *Mass Communication Theory.* London: Sage.

McRobbie, A. 1991. *Feminism and Youth Culture: From Jackie to Just Seventeen.* Basingstoke, UK: Macmillan.

– 1994. *Postmoderism and Popular Culture.* London: Routledge.

Mead, G.H. 1934. *Mind, Self and Society.* Chicago: University of Chicago Press.

Measey, L. 1972. 'The Psychiatric and Social Relevance of Tattoos in Royal Navy Detainees.' *British Journal of Criminology* 12: 182–6.

Menard, S. 1995. 'A Developmental Test of Mertonian Anomie Theory.' *Journal of Research in Crime and Delinquency* 32, 136–74.

Mennell, S. 1992. *Norbert Elias: An Introduction.* Oxford: Blackwell.

Merleau-Ponty, M. 1962. *The Phenomenology of Perception.* London: Routledge and Kegan Paul.

Merton, R. 1938. 'Social Structure and Anomie.' *American Sociological Review* 3: 672–82.

Messner, M. 1992. *Power Play: Sport and the Problem of Masculinity.* Boston: Beacon Press.

Miethe, T., M. Hughes, and D. McDowell. 1991. 'Social Change and Crime Rates: An Evaluation of Alternative Theoretical Approaches.' *Social Forces* 70: 165–85.

Mifflin, M. 1997. *Bodies of Subversion: A Secret History of Women and Tattoo.* New York: Juno Books.

Miles, S., D. Cliff, and V. Burr. 1998. 'Fitting In and Sticking Out: Consumption, Consumer Meanings and the Construction of Young People's Identities.' *Journal of Youth Studies* 1: 81–120.

Miller, L. 2000. 'The Poverty of Truth-Seeking: Postmodernism, Discourse Analysis and Critical Feminism.' *Theory and Psychology* 10: 313–52.

Miller, L., and O. Penz. 1991. 'Talking Bodies: Female Bodybuilders Colonise a Male Preserve.' *Quest* 43: 148–63.

Mills, C.W. 1940. 'Situated Actions and Vocabularies of Motive.' *American Sociological Review* 5: 904–13.

– 1956. *The Sociological Imagination.* New York: Oxford University Press.

Morgan, D. 1993. 'You Too Can Have a Body Like Mine: Reflections on the Male Body and Masculinities.' In S. Scott and D. Morgan, eds, *Body Matters.* London: Falmer Press.

Morse, A. 1977. *The Tattooists.* San Francisco: Albert Morse.

Muggleton, D. 1998. 'The Post-Subculturalist.' In S. Redhead, ed., *The Clubcultures Reader,* 167–85. Oxford: Blackwell.

– 2000. *Inside Subculture: The Postmodern Meaning of Style.* Oxford: Berg.

Myers, J. 1997. 'Nonmainstream Body Modification.' In P. Adler and P. Adler, eds, *Constructions of Deviance,* 516–32. New York: Wadsworth.

Newman, G. 1982. 'The Implication of Tattooing in Prisoners.' *Journal of Clinical Psychiatry* 43: 231–4.

Novak, P. 2000. 'Tattoos: No Longer Just for Sailors.' *Calgary Herald,* 13 January: N2.

O'Bireck, G. 1996. *Not a Kid Anymore: Canadian Youth, Crime, and Subcultures.* Toronto: Nelson.

Ollenberger, J., and H. Moore. 1992. *A Sociology of Women.* Englewood Cliffs, NJ: Prentice-Hall.

Paine, J. 1979. 'Skin Deep: A Brief History of Tattooing.' *Mankind* 6: 18–45.

Park, R., and E. Burgess. 1925. *The City.* Chicago: University of Chicago Press.

Parsons, T. 1937. *The Structure of Social Action.* New York: McGraw-Hill.

Philip, M. 1990. 'The 6% Solution.' *FUSE* 14: 28–9.

Pitts, V. 1998. 'Reclaiming the Female Body: Embodied Identity Work, Resistance and the Grotesque.' *Body and Society* 4: 67–84.

Polhemus, T. 1994. *Street Style: From Sidewalk to Catwalk.* London: Thames and Hudson.

– 1996. *Style Surfing: What to Wear in the 3rd Millennium.* London: Thames and Hudson.

Pollak, O., and E. McKenna. 1945. 'Tattooed Psychotic Patients.' *American Journal of Psychiatry* 101: 673–4.

Polsky, N. 1967. *Hustlers, Beats, and Others.* Chicago: Aldine.

Potter, J. 1996. *Representing Reality: Discourse, Rhetoric and Social Construction.* London: Sage.

Pronger, B. 1990. *The Arena of Masculinity: Sports, Homosexuality and the Meaning of Sex.* New York: St Martin's Press.

Prus, R. 1987. 'Generic Social Processes: Maximizing Conceptual Development in Ethnographic Research.' *Journal of Contemporary Ethnography* 16: 251–91.

– 1996. *Symbolic Interaction and Ethnographic Research: Intersubjectivity and the Study of Human Lived Experience.* Albany: State University of New York Press.

– 1997. *Subcultural Mosaics and Intersubjective Realities.* Albany: State University of New York Press.

Prus, R., and S. Irini. 1980. *Hookers, Rounders, and Desk Clerks: The Social Organisation of the Hotel Community.* Salem, WI: Sheffield.

Prus, R., and C. Sharper. 1991. *Road Hustler: Hustlers, Magic, and the Thief Subculture.* New York: Kaufman and Greenberg.

Rail, G. 1998. *Sport and Postmodern Times.* Albany: State University of New York Press.

Redhead, S. 1993. *'Rave Off': Politics and Deviance in Contemporary Youth Culture.* Aldershot, UK: Avebury.

– 1997. *Subculture to Clubcultures: An Introduction to Popular Cultural Studies.* Oxford: Blackwell.

– 1998. *The Clubcultures Reader: Readings in Popular Cultural Studies.* Oxford: Blackwell.

Richie, D., and I. Buruma. 1980. *The Japanese Tattoo.* New York: Weatherhill.

Rintala, J. 1995. 'Sport and Technology: Human Questions in a World of Machines.' *Journal of Sport and Social Issues* 19: 6–75.

Robinson, J. 1998. *The Quest for Human Beauty: An Illustrated History.* New York: W.W. Norton and Co.

Rosenblatt, D. 1997. 'The Antisocial Skin: Structure, Resistance, and "Modern Primitive" Adornment in the United States.' *Cultural Anthropology* 12: 287–334.

Rosneau, P. 1992. *Postmodernism and the Social Sciences.* Princeton, NJ: Princeton University Press.

Rubin, A. 1988. *Marks of Civilization: Artistic Transformations of the Human Body.* Los Angeles: Museum of Cultural History.

St Clair, L., and A. Govenar. 1981. *Stoney Knows How: Life as a Tattoo Artist.* Lexington: University of Kentucky Press.

St Martin, L., and N. Gavey. 1996. 'Women's Bodybuilding: Feminist Resistance and/or Femininity's Recuperation?' *Body and Society* 2: 45–57.

Salumets, T. 2001. *Norbert Elias and Human Interdependencies.* Montreal and Kingston: McGill-Queen's University Press.

Sampson, R., and J. Laub. 1993. *Crime in the Making: Pathways and Turning Points through Life.* Cambridge, MA: Harvard University Press.

2001. 'Turning Points in the Life Course: Why Change Matters to the Study of Crime.' In R. Smandych, ed., *Youth Crime: Varieties, Theories, and Prevention,* 57–79. Toronto: Harcourt.

Sanders, C. 1988. 'Marks of Mischief: Becoming and Being a Tattooed Person.'
    Journal of Contemporary Ethnography 16: 395–431.
– 1989. *Customizing the Body: The Art and Culture of Tattooing.* Philadelphia: Tem-
    ple University Press.
– 1991. 'Memorial Decoration: Women, Tattooing, and the Meanings of Body
    Alteration.' *Michigan Quarterly Review* 30: 146–57.
Sanford, W. 1992. 'Body Image.' In Boston Women's Health Book Collective,
    eds, *The New Our Bodies, Ourselves,* 23–30. New York: Touchstone.
Sardiello, R. 1998. 'Identity and Status Stratification in the Deadhead Subcul-
    ture.' In J. Epstein, ed., *Youth Culture: Identity in a Postmodern World.* Oxford:
    Blackwell.
de Saussure, F. 1960. *Course in General Linguistics.* London: Peter Owen.
Scheff, T. 1966. *Being Ill: A Sociological Theory.* Chicago: Aldine.
– 1983. 'Towards Integration in the Social Psychology of Emotions.' *American
    Review of Sociology* 84: 1317–34.
– 1990. *Microsociology: Discourse, Emotion, and Social Structure.* Chicago: University
    of Chicago Press.
– 2001. 'Unpacking the Civilizing Process: Interdependence and Shame.' In
    T. Salumets, ed., *Norbert Elias and Human Interdependencies.* Montreal and
    Kingston: McGill-Queen's University Press.
Schutz, A. 1967. *The Phenomenology of the Social World.* Evanston, IL: Northwestern
    University Press.
Scott, M., and S. Lyman. 1968. 'Accounts.' *American Sociological Review* 33: 46–62.
Scott, S., and D. Morgan. 1993. *Body Matters.* London: Falmer Press.
Scotton, G. 2000. 'The World Beats a Path to Smilin' Buddha.' *Calgary Herald,*
    14 February: C2.
Seaton, E. 1987. 'Profaned Bodies and Purloined Looks: The Prisoner's Tattoo
    the Researcher's Gaze.' *Journal of Communication Inquiry* 11: 17–25.
Sedgwick, E. 1994. *Tendencies.* Durham, NC: Duke University Press.
Segal, L. 1994. *Straight Sex: The Politics of Pleasure.* London: Virago.
Seidman, S. 1994. *Contested Knowledge: Social Theory in the Postmodern Era.* Oxford:
    Blackwell.
Sennett, R. 1977. *The Fall of Public Man.* New York: Knopf.
– 1998. *The Corrosion of Character.* New York: Norton.
Shaffir, W. 1999. 'Doing Ethnography: Reflections on Finding Your Way.' *Journal
    of Contemporary Ethnography* 28: 676–86.
Shaw, C., and H. McKay. 1927. *Juvenile Delinquency and Urban Areas.* Chicago: Uni-
    versity of Chicago Press.
Sheard, K. 1999. 'A Stitch in Time Saves Nine: Birdwatching, Sport, and Civilis-
    ing Processes.' *Sociology of Sport Journal* 16: 181–205.

Shilling, C. 1993. *The Body and Social Theory*. London: Sage.

– 1997. 'The Body and Difference.' In K. Woodward, ed., *Identity and Difference*, 63–121. London: Sage.

Shogan, D. 1999. *The Making of High Performance Athletes: Discipline, Diversity, and Ethics*. Toronto: University of Toronto Press.

Simmel, G. 1957. 'Fashion.' *American Journal of Sociology* 62: 215–30.

– 1964. *Conflict and the Web of Group Affiliations*. New York: Free Press.

– 1971. *The Sociology of Georg Simmel*. Glencoe, IL: Free Press.

Smandych, R. 2001a. *Youth Crime: Varieties, Theories, Prevention*. Toronto: Harcourt.

– 2001b. *Youth Justice: History, Legislation, Reform*. Toronto: Harcourt.

Sontag, S. 1991. *Illness as Metaphor: AIDS and Its Metaphors*. Harmondsworth, UK: Penguin.

Spencer, H. 1908. *The Principles of Sociology*. New York: Appleton.

Stafford, B. 1991. *Body Criticism: Imagining the Unseen in Enlightenment Art and Medicine*. Cambridge, MA: MIT Press.

Statistics Canada. 2001. www.statcan.ca/english/Pgdb/popula.htm.

Stebbins, R. 1992. 'Concatenated Exploration.' *Quality and Quantity* 26: 435–42.

– 1996. *Tolerable Differences: Living with Deviance*. Whitby, ON: McGraw-Hill.

– 1997. 'Lifestyle as a Generic Concept in Ethnographic Research.' *Quality and Quantity* 31: 347–60.

Steward, S. 1990. *Bad Boys and Tough Tattoos: A Social History of the Tattoo with Gangs, Sailors, and Street Corner Punks*. New York: Haworth Press.

Strinati, D. 1995. *An Introduction to Theories of Popular Culture*. New York: Routledge.

Sutherland, Edwin. 1937. *The Professional Thief*. Chicago: University of Chicago Press.

Sweetman, P. 1999. 'Anchoring the (Postmodern) Self? Body Modification, Fashion, and Identity.' *Body & Society* 5: 51–76.

Sykes, G., and D. Matza, 1957. 'Techniques of Neutralisation.' *American Sociological Review* 22: 837–49.

Tanner, J. 2001. *Teenage Troubles: Youth and Deviance in Canada*. 2nd edition. Toronto: Nelson.

Taylor, S. 1983. 'Adjustment of Threatening Events: A Theory of Cognitive Adaptation.' *American Psychologist* 38: 1161–73.

Thornton, S. 1995. *Club Cultures: Music, Media, and Subcultural Capital*. Cambridge, MA: Polity.

Thrasher, F. 1927. *The Gang*. Chicago: University of Chicago Press.

Tittle, C. 1995. *Control Balance: Toward a General Theory of Deviance*. Boulder, CO: Westview Press.

Todd, L. 1990. 'Notes on Appropriation.' *Parallelogramme* 16: 24–33.

Tomlinson, J. 1991. *Cultural Imperialism.* London: Pinter Publishers.

Trice, H. 1993. *Occupational Subcultures in the Workplace.* Ithaca, NY: ILR Press.

Trinh, T. 1991. *When the Moon Waxes Red: Representation, Gender, and Cultural Politics.* New York: Routledge.

Turner, B. 1984. *The Body and Society.* London: Sage.

Turner, V. 1969. *The Ritual Process.* Ithaca, NY: Cornell University Press.

Tyler, S. 1986. 'Postmodern Ethnography: From Document of the Occult to Occult Document.' In J. Clifford and G. Marcus, eds, *Writing Culture.* Berkeley: University of California Press.

Vail, A. 1999. Tattoos Are Like Potato Chips ... You Can't Have Just One: The Process of Becoming a Collector.' *Deviant Behavior* 20: 253–73.

Vale, V., and A. Juno. 1989. *Modern Primitives: An Investigation of Contemporary Adornment and Ritual.* San Francisco: Re/search Publications.

Van Dijk, T. 1993. 'Principles of Critical Discourse Analysis.' *Discourse and Society* 4: 249–83.

Van Krieken, R. 1998. *Norbert Elias.* New York: Routledge.

Verberne, T. 1969. 'The Personality Traits of Tattooed Adolescent Offenders.' *British Journal of Criminology* 9: 172–5.

Vigarello, G. 1995. 'The Life of the Body in Discipline and Punish.' *Sociology of Sport Journal* 12: 158–63.

Wade, T., and A. Brannigan. 1998. 'The Genesis of Adolescent Risk-Taking Behaviour: Pathways through Family, School, and Peers.' *Canadian Journal of Sociology* 23: 1–19.

Wallerstein, I. 1974. *The Modern World System.* New York: Academic Press.

Webb, S. 1979. *Pushing Ink: The Fine Art of Tattooing.* New York: McGraw-Hill.

Weber, M. 1930. *The Protestant Ethic and the Spirit of Capitalism.* London: Allen and Unwin.

White, P., and K. Young. 1997. 'Health and the New Age Ascetic.' In P. Donnelly, ed., *Taking Sport Seriously: Social Issues in Canadian Sport,* 106–10. Toronto: Thompson.

– 1999. *Sport and Gender in Canada.* Toronto: Oxford University Press.

White, P., K. Young, and J. Gillett. 1995. 'Body Work as a Moral Imperative: Some Critical Notes on Health and Fitness.' *Loisir et Société* 18: 159–83.

Whyte, W. 1943. *Street Corner Society.* Chicago: University of Chicago Press.

Widdicombe, S., and R. Wooffitt. 1995. *The Language of Youth Subcultures: Social Identity in Action.* Hemel Hemstead, UK: Harvester Wheatsheaf.

Williams, R. 1963. *Culture and Society 1780–1950.* Harmondsworth, UK: Penguin.

– 1965. *The Long Revolution.* Harmondsworth, UK: Penguin.

– 1976. *Keywords: A Vocabulary of Culture and Society.* London: Fontana.

– 1977. *Marxism and Literature.* Oxford: University of Oxford Press.

Williams, S., and G. Bendelow. 1998. *The Lived Body: Sociological Themes, Embodied Issues.* London: Routledge.

Willis, P. 1978. *Profane Culture.* London: Routledge and Kegan Paul.

– 1980. 'Notes on Method.' In S. Hall, ed., *Culture, Media, Language,* 88–96. London: Hutchinson.

–1997. 'Theoretical Confessions and Reflexive Method.' In K. Gelder and S. Thornton, eds, *The Subcultures Reader,* 246–53. New York: Routledge.

Wilson, B., and R. Sparks. 1996. '"It's Gotta Be the Shoes": Youth, Race and Sneaker Commercials.' *Sociology of Sport Journal* 13: 398–427.

Wolf, N. 1990. *The Beauty Myth.* London: Chatto and Windus.

Woodward, K. 1997. *Identity and Difference.* London: Sage.

Wouters, C. 1989. 'The Sociology of Emotions and Flight Attendants: Hochschild's Managed Heart.' *Theory, Culture, and Society* 6: 95–123.

Wroblewski, C. 1992. *Tattooed Women.* London: Virgin Publishing.

Young, K. 1993. 'Violence, Risk, and Liability in Male Sports Culture.' *Sociology of Sport Journal* 10: 373–96.

– 1997. 'Women, Sport, and Physicality.' *International Review for the Sociology of Sport* 32: 297–303.

– 2000. 'Sport and Violence.' In J. Coakley and E. Dunning, eds, *Handbook of Sports Studies,* 382–409. London: Sage.

Young, K., and L. Craig. 1997. 'Beyond White Pride: Identity, Meaning and Contradiction in the Canadian Skinhead Subculture.' *Canadian Review of Sociology and Anthropology* 34: 175–206.

Young, K., P. White, and W. McTeer. 1994. 'Body Talk: Male Athletes Reflect on Sport, Injury, and Pain.' *Sociology of Sport Journal* 11: 175–94.

Index